"Jim Belcher shows that we don't have to choose between orthodox evangelical doctrine on the one hand, and cultural engagement, creativity and commitment to social justice on the other. This is an important book."

Tim Keller, Redeemer Presbyterian Church, New York City

"*Deep Church* is the book we need—it's a genuine third way. Jim Belcher is poised like no other to evaluate the emerging movement: he knows theology, he loves the church, he cares about twentysomethings, he knows the entire emerging movement, and he remains faithful to theological orthodoxy. Most of all, *Deep Church* avoids the clamor for extremes. There are only two or three really good books about the emerging movement, and this is the best analysis I've seen."

Scot McKnight, Karl A. Olsson Professor in Religious Studies, North Park University

"Jim Belcher's book is the first to be truly gracious to both of these oft-contentious perspectives, suggesting a fair and honest critique of both. Belcher has clearly done his homework, and lives—as a lead pastor of a church plant—with one foot in the Reformed, traditional camp, and one foot in the emerging church. This is a great read for any who are tired of straw man arguments and polarization."

Mark Oestreicher, president, Youth Specialties

"Rising above the usual shallow, facile critiques of the emergent church movement, Jim Belcher has written for us a book that, indeed, goes deep. Jim took the time to listen to emergent voices, and as a result, he appreciates the movement for what it is. And his admonitions ring true. While Jim and I have theological differences, I can heartily recommend *Deep Church* as an invigorating study of and healthy corrective to both the emergent and traditional church."

Tony Jones, author of *The New Christians: Dispatches from the Emergent Frontier*

"Working out his ideas in the crucible of pastoral ministry, Jim Belcher proposes fascinating new ways to arbitrate today's disputes by appealing to the Great Tradition. Read it and learn how your church can go deeper."

Collin Hansen, editor-at-large, *Christianity Today,* and author of *Young, Restless, Reformed: A Journalist's Journey with the New Calvinists*

"*Deep Church* is a narrative of one man's journey of spiritual discovery involving at core a search for a place to stand. Whether you can fully agree with Jim's findings or not, you will find this book to be an accessible, well-articulated, deeply personal and (thankfully) theologically irenic apologetic for the emerging church."

Alan Hirsch, author of *The Forgotten Ways*

"Jim Belcher points a way that ties orthodox theological moorings with creative thinking and missional engagement, providing a helpful guide to thinking about church."

Ed Stetzer, president of LifeWay Research

"Jim Belcher judiciously assesses the divide between liberal and conservative factions of evangelicalism. Lucidly analyzing the strengths and weaknesses of the emerging church as well as of the traditionalists who critique it, Belcher offers an inspirational 'third way,' the 'deep church,' that synthesizes the best of both."

Crystal L. Downing, author of *How Postmodernism Serves (My) Faith*

"*Deep Church* is a carefully balanced and helpfully critical analysis of the emerging church and the numerous negative reactions against it. It is a fair-minded, truly gracious undertaking that speaks the truth in love and charts a clear third way. . . . Only a thoughtful pastor who knows Scripture, the Christian tradition and the modern challenges to mission could write such an excellent book."

Dr. John H. Armstrong, president, ACT 3, and author of *Your Church Is Too Small*

"Jim Belcher's *Deep Church* calls our attention to the pressing issues of our day to create a 'third language' conversation between the traditional and emergent church movements. *Deep Church* provides a healthy theological wrestling full of pragmatic wisdom, bringing a renewed perspective of birthing a church today. I highly recommend this book to pastors and lay leaders alike, to consider what the church, God's artwork, is called to become in the coming days."

Makoto Fujimura, artist and author of *Refractions: A Journey of Art, Faith and Humanity*

"In *Deep Church,* Jim Belcher has given us great thoughts about how a church can walk the tightrope between emerging and traditional, between sound doctrine and openness to our culture, between modernism and postmodernism, and between 'belonging before believing' and the importance of 'community in the conversion process.'"

Howard Ahmanson, president, Fieldstead and Company

DEEP CHURCH

A Third Way Beyond Emerging and Traditional

JIM BELCHER

FOREWORD BY RICHARD J. MOUW

IVP Books

An imprint of InterVarsity Press
Downers Grove, Illinois

InterVarsity Press
P.O. Box 1400, Downers Grove, IL 60515-1426
World Wide Web: www.ivpress.com
E-mail: email@ivpress.com

InterVarsity Press® is the book-publishing division of InterVarsity Christian Fellowship/USA®, a movement of students and faculty active on campus at hundreds of universities, colleges and schools of nursing in the United States of America, and a member movement of the International Fellowship of Evangelical Students. For information about local and regional activities, write Public Relations Dept., InterVarsity Christian Fellowship/USA, 6400 Schroeder Rd., P.O. Box 7895, Madison, WI 53707-7895, or visit the IVCF website at <www.intervarsity.org>.

All Scripture quotations, unless otherwise indicated, are taken from the Holy Bible, New International Version®. NIV®. Copyright ©1973, 1978, 1984 by International Bible Society. Used by permission of Zondervan Publishing House. All rights reserved.

While all stories and illustrations in this book are true, some names and identifying details have been changed to protect the privacy of the individuals involved. Personal conversations are cited with the permission of the speakers.

Design: Cindy Kiple
Cover images: iStockphoto
Interior image: x: Dmytro Konstantynov/iStockphoto

ISBN: 978-0-8308-3716-8

Printed in the United States of America ∞

Library of Congress Cataloging-in-Publication Data

Belcher, Jim, 1965-
   Deep church: a third way beyond emerging and traditional/Jim
   Belcher.
     p. cm.
   Includes bibliographical references.
   ISBN 978-0-8308-3716-8 (pbk.: alk. paper)
   1. Church. I. Title.
   BV600.3.B45 2009
   262'.26 —dc22
                           2009021520

| P | 19 | 18 | 17 | 16 | 15 | 14 | 13 | 12 | 11 | 10 | 9 | 8 | 7 | 6 | 5 | 4 | 3 |
| Y | 24 | 23 | 22 | 21 | 20 | 19 | 18 | 17 | 16 | 15 | 14 | 13 | 12 | 11 | 10 | 09 |

CONTENTS

FOREWORD

Richard J. Mouw

Deep Church is an answer to my prayers. Let me explain why.

A young "emergent" pastor told me recently that seminaries have become irrelevant. While he conceded that my own seminary is not quite as bad as the rest, the truth is that all of our theological schools are, to use his term, "dinosaurs." When I asked him what led him to this assessment, he responded that everything that we do in theological education—curricula, programs, strategic planning—"it's all a product of modernity." Since my own seminary has recently been revising our strategic plan, I decided to push him for clarification on that particular subject. "Strategic planning is all about rationality," he said. "My generation is more interested in envisioning."

The conversation did not last much longer, and I came away with a bit of irritation about what I saw as his rhetorical overkill and his posing of false choices. Why, for example, can't strategic planning itself be informed by a healthy dose of "envisioning"?

A few days later, however, my irritation was directed in a very different direction when I read yet another attack by an evangelical theologian on the "heresies" and "apostasy" of that young pastor's brand of "emergent church" thinking. Here too I worried about rhetorical overkill. I know about too many emergent congregations where people are coming to a genuine faith in Christ and being encouraged to study the Scriptures and to seek new paths of obedient discipleship. And this at a time when many traditional denominations are once again reporting significant membership losses.

◆ ◆ ◆

I came away from those two encounters—the conversation and the written critique—with a prayerful desire for a "time out" in the rhetorical shouting match, so that we can relax a bit and really listen to each other.

This fine book by Jim Belcher is an answer to my prayer. He has given us an articulate guide to the territory, paying careful attention to the people who are having such a difficult time listening to each other. And he does this as an honest seeker, a "participant observer" who reports candidly about his creative efforts at ministry—including some of the false starts he has made along the way.

Jim's call for the formation of a deep church speaks profoundly to those of us who stand with him as insider-outsider types in the current debates. His orthodox theological credentials are beyond challenge, yet he also knows that we desperately need to find new ways of being church. Jim Belcher does not pretend to have all the answers. But he demonstrates in these pages that he is a marvelously reliable guide—indeed I know of none better—for our much-needed efforts to go deeper as churches by mining the depths of the gospel for creative and faithful ministry in the strange and exciting new world of the twenty-first century.

Richard J. Mouw

INTRODUCTION

Is a Third Way Possible?

The evangelical church is deeply divided. Although evangelicalism has always been diverse, in recent years this fragmentation has threatened to pull the movement apart. Two groups, the traditional and emerging camps, are at the heart of the impending split. In the late 1990s some young evangelicals (now called the emerging church), unhappy with the reality and direction of the church, began to protest. In their writing and speaking they found fault with many elements of evangelicalism. They organized conferences, wrote books and started new churches to make their voice and opinions heard. It has become a movement with great momentum, energy and resources. It has, however, elicited a strong pushback from the traditionalists in the evangelical church.

Ironically, thirty years ago the protest was pioneered by the traditional wing of evangelicalism. Unhappy with what the Western church had become—anti-intellectual, entertainment-driven, success-focused—the traditional church condemned the worst elements with books like *Dining with the Devil*, *The Evangelical Forfeit*, *Selling Jesus* and *No Place for Truth*.[1] These books primarily attack what Robert Webber calls the pragmatists, those who pioneered seeker-sensitive worship that stripped traditional worship of historical and liturgical elements.[2] The pragmatists also had adopted a business paradigm to structure and run the church, a psychological model of counseling and church-growth philosophy drawn from marketing theory, all of which the traditionalists condemn.

While this critique was in full swing, the newest generation of evangelicals, termed "the younger evangelicals" by Robert Webber, joined in the protest. In the twenty-first century, some of these younger evangelicals have become known as the emerging church. They too decry the pragmatists' penchant for entertainment, individualism, unconcern for social justice and narrow theology of salvation—to name just a few points.

Though the emerging church shares much in common with the traditional church, they also include the more conservative wing of evangelicalism in their critique. And the traditional church has begun to fire back. Unlike the pragmatists, whose reaction to the emerging church has been minimal, the traditional church has gone after the emerging movement through books, conferences and blogs. After almost a decade the two sides now are at loggerheads, and it seems the rift will not be healed anytime soon.

The emerging church is composed of many different authors, pastors and church traditions, and therefore does not speak with one voice. What unifies them, in part, is their view that something is wrong with the evangelical church. They are seeking wholesale change, not just reform. But not everyone in the movement agrees on what this change should be.

To be fair, the traditional camp is not monolithic; it cuts across denominational and theological lines.[3] But the groups comprising traditional evangelicalism share similar views of culture, epistemology and the church. They also hold a fairly unified analysis of the emerging movement.[4] Therefore, in this book I group them all under the rubric of "the traditional church."

SPEAKING A DIFFERENT LANGUAGE?

At the height of the tension between the emerging and traditional churches, Tony Jones and Doug Pagitt, who are part of Emergent Village,[5] reached out to a leader in the traditional camp, John Piper. Since they all lived and ministered in Minneapolis, it made sense to bridge the gap. They met for lunch and discussed their differences and commonalities. Since that meeting, both sides have written a description of their experience. It is fascinating to read how amazingly different the two accounts are. It paints a vivid picture of the gap between the two sides.[6]

Piper, senior pastor of Bethlehem Baptist Church in Minneapolis, came away convinced that Jones and Pagitt believe that "committed relationships trump truth."[7] This is dangerous, from Piper's perspective, because it assigns Scripture to a secondary status. As Jones and Pagitt tried to explain how they know ultimate truth in life, Piper was thinking to himself: "I just don't understand the way these guys think. There are profound epistemological [the theory of how we know] differences— ways of processing reality—that make the conversation almost impossible, as if we were just kind of going by each other."[8] After the lunch Piper concludes, "We seem to differ so much in our worldviews and our ways of knowing that I'm not sure how profitable the conversation was or if we could ever get anywhere." Piper left shaking his head, wondering what exactly Jones and Pagitt believed on the important theological topics. They just would not be pinned down. "I came away from our meeting frustrated and wishing it were different but not knowing how to make it different."[9]

Tony Jones has also written about this meeting in his book *The New Christians*. His perspective on the same meeting could not be more different. After seeing promotional literature for a conference Piper was hosting that was critical of the emerging movement, Jones offered to meet with Piper as a kind of "olive branch." Jones wanted to make clear that both sides "share a commitment to proclaiming Christ." He writes that Piper is a "gentle-looking man, but his theology is anything but gentle." "He believes that God's anger burns with holy fire against human sin. Words like *wrath, hate* and *blood* peppered his sentences as we dined." The meeting seemed tense from the start. Piper, remembers Jones, "began by admitting that he'd never heard of me before, and that he really didn't have anything against emergent Christians per se." His problem was with Brian McLaren, another emergent author, who has questioned the version of the doctrine of atonement that Piper holds dear.

When Pagitt, who is Jones's pastor, asked Piper, "Maybe we can find ways to work together," Piper said it would be impossible without agreement on essential doctrines like the atonement. Because Pagitt and Jones don't hold to Piper's view of atonement, they are "rejecting the gospel *in toto*, and so, by logical extension, [they] are not . . . Christian." When Jones pushed back that through the millennia billions of Christians have not had the same view of atonement that Piper holds today, "The pastor paused, looked at me, and said, 'You should never preach.' " Jones tried to explain that for him the gospel was mainly about reconciliation. It is more than a "fixed point of doctrine that is the litmus test of all ministry," he said. "Everything we do in the emergent church is surrounded by an envelope of friendship, friendship that is based on lives of reconciliation." "In fact," Jones concluded, returning Piper's slight, "I'm not sure it's even possible to be an orthodox Christian if you're not living a life of reconciliation."[10]

This exchange vividly makes clear how far apart the two sides are on issues of theology, epistemology and the nature of the church. There appears to be little common ground. Unity seems impossible. Can the two sides get along? Are they really this far apart? Can they work together to build evangelicalism, or are their differences irreconcilable?

IS THERE A THIRD WAY?

Most observers of this conflict are caught somewhere in between. Many recognize that something has gone wrong with the pragmatic wing of evangelicalism, and they want something different.[11] They desire more depth in worship, a stronger sense of belonging and greater impact in the world. When Bill Hybels, a pioneer of the pragmatic, seeker-driven church, admitted that he had been wrong, that his church had not done a good job at discipling people, his critics felt vindicated.[12] They knew something was wrong and are convinced that a biblical view of the church can be a reality.

But those caught in the middle are confused. They see two groups, the traditional and emerging camps, echoing their sentiments about pragmatic worship. Both accuse the Western church of being shallow, ahistorical and more focused on pragmatic issues than on real transformation and cultural renewal. Both sides are calling on the church to recover its heritage—the breadth and depth of Christian theology, worship and practice—and be informed by a missional ministry in the postmodern world, all to the glory of God. Yet the two sides can't get along. They are hostile to each other, using their writings and conferences to denounce the other side.

The vast majority of people are confused by the debate. Many have read emerging authors, agreeing with their assessment of the problem and aspects of what they are proposing. But they also have read traditional authors and are drawn to parts of their vision of the church as well. The majority want to learn from both sides. Why don't they get along? After all, don't they want the same thing—a deeper, more robust evangelical church that profoundly affects people and the world? But on the other hand, there must be a reason for all the distrust on both sides. Is it possible the two camps aren't teaching the same gospel and should not be together? Maybe they do have different starting points and different stories. Those in the middle want to find out.

WHO THIS BOOK IS FOR

This book is written for those who are caught in between. They are unhappy with the present state of the evangelical church but are not sure where to turn for an answer. They like some of what the emerging and traditional camps offer, but they are not completely at ease with either. The public conflict makes this anxiety worse, and these people don't know who to trust or believe. What if both are off target? Is there a third option, a via media? I believe there is a third way. It is what C. S. Lewis called the "Deep Church."[13] *Deep church* is a term taken from Lewis's 1952 letter to the *Church Times* in which he defended supernatural revelation against the modernist movement. He wrote, "Perhaps the trouble is that as supernaturalists, whether 'Low' or 'High' Church, thus taken together, they lack a name. May I suggest 'Deep Church'; or, if that fails in humility, Baxter's 'mere Christians'?"

Second, this book is written for those on the outside who want to understand the debate. They are new to the conversation and want to understand what all the fuss is about. They have heard of the emerging church but have no idea what the term stands for or what it is advocating. The whole conversation seems foreign and is outside their church reality. Why is this debate important? How does it affect their church world? Should it concern them? This book will explain the contours of the conversation, what the emerging church is and desires, and why it has created such a strong pushback from the traditional church.

Third, this book is written for seminarians, those who are attempting to work out their ecclesiology—their theological view of the church, its purpose, structure and goals. Seminary is a great time to test inherited beliefs, dig deeper and then slowly work out in greater depth biblical convictions about ministry. This book lays out the options, the two sides of the debate, so seminarians can get a handle on what they believe Christianity and the church is all about.

Finally, this book is for pastors who have been in the ministry for a while and have begun to question how ministry is practiced in their context. Many pastors who reach this midlife ministry crisis end up burning out and even leaving the ministry. I don't want to see this happen. Some pastors are disillusioned with aspects of evangelicalism. They are searching for pastoral models that can refire their ministry, their calling and their church. Though they may not know how to achieve it, they know they want a deep church, one that is profoundly meaningful to them and their community, and brings glory to God. This book is for them.

SUMMARY OF THE JOURNEY AHEAD

In chapter two I will define the emerging church, their protest and their plan for change, highlighting seven areas in which they are dissatisfied with the traditional church. Much of this will rub the traditionalists the wrong way; all reform movements tend to do this. The question is whether or not they are correct. In chapter three, we will examine whether their protest threatens or strengthens the unity of the church. Do they have the same story, or are they too far apart to ever work together for the kingdom? If unity is possible, what is it based on?

In chapters four through ten we will look at the seven major protests of the emerging church in greater detail. In each chapter I have chosen to focus on one author whose work has generated the most pushback or has best articulated an emerging viewpoint being addressed. Though this limits me from capturing the breadth and diversity of the emerging voices, it allows me to dig deeper, listen well and respond in a way that is more helpful to the conversation.[14] It is much harder to set up a straw man when dealing with one author's views.

We will see that in each of these seven protests the authors have a well-thought-out critique and plan for renewal. We will also listen to the traditional church and its pushback, assessing whether the critique is accurate. Then I will demonstrate the strengths and weaknesses of both groups, and move beyond them to a third way, the deep church. I will tell stories from the church I pastor, Redeemer Presbyterian Church in Newport Beach, California, and other churches like it, as examples of how to live out deep church.[15] Please note that although chapters four to ten build on each other slightly, they don't *necessarily* have to be read in order. Feel free to skip a chapter and then return to it later on or read the chapters that most interest you first. In the end, they all make up the deep church.

But before we begin this exciting journey, I want to begin with my story and why this topic is so relevant, important and meaningful to me. It's personal.

Part 1

MAPPING NEW

TERRITORY

1   THERE FROM THE START

How to Be an Insider and an
Outsider at the Same Time

In the early 1990s I was working on my Ph.D. in political philosophy at Georgetown University. I lived blocks from the university, in the basement apartment of a wealthy woman who was in her late seventies. I walked her dog twice a day for free rent. Not a bad gig for a poor graduate student. Katharine Graham, the owner of the *Washington Post*, lived two doors down. Senators were denizens of the neighborhood. Tree-lined streets, lampposts, gorgeous homes and townhouses, and picturesque parks describe Georgetown well. It was a coveted place to live. And when the leaves fell it was downright storybook.

I was sitting in the second-story apartment of my good friends Jonathan and Allyson Whittle, just a few blocks from my house. It was Halloween night, and we were observing Tom Cruise and Demi Moore as the filming of the movie *A Few Good Men* took place on the street below, which was fascinating to watch. Autumn had arrived and there was a crispness in the air. I had never been more content or happy living in a neighborhood. We sat for hours that night, talking as we watched Hollywood director Rob Reiner direct his stars on the street below. It was a fun time. We laughed a lot: the laughter reflected our deep gratitude for the community we were experiencing. My greatest memories of my two years in Georgetown are not the classes or the long days of study, which were satisfying, but the community, the fellowship we built.

After a lonely first semester, I met Jonathan and Allyson in a class on the politics of Latin America. They were graduates of Westmont College in Santa Barbara and recently married; they were both working on masters' degrees at Georgetown. We connected right away and began hanging out. They were genuine, authentic and interesting. It was the start of community. Slowly we began to meet other Christians, some grad students like us and others working on Capitol Hill. We were all hungry for a meaningful sense of belonging. The university and the city can be a lonely, overly competitive place. We started meeting together on Friday nights at Jonathan and Allyson's apartment. Within six months this informal gang had grown to about twelve people. Added to our number was an international couple from Chile. They had this wonderful cultural habit of kissing everyone on both cheeks when they said goodbye. After a while we all picked up this habit, even if the Chileans weren't there. It seemed so ancient, so biblical. But also very cosmopolitan. Our goodbyes took a lot longer.

Normally, we would gather after dinner, people trickling in throughout the evening, to talk, enjoy one another's company, discuss what we were learning in class, argue about politics and dream about the future. It was a time filled with hope, with great expectations. Although God was not always on our lips, he was never far from our minds. We were attempting to live boldly, full of conviction, making a difference—all to the glory of God.

I recall the sad June day when I had to say goodbye, my classes done, and drive my car back to California. I knew I would miss my friends; this kind of community is hard to replace. It was a once-in-a-lifetime experience where everyone is at the same stage in life, has similar needs and fears, and loves being together. At the time, I thought this is how it would be all the time. I did not realize how exceptionally hard it is to find or build this type of community.

Shortly after I returned to California, I realized something was missing. I was glad to be back in the California sun and to be near the ocean.

I had spent two years there, before Georgetown, attending Fuller Seminary in Pasadena. I fell in love with the warm weather, the foothills and the beaches. So I was glad to be back. This New England boy is right at home in California. I love summer twelve months a year, and I was thrilled to be near my girlfriend, Michelle (now my wife). But something was missing. Though we attended a thriving two-hundred-person college-graduate group at our church, it seemed superficial. The teaching was solid, but the community weak. We would come together on Sunday and maybe on Wednesday night, but the conversation never got too deep. It was more about having fun for most people.

The more I related my experiences in D.C., the more Michelle and I despaired of belonging to something as powerful in Pasadena. I remember hearing radio teacher Chuck Swindoll, who pastored in Fullerton, California, describe Southern California people as "a mile wide and an inch deep." Michelle, who was a native, commented, "This is so true." So one cloudy Sunday night, the fire crackling on the gigantic hearth, we sat together eating dinner alone in my house, nestled in the hills overlooking Pasadena. We began to dream about creating deep fellowship like I had experienced at Georgetown. Or like the kind Francis Schaeffer, the Christian missionary and apologist, developed at L'Abri in Switzerland.[1] We decided we would start by inviting a few friends, mostly leaders in the college group, to my place on Sunday night. We would build a fire and light some candles, and I would explain our goal—to brush aside the superficial and develop genuine family.

So that first Sunday night, a few weeks later, I began the discussion— with trepidation. After a story about a painful incident in my life, I launched the discussion by asking what purpose suffering plays in the Christian life. Not so much why God allows hard times, but how he uses them in our lives to grow us. If God can use these experiences for good in our lives, I asked, why do we get so mad at him for allowing them to happen? Why don't we rejoice in suffering, as the epistle of James says we should? Honestly, I don't remember much more about the conversation except that for the next four hours I led a discussion that crackled with enthusiasm, authenticity and depth. My initial anxiety proved ill-founded. It was like offering bread to people who had not eaten in weeks. They devoured everything. They were hungry for meaning and for a sense of belonging. After prayer, we said goodnight, hugged (no kiss on the cheek yet) and could not wait till next Sunday. Something beautiful had been born.

The next week, our four friends brought a few more people. This pattern went on for weeks. Within two months we had close to fifty people, crammed into every available space, sitting around the raging fire, with the valley lights sparkling below. Each Sunday night I picked a topic related to Christian growth and inner change and opened with a fifteen-minute introduction that set up the problem for the night's discussion. We then spent the next three or four hours in intense conversation, trying to find a solution, attempting to make Christianity relevant to our deepest needs. I would guide the process, asking questions, steering it back when it went on tangents or someone tried to dominate. The atmosphere was electric, filled with an amazing energy, a desire to be real. It was a rare Sunday when people did not stay past midnight.

Over the next year we discovered how hungry we were for authenticity. We were tired of playing church, going through the motions. We wanted something to touch us at our deepest levels, a faith that dealt with our guilt, shame and disappointments. The more these conversations, so raw in their honesty, pointed us to the gospel—to Jesus' announcement that a new day has dawned and that we could enter his kingdom by trusting in what he had done on our behalf—the more the scales came off our eyes. For the first time we were experiencing grace. So many of us had grown up thinking Christianity was about morality and being good. It was an ideal we could never live up to; many of the group had stopped trying even though they still went to church. Some had dropped out of church, not willing to attempt the impossible anymore. We came to realize that we can live the Christian life only after our hearts have been transformed by Christ. Grace then compels us to obedience. This is grateful living. We saw people move from discouragement, a feeling of deep failure in their Christian walks, to genuine hope.

Hope, so often extinguished by the disappointments and failures of life, began to return, slowly. People were being set free. What we all discovered together was that in his death, Jesus not only destroyed the power and fear of death, but paid the price for our sins. In doing this he set us free from so many of the idols that enslave us, hold us down, keep us from experiencing the life God has for us. The effect was so great on so many people that revival is the only word that captures what was going on. Lives were changed forever. I still hear from some of the participants who say that those Sunday nights were the most meaningful time in their entire life. It was incredible.

A year after we started meeting in our house, the landlord put an end to it. He did not want the foot traffic damaging his carpet. After much agonizing, we decided to move the group onto the church campus. No one had a house big enough to contain the group. I was afraid that the institution would kill the revival. I loved our church, but at an arm's length. At one hundred years old our church, the largest in Pasadena, stood as a beacon of orthodoxy. It had much to commend and was bursting with activity and growth. But it had adopted some of the worst aspects of the megachurch movement—focusing more on programs than people, stressing morality more than Christ, employing a CEO style of leadership and having no interest in starting new churches. It had planted only one church in one hundred years. Knowing all these problems existed at the church, we reluctantly brought the ministry onto the campus with the full support of the pastoral staff. Within a few years, the group had grown to a couple hundred young adults.

INSIDER

At the time I was pastoring this vibrant group, I thought what we were doing was completely unique in the larger church world. I believed we were the only ones in the world who recognized the problems in the traditional church and were attempting something new. I did not understand that there were hundreds of young pastors who had grown up in the traditional (and pragmatic) church and were not satisfied. They were eager to try something different. They too were starting to pioneer new models of ministry centered on dialogue, authenticity, community and an outward focus. Many of these young pastors and practitioners were writing in a new journal called *re:generation quarterly*.[2] It was a clearing house for young evangelical leaders. Drew Ladner, who was part of our Friday night group in Georgetown, helped start the journal. He contacted me at the start of the journal to write something, which I did.[3]

By the mid-1990s young church planters like Dieter Zander and Tim Celek were writing books describing this new style of ministry, which was more contextualized to the culture, focused on building community and characterized by a more informal, honest style of preaching.[4] Even the worship music, influenced by the Seattle grunge scene, was edgier. Originally, this new style of ministry was called "Buster" or "Gen X." These were sociological terms applied to the generation that followed the post–World War II baby boomers. Eventually, this kind of ministry would be referred to as "emerging." (I will continue to use Gen X until my narrative reaches the year 2001, when the words *emerging* and *emergent* were coined.)

In an attempt to stay in touch with what was going on in the evangelical world, I continued to read everything that was being written about Gen X ministry. Many of the trends being discussed in these books, we were already doing in our ministry—discussion-based teaching, small groups, engaging the culture, liturgy, a return to singing hymns.

Although a few people, like Dieter Zander, planted Gen X churches from scratch, the trend was to start alternative worship services within larger churches, targeted at the Gen X generation who were unsatisfied with the worship tendencies of the boomer generation. In 1996 I teamed with Mark ("Marko") Oestreicher, who was then leading the junior high ministry and associate pastor of education at our church (and my immediate boss), to begin an alternative service. The college pastor, Kara Powell, joined the team as well. Prior to launching this new service, Marko had heard about Gen X 2.0, a conference being held at Mount Hermon Christian Conference Center, near Santa Cruz, for large churches who wanted to start a Gen X alternative service.[5]

This conference brought together some of the young Gen X pioneers like Chris Seay, Doug Pagitt, Dan Kimball and Mark Driscoll. For Driscoll, who, in his twenties, had just started a church in Seattle called Mars Hill, this was his first speaking assignment at a large conference. Mars Hill then had less than 150 attendees; today it has over eight thousand. He spoke on cultural changes and how the church needed to respond differently than it had in the past. His main point, if I recall accurately, was that the reigning worldview of the West, Enlightenment scientific rationalism, was crumbling, and a new worldview was emerging from the rubble, something called postmodernism (see chapter four). Modernism, he said, could be characterized by a great building constructed on top of science and rationalism. The modern city demonstrated power, efficiency—the conquering of nature, ignorance and poverty. But after two hundred years modernism was beginning to crumble. It no longer satisfied the deepest longings of the human spirit. In fact, it destroyed the inner life of men and women.

People in the West are now looking for other philosophies and worldviews on which to base their inner lives. For this reason spirituality, world religions and the New Age are growing in popularity. According to Driscoll, *postmodernism* is the term for life after the failure of the Enlightenment. Postmoderns are not constructing a city but building an underground community, one that undermines the foundation of modernism. It is developing a radically different environment of inclusion instead of exclusion, community in place of individualism, service instead of power. Postmodernism rejects the narrative of universal truth based on reason, proposing instead that truth is local, found in communities of meaning.

Mark called for churches to wake up to these cultural earthquakes and begin changing their ministries to reach people caught in the maelstrom. His lecture was the buzz of the conference. Many pastors had just heard of postmodernism and could not explain it well, but they resonated with Mark's talk. They may have only grasped this message on an intuitive level, but it was real to them nonetheless. "Finally," a typical conversation went, "someone is describing the world in which we live and minister." Interestingly, Mark says in his book the *Confessions of a Reformission Rev.* that this talk was so well received that it became the conference center's most requested tape of the year and launched him on a national speaking tour.[6] He joined up with other young leaders in this Gen X movement, speaking at conferences and churches around the county. He was part of a group named Terra Nova, which included Doug Pagitt, Dan Kimball and Brian McLaren, all well-known names in this movement. (The group eventually changed its name to Emergent Village.)

I enjoyed Gen X 2.0. But I felt the conference spent too much time on technique—that is, what kind of ministry would reach this new genera-tion—and not enough time on the core doctrines of Scripture that young people needed to hear to set them free. But I realized that something indeed was afoot. My generation was not satisfied with how church was presently done. I also understood that what we were doing in Twenty-Something Fellowship (the name we used when we moved to the church campus) was being done in churches all around the county. We were not unique!

In 1997, shortly after Gen X 2.0, we launched our new alternative service, The Warehouse. We had figured out the recipe for a Gen X ser-vice inside a large church and it was working. Like other similar services, we used interactive teaching, table discussions after the sermon, video clips of music and movies, and the arts. The team of four pastors shared the teaching, avoiding dependence on one personality. The music was loud and energetic, more like a rock concert than anything else.

This was a time of great learning for me. Michelle and I had been mar-ried for two years. I was working at the church half-time, running the young adult ministries, and was also teaching as an adjunct professor at Azusa Pacific University. I wrestled with whether God wanted me to be a professor or a pastor. It would be another four years before I got clarity on my calling.

As exciting as it was to be a professor and a pastor, sometimes the strain got to be too much. I recall contacting Jim Denison, one of the original members of the group at our house; he had just recently started a church in Pasadena.[7] I asked him to meet me in the pub of the old Huntington Hotel to talk. When I shared my burdens and frustrations about ministry and life, he empathized right away because he was having a tough go with his young church.

We decided to meet every Tuesday night to talk and share ministry war stories. Eventually, we invited a few more of our friends, all young pastors in the area, to join us. We dubbed ourselves "the Huntington Group" and met each week at the Huntington to eat, smoke cigars and talk practical theology. It was an amazing group of young and up-and-coming pastors. We talked about the church, the best ways to structure ministries, how to preach effectively, and how to make Christianity real in our lives and to the people we were leading. We were young and idealistic, trying to devise the perfect church, or at least one that was better than what we had known. In some ways it was like boot camp for future church planters. In fact, four of the six members have gone on to church planting.[8] The most well known, Rob Bell, is founding pastor of Mars Hill Bible Church in Grand Rapids, Michigan, and author of several bestselling books.[9]

This group was formative for two reasons. First, some of the participants are now influential voices in the emerging conversation. Second, many of the questions we had—how to connect our faith to our changing world, how to make Christianity understandable to our culture, how to build community in an individualistic world, how the church should impact the city—are being asked by the emerging church today. Much of what I will be discussing in this book first had a hearing in the Huntington Group.

People ask me if I am part of the emerging church movement. That is a tough question to answer. In many ways I have been an insider to the discussion since its inception. Many of my friends and former ministry colleagues are major players on the emerging stage. They are writing books, speaking at conferences and setting the agenda for this movement. Their questions are the same ones that I struggled with fifteen

years ago. I like the fact that others in the conversation are trying to rediscover what the church should look like, how it should impact the culture around it, what it means to be a Christian in a world moving from
modernism to postmodernism. The writers of the emerging church have
done a great job assessing the problems in the traditional church, and
many of their answers are right on target. Thus I resonate with this part
of the emerging church conversation. But at the same time, I have had
and continue to have serious qualms about some of the answers to the
questions they have raised.

OUTSIDER

As much as I feel like an insider to the conversation, I also feel at times
like an outsider because of some reservations I have with aspects of the
emerging conversation. My mentor at Fuller Seminary, President Richard Mouw, taught me to call these "Calvinist misgivings."

During my wife's first pregnancy, we would walk for about an hour
each day in one of our town's most picturesque neighborhoods. As we
walked, admiring the beautiful homes and their landscaping, we would
talk about my misgivings. By this time, I had left the staff of the church.
We had learned much from our years there and are deeply grateful for
the experience. While we were not sure of our next steps, we were sure
of the reasons why we left.

At the top of our list was generationally targeted ministry, or what
is often called life-stage ministry. The church-growth movement calls
it the "homogeneous unit principle." Both seeker churches and new
Gen X ministries had adopted this principle, which is still popular in
some emerging circles.[10] In life-stage ministry each generation has its
own pastor and targeted ministries—in effect becoming a church
within a church. This was true for our Twenty-Something Fellowship.
But we discovered that life-stage ministry segregates the church. Add
to this the creation of worship services with a musical style targeted to
a particular age group and the church is no longer what it is supposed
to be—a family with all ages worshiping together. Different groups

using the same facility is not the same thing.

Although our ministry to young adults benefited many people, we came to see myriad weaknesses in this "church within a church" model. Our Twenty-Something Fellowship did not allow us to be mentored by and receive wisdom from the older generations. Neither did we have the opportunity to influence and serve those younger than ourselves. Something was missing, and we knew it. We decided that age segregation impoverished both individuals and the community. It became too big of an issue to work around. Although the thinking on this has shifted slightly in emerging circles, there is still a pretty strong commitment to the homogeneity principle, starting churches of people who are similar ages and similar cultural and demographic backgrounds. This is often accomplished through worship music. For example, super-loud music tends to alienate older generations. Thus an intergenerational church is precluded even if the homogeneous unit principle is not formally adopted.[11]

A second misgiving was the need for roots. As evangelicals we felt rootless, cut off from much of the church. We longed to feel part of something greater than our little movement. We wanted connection to the past. We hungered to be part of the ancient church with all its depth, splendor and mystery. This meant that we needed to be attached to more than nondenominational churches.

We began to think about being attached to a denomination that provided mentoring and oversight. We knew that denominations had fallen out of favor with many in Gen X circles. We also knew that denominations are not perfect. But what was the alternative? Independent churches doing their own thing? Where was the oversight, the mentoring, the accountability? When the pastor went off the rails, who would protect the congregation? Who would protect the perfectly good pastor whom some in the congregation wanted to fire? Without oversight from a denomination, a church split was inevitable. And splits happen all the time, leaving in their wake broken pastors and disenchanted congregations. There must be something better.[12]

We also longed to be part of a denomination that could train, inspire and mentor us. As a young pastor with so much to learn, I wanted to find a denomination that took ordination seriously. Not only because pastoring is an important and vital calling, but because I needed the coaching. This aspect of mentoring was not a Gen X strength. Many voices within it seemed to be rejecting ordination, denominations and church connectionalism. At the time, it did not provide the roots we were looking for.

This desire to be connected to something bigger than ourselves not only led us to thinking about historic connection, it also got us talking about ancient worship. As much as we appreciated the attempt of Gen X worship to be culturally relevant, less performance driven and more authentic, we still had misgivings. Day and in day out, as we walked those beautiful tree-lined streets, my wife and I assessed the strengths and weaknesses of Gen X worship. We began to dream about the kind of worship service we longed for. And the more we dreamed the more we felt like outsiders to the Gen X movement.

We had misgivings about the worship of the early Gen X movement. It seemed overly contextualized. In an attempt to reach the culture around it, the worship looked too much like the world and was not countercultural enough. Gen X worship seemed like a hipper version of the boomers' seeker worship. We desired worship that had depth, the kind that comes when a service is rooted in the two-thousand-year history of Christianity. We hungered for solid food, something that would connect us to the past but change us for the future. We wanted reverence as much as joy, to experience the connection of head and heart in worship, and to be involved, not as spectators, but as full participants with others in the body of Christ in worship.

Our final misgiving was the lack of gospel centeredness that we noticed in Gen X gatherings. There was much talk of obedience, mission and the need to reach the culture, but little discussion on the centrality of the cross for forgiveness and the enabling power of grace to live for Jesus. I remember being frustrated at the Gen X 2.0 conference by how little the speakers discussed the gospel, the very power to transform people and nurture powerful incarnational community. It was about this time that I wrote an article for *re:generation quarterly*, which was my attempt to call the movement back to gospel centeredness. (See note two in this chapter.)

As my wife and I talked about our dreams, we would often wonder if this type of church would be welcomed by people now living in a postmodern context. Does anyone else long for ancient depth, mystery and gospel centeredness? I remember a conversation I had with a young college student at that time. When I told her about our desire for a church that sings hymns, recites set prayers, has Communion every week, and is intergenerational and gospel centered, she replied, "That church is going to fail. It is going to attract only *really* old people who have worshiped that way when they were younger."

DEEP CHURCH

Through many conversations with Michelle I began to feel like an outsider to Gen X ministry and what is now the emerging conversation. At the time I was not sure how to reconcile my misgivings with a movement I had so much in common with. But I knew it did not mean a return to the traditional church either. We had much in common with both but were well aware of their weaknesses. What I did not realize at the time is that the ambiguity I was feeling, caught between two models of ministry, meant that we were working out a third way, the deep church.

So one afternoon about four months after our first child was born, we went out for our walk, this time pushing a stroller. I remember the day well. It was the first week of December and the leaves were just beginning to fall.

"Now don't freak out at this idea," I said to Michelle.

"Why would I do that?" she queried.

"Because I have a pretty crazy idea of where God might be leading us, and it has not been on our radar screen of possible ideas. I think," I continued hesitantly, "God is leading us not to *find* this church we have been describing but to *start* this church."

Wow. I had said it. How crazy was that, particularly with a new mouth to feed?

But instead of reacting in horror at the thought of taking this huge spiritual and financial risk, she surprised me. "I think we should do it, and I think your passions and gifts make you suited to pull it off." And that is how it all began.

The next day I contacted the Presbyterian Church in America (PCA), a thirty-five-year-old denomination with roots that go back to the sixteenth century and beyond, to the early church fathers. I inquired about church planting. I knew from some of my seminary professors that although the PCA had lots of faults, it would be a good theological fit for me and it was aggressively starting new churches. They welcomed my efforts. Three weeks after my initial conversation with the church-plant coordinator, Michelle and I were in Atlanta for their weeklong church-planter assessment center. The goal of this intense week was to determine whether we had the gifts and ability to successfully start a church, most likely in a brand new territory with a limited number of contacts. In that intense week, along with twelve other prospective church planters and their wives, they put us through exercise after exercise to see if we had the gifts, temperament and ability to handle the overwhelming stress of starting a church. It was grueling, mentally and physically, just like starting a new church would be. They knew what they were doing. A number of candidates did not receive a passing grade. Those who passed almost always went on to successfully launch a church.

Over the next year, as we raised money, gathered a core group of people to help us, and figured out what our church's values and commitments would be, we began working out the deep church.

One conversation has stayed with me. As I talked with another pastor in our denomination, describing to him the kind of church we wanted to plant, he said matter-of-factly, "Oh, you are describing Redeemer Presbyterian Church in New York City, which was started by Tim Keller ten years earlier." Now, I had heard about Tim Keller for years and loved his preaching.[13] But I did not realize that the kind of church we wanted to create was already being modeled by his church and the churches he has helped start, which are now part of the Redeemer Movement of churches throughout the country. Over the next few months I cultivated friendships with a number of the pastors of these churches. Many sent me information, sample worship bulletins, curriculum and vision statements, all of which were invaluable as we worked out our third way in Orange County.

Seven years later, I remain an insider and an outsider to the emerging conversation. There are many areas of emerging theology and ministry with which I wholeheartedly agree. They desire many of the things I embrace, and they dislike many of the things I don't like about evangelicalism. But I also have deep misgivings about areas of their thought and practice. I am caught in between, and am comfortable with this ambiguity. It allows me to learn from both the traditional church and the emerging church as I follow a different route—the deep church.

2

DEFINING THE
EMERGING CHURCH

In January 2006, I audited a two-week intensive class at Fuller Seminary on the emerging church. Alumni can audit up to two classes a year at the seminary for continuing education purposes. The class was taught by Eddie Gibbs and Ryan Bolger, two Fuller professors who had just published *Emerging Churches: Creating Christian Community in Postmodern Cultures.*[1] They had spent five years researching the movement, and this was the first class they taught using their new research. There was a buzz in the air on the first day, like opening night of a good movie.

Halfway through the first day I got a strong sense of whiplash and déjà vu all at once. Bolger began by saying that for emerging church leaders, traditional and pragmatic churches have gotten it all wrong. These churches are no longer effective in reaching the culture. They no longer speak the language of the culture, and they don't create the kind of authentic community that attracts someone in this post-Christian environment. So I wrote in my notes, "traditional bad, seeker bad, emerging good."

Back in 1990, while a student at Fuller, I took Peter Wagner's church-growth class. Many thinkers in the traditional church whom I respected were critical of Peter Wagner and the whole concept of church growth. Writers like Michael Horton and Os Guinness were warning of the dangers of the church-growth movement, which is wedded to pragmatism and is an apology for the seeker-sensitive movement.[2] I took the class because I wanted to hear from missiologist Peter Wagner firsthand. (I believe that even when I disagree with others I can still learn from them.) And I learned many sound, biblical principles of healthy church growth and multiplication. Fundamentally, I agreed with Wagner that God cares about growing churches and that, by and large, spiritually healthy churches will increase in both grace and numbers. Yet I remained uncomfortable with some of his pragmatism regarding the seeker movement.

For example, he held up a ten-thousand-member church in Los Angeles as a positive model for church growth. He praised its success and its willingness to put church-growth principles into practice. Yet he failed to mention that it based its entire ministry on prosperity theology—the gospel of health and wealth. The fact that it had grown big did not necessarily mean it honored God. Growth does not always equal biblical faithfulness. Throughout the semester Wagner seemed to be saying that traditional churches were bad and seeker churches were good just because the latter had followed certain church-growth principles and were large. This made me nervous.

Here is my déjà vu moment. Once again I was listening to a Fuller professor (Ryan Bolger) saying that though traditional churches had failed to reach their culture, a new church movement would. Peter Wagner had said this twenty years earlier.

But I also experienced whiplash. Bolger was saying that not only were the traditional churches irrelevant; the seeker movement was as well. This surprised me. Sixteen years ago the seeker movement was being trumpeted; now it was described as a mistake. I raised my hand, rubbing the back of my neck and trying to regain my balance, and asked for an explanation of this curious phenomenon. Eddie Gibbs liked my question. In fact, he was anxious to answer it, almost as if he were a man who wanted to come clean about his past: "Our thinking," he said, "has changed over the past decade at Fuller. We no longer think the seeker movement was right. We don't see the seeker movement as relevant to this generation or future ones. Too much has changed in the culture. It has now become more postmodern. And if the church does not change along with it, the church will no longer be effective in reaching people for Christ." I respect his honesty. He was willing to admit that many of the Fuller faculty had changed their mind.

Bolger's explanation was more pragmatic than the one Gibbs gave. Bolger is less willing to say that the seeker movement was wrong. According to Bolger, "The seeker movement was what was needed for the mall culture but now a new church is needed to reach this post-consumeristic culture." I understand what he was saying. I agree with the importance of contextualization. But his response was a little too quick for me. I think he was trying to be nice, not wanting to say the church-growth movement was wrong or theologically off-track. But what makes me nervous is that his response comes close to making ministry decisions solely on pragmatic grounds—what works best at the time and nothing more. I am sure this is not what he means. I think he was just being generous. I like that about him.

As I sat through the rest of the two-week intensive class, one question consumed me. Were they saying that emerging ministry just worked better? In other words, was it all about technique, or was it rooted in a deeper theology that the church needed to reenvision or at least recapture? And if it was more than just technique or strategy, what theological convictions define the movement? This is important because if this whole conversation is about adopting new methods to reach a changing cultural environment, then the emerging dialogue is not so revolutionary. It is a conversation of contextualization, not wholesale change, which may be helpful but certainly is not something for the traditional church to get that upset about. After all, missionaries, even from traditional churches, have always held different convictions about communicating the gospel in a way that can be heard by a local culture.

But as the class carried on I got the strong impression that what Gibbs and Bolger were talking about was more than methods, though this is part of it. It has to do with seeing the church and how it relates to the world in a whole new light. It is this contention that has caused so much

controversy. When someone in the emerging church calls for the total
recalibration of the church, they are saying that the traditional church
has been wrong—that its understanding of the church is unbiblical. This
causes a stir. To understand what this recalibration means, we need to
understand more about the emerging church. We need to define it as a
movement, particularly its theology. The best way to do this is to look at
what the emerging movement is against—the things they are protesting
and the reasons why they are calling for change.

PROTESTANT MEANS PROTEST

It doesn't take long in reading the literature of the emerging church to
realize that protest is at the heart of their teaching. They are unhappy
with the evangelical church. *Stories of Emergence*, a collection of essays that
stress the emerging movement's deep dissatisfaction with the traditional
church, is the best place to see this protest on display.[3] I don't think there
is a chapter in the book where protest is not a major theme.

After class on that first day, I went home to read Gibbs and Bolger's
book. I wanted to see what their research had uncovered. Protest jumped
off the page. After hundreds of interviews Gibbs and Bolger found that
agitation was a common theme. The task of these emerging churches,
they contend, is one of "dismantling first and then . . . rebuilding." They
realize that this makes the traditional church uneasy. But, they add, the
rebuilding stage cannot be rushed. The work of undoing is essential.
"What to some may appear to be pointless complaining is part of a larger
process of dismantling ideas of church that simply are not viable in postmodern culture."[4] The emerging church even calls the church to deconstruct itself before it reconstructs itself for ministry in a postmodern
climate.

The literature of the emerging church uses words like *deconstruct*,
wholesale change, *recalibration* and *dismantle* to describe what is needed.
Brian McLaren even calls for a "rebooting" of the Christian faith to reach
a postmodern culture. Before this takes place, the church must "debug"
itself of the viruses that it picked up during modernity.

In trying to understand what needs to be debugged, I have spent hours reading emerging blogs, reading all the books I could get my hands on, and talking to my friends and former colleagues in the movement. I visited many emerging churches and have attempted to get a handle on what they most dislike with the traditional church. Doing this has helped me define, in part, the movement. Discovering what someone is *against* is not the same thing as saying what they are *for*, but it does provide a good snapshot of what they care about. And from there we can figure out what they positively envision. In an attempt to boil down all their dissatisfaction with the traditional church, I have come up with seven main categories of protest in the literature, on the blogs and in conversation. Certainly there are more than seven, but these are helpful in summarizing emerging beliefs.

My goal is to present a well-rounded picture of the emerging community's convictions. Seeing the breadth of their protest not only allows us a greater chance to learn from them but also protects us from focusing on one or two easy targets. While most critics focus on emerging views on postmodernism, the movement goes way beyond views of epistemology and hermeneutics (as important as those are) and includes opinions on preaching, culture and community. I think the seven categories I have chosen capture the breadth of emerging criticism and demonstrate their attempt to be systematic in their call for change. I like what Scot McKnight said in a recent lecture. It is a good warning for us.

> If you narrow the emerging movement to Emergent Village, and especially to the postmodernist impulse therein, you can probably dismiss this movement as a small fissure in the evangelical movement. But, *if you are serious enough to contemplate major trends in the Church today, at an international level, and if you define emerging as many of us do—in missional, or ecclesiological terms, rather than epistemological ones—then you will learn quickly enough that there is a giant elephant in the middle of the Church's living room. It is the emerging church movement and it is a definite threat to traditional evangelical ecclesiology.*[5]

If there is an elephant in the room, the traditional church needs to take it seriously. We can do this by looking at the entire argument they are making.[6]

WHAT IS THE EMERGING CHURCH PROTESTING?

1. Captivity to Enlightenment rationalism. First, the emerging authors stress that the traditional church has become captive to Enlightenment rationalism. The Enlightenment, which began in the seventeenth century, was a philosophical movement that based truth not on revelation but on natural reason. Its growing strength threatened the traditional church. In an attempt to defend the faith to the cultural despisers of the day, the church began to use the philosophical arguments of the day to support its doctrines, looking to reason, often detached from revelation, to secure itself in the world. Over time, say the emerging writers, the traditional church began to look increasingly like Enlightenment-spawned modernism; it had no way of differentiating itself, of standing apart from the worldview of the culture. The church took on the role of chaplain to modernism, mostly condoning individualism, rationalism and pragmatism, pillars of Enlightenment thought. The end result is either the social gospel of the mainline denominations or the tribalism of fundamentalism. Both extremes claimed to be biblical, but their final justification was the self-evident truth of reason and common sense. According to many in the emerging conversation, these two options keep the church from its call to be countercultural.

The traditional church's alignment with the Enlightenment, which has been discredited, invalidates its own position, according to emerging writers. Thus the emerging movement calls the church to reject modernism and embrace the postmodern project of deconstructing the Enlightenment. Though most are not hard postmodernists—that is, they still believe in revelation—they value the negative project of postmodernism: the part that dismantles rationalism. Although some in the emerging camp find value in postmodernism's positive project—the rebuilding after the deconstruction—many emerging writers look less to postmodernism for re construction and more to the biblical vision of the church as resident alien.

2. A narrow view of salvation. The emerging protest argues that the traditional church has focused too much attention on *how* an individual becomes saved and not enough on how he or she *lives* as a Christian. Putting too much focus on justification, traditionalists have not stressed the sanctification process enough. The church has been overly dependent on the way of salvation in the epistles and has not paid enough attention to Jesus' teaching on the kingdom of God in the Gospels. The critics say the good news is more than forgiveness from sins and a ticket to heaven; it is the appearance of the kingdom of God. Jesus invites people to enter it and thus live differently.

The Sermon on the Mount is a favorite biblical passage. Once people enter the kingdom, they realize they are brought into the family of God in order to be sent out. The church is called to mission, that is, sent into the world. When the stress is only on how people are saved from sin, Christianity turns into nothing more than "fire insurance" for the end of life. It does not teach how we are to live and witness in the here and now. Many emerging writers, reacting to the end-times theology of their fundamentalist past, call the church to care as much about earth as they do about heaven. This can't be done until the church rejects its narrow view of salvation and adopts a broader view, the kingdom of God, which encompasses not only salvation of individuals but God's reclamation of the whole world, including the material world.

According to Dan Kimball, "the term 'the emerging church' simply meant churches who were focusing on the mission of Jesus and thinking about the Kingdom in our emerging culture."[7] Missional churches become passionate, he contends, about seeing the gospel of Jesus communicated and lived out to emerging generations.

3. Belief before belonging. The emerging church is critical of the traditional view that a person must believe the correct theology before they are welcomed into the church. They reject using doctrine as a gatekeeper, which keeps seekers out of the church. They want an open-border mentality where people are free to come and go, ask questions, engage eternal issues, and get to know God through being part of the community. They believe that the traditional church has eclipsed the mission of the church by setting up all kinds of boundaries to keep people in and to keep other people out. They are calling for a new way of doing evangelism that includes the importance of community. For the emerging camp, belonging precedes belief.

4. *Uncontextualized worship.* Another common protest from emerging writers is that worship in the traditional church does not speak to the culture around it. Using music and traditions that are hundreds of years old, making no attempt to speak to the present culture and setting a posture that is against the world, traditional churches have become incapable of reaching the culture for God. The traditional church is not being faithful to the biblical call to worship before the nations. There simply is no way traditionalists can effectively communicate the message of Christianity to a postmodern world.

5. *Ineffective preaching.* Many emerging leaders have serious reservations about old-style preaching and are calling for new tactics of making disciples. Doug Pagitt speaks for many in the emerging church when he says that old-style preaching, or "speaching" as he calls it, is no longer an effective method of spiritual formation.[8] He observes that this old style of preaching—where the pastor is the fount of all knowledge, where rationalism trumps experience and where people are not involved in learning—has reduced spiritual formation to head knowledge. He calls for spiritual formation in which we learn from each other, in which people are changed through many different experiences and modes, in which more than knowledge is needed to change us.

6. *Weak ecclesiology.* The only way to discover a new kind of church is to reject the old ecclesiology that handcuffs the traditional church, robbing it of its biblical faithfulness and effectiveness. *Ecclesiology* is the study of how the church is structured, ordered and led. It includes officers and rules. Emerging writers have not shied away from tackling the sticky question of ecclesiology. According to some in the emerging church, the traditional church is more concerned with form than mission. It cares

more about institutional survival—protecting the growth and assets of the church—than being the sent people of God.

7. Tribalism. The traditional church is unwilling to engage the culture and be salt and light, according to the emerging critique. The new voices, often reacting against their culturally narrow fundamentalist upbringing, blame the traditional church for being sectarian, having no desire to reach people in postmodern culture, being uninterested in the biblical call to be creative in the arts and being sold out to "Christendom," a much discussed topic. This desire for power at the heart of Christendom has led, the emerging authors say, to a negative, critical stance toward the world. The church is known for what it is against more than what it is for. It has lost its ability to be countercultural, to model a different way of life and to actually create beauty.

HOW BIG IS THE TENT?

A few years ago I taught an adult education class on the emerging church. After I laid out the seven characteristics in one of my talks, the response was pretty positive. Most people in the class agreed that these were problems in the traditional church.

"So, what is so controversial about the emerging church?" someone asked. "Well," I said, "I don't think it is so much the areas of protest that are controversial as much as the solutions the emerging church is putting forward." I went on to say, "Some of their answers are controversial. But not all of them. As we look at these seven areas in more detail, we will get a better idea about what has caused such a pushback from the traditional church." But then I added,

> What makes this conversation difficult to follow is that the emerging church, while it may agree on the problems of the traditional church, is not completely unified on how to address these deficits. In other words, it does not speak with one voice. There are many different camps in the emerging movement, some closer to the traditional church in all seven categories and some far away. Adding to

the problem is that a few well-known writers are seen as speaking for the whole movement. Thus when they are condemned, most people in the traditional church assume the whole movement is suspect. In order to understand the emerging church, then, we also need to know what groups compose its constituency and how their responses differ to the seven areas of protest. Another way of asking this question is, "How big is the tent and who is under it?"

This is a hotly contested topic. In some ways it comes down to who defines *emerging*, which determines who is in and who is out (a very unemergent thing, I must add). But in reality, definitions by definition exclude. Some are in and some are out. And until we decide what the term means, it is very hard to dialogue with it in any meaningful way.

Dan Kimball, one of the first to use the word *emerging* in a book title, seems to hold a fairly big-tent view; he includes all those churches who see the call of the church as missionally engaging the changing culture around them. Dan focuses on the church's call (sent missionally into the culture) and ecclesiology (form and structure). Others think this definition is too broad.

The other day I was having coffee with Ryan Bolger and asked him to define *emerging,* and who is in and out based on it. "Do you agree," I asked, "with Dan's big-tent view? Or do you still hold to your more narrow definition that appeared in your book?" In his book *Emerging Churches,* he and Eddie Gibbs were adamant that emerging churches were small (under seventy-five), had leaderless groups and let every person have a say in worship. This not only set them apart from traditional churches but also from the larger Gen X churches that were hipper versions of seeker churches, where all the action takes place up front. Did he still exclude them from the emerging camp? His answer surprised me.

"It is about ecclesiology," he said. "I am not as concerned about denominations, particular views on postmodernism or even theology as much as I am about being a church that is missional, that cares for the poor and builds authentic community." So when I mentioned a few well-known large churches with up-front worship formats and attractive models of ministry, he nodded, as if to affirm them. Ryan was less concerned about their style of worship than their ecclesiology, hospitality and mercy ministry. He felt that these churches were making great strides in all these areas. Thus they could be called emerging.

I left our coffee time not sure if he was changing or merely expanding his definition of *emerging*. If both Dan's and Ryan's definitions are accurate, the emerging tent is fairly large. It is bigger and more encompassing than some of the early emerging voices allowed (who reduced it to small home gatherings), and it certainly is a lot bigger than most traditional voices think (who reduce it to epistemology or Emergent Village or Brian McLaren). In many people's minds, Brian McLaren is the emerging church. But Kimball and Bolger contend the movement is so much larger, encompassing a large swathe of the evangelical world.[9]

THREE MAIN GROUPS IN THE EMERGING FAMILY

While the critics of the emerging church have narrowed the emerging movement to one or two writers, those in the emerging church have a much broader tent. As I have wrestled with this, I have been helped by church planter Ed Stetzer. He lays out three broad categories or groups that he contends make up the emerging tent, regardless of the size of the church or gathering: "relevants," "reconstructionists" and "revisionists." Summarizing the three positions, he comments, "I believe that some [relevants] are taking the same Gospel in the historic form of church but seeking to make it understandable to emerging culture; some [reconstructionists] are taking the same Gospel but questioning and reconstructing much of the form of church; some [revisionists] are questioning and revising the Gospel and the church."[10] Let's look at these three camps.

Relevants. Relevants, Stetzer says, are theologically conservative evangelicals who are not as interested in reshaping theology as they are in updating worship styles, preaching technique and church leadership structures. They are often deeply committed to biblical authority and preaching, male pastoral leadership, and other values in common in evangelical circles. Relevants are "trying to make their worship, music and outreach more contextual to emerging culture." Rock Harbor Church in Costa Mesa, Mars Hill Church in Seattle and Vintage Faith Church in Santa Cruz fit this description. As different as these churches may be, in many ways they would fit nicely in the traditional camp, especially in areas of biblical inerrancy, acceptance of the Nicene Creed and the importance of the institutional church. Many in the "Young, Restless and Reformed" camp would also fit under this heading.

Reconstructionists. Reconstructionists, according to Stetzer, "typically hold to a more orthodox view of the Gospel and Scripture" but are rethinking the current form of the church and its structure. They contend that the traditional and even seeker models of the church are often unbiblical and surely irrelevant to meet the challenges of a changing culture. Often influenced by Anabaptist, Mennonite and more mainline models of the church, they are experimenting with informal, incarnational and organic church forms such as house churches and new monastic communities. They stress that the church is sent, are aggressively planting churches, call for the church to be "a resident alien," and want the form of the church to be less hierarchical and based more on a servant model. They look to the pre-Constantinian early church as their model. Reconstructionist leaders look to such people as Neil Cole, Australians Michael Frost and Alan Hirsch, and George Barna and Frank Viola for inspiration.[11]

Revisionists. Revisionists get most of the attention. According to Stetzer, they are open to questioning key evangelical doctrines on theology and culture, wondering whether these dogmas are appropriate for the postmodern world. Revisionists look to leaders from Emergent Village, particularly Brian McLaren, Tony Jones and Doug Pagitt. Revisionists, contends Stetzer, are questioning issues "like the nature of the substitutionary atonement, the reality of hell, the complementarian nature of gender, and the nature of the Gospel itself."

When most people think about the emerging conversation, the revisionists come to mind.[12] They get most of the media. Why? Some of this has to do with high-profile writers like Brian McLaren. He has written a dozen books and speaks at many emerging events. He is also very provocative, often saying things to get a rise or start the conversation. Another factor is the visibility of the revisionists' Emergent Village.[13] Many equate the emerging movement with Emergent Village. Dan Kimball recalls that at the same time that *emerging* was being used to describe the larger movement, the name "Emergent" came into existence, thus creating confusion. He says, "The term 'emergent' was first used formally on June 21, 2001, when Tony Jones, Brian McLaren and Doug Pagitt met and had a conference call with some others to come up with a name for a new network they were starting."[14] They chose the name Emergent Village. Dan stresses that the emerging church is much broader than Emergent Village. They are related but aren't identical, which is important.

The day after the name Emergent Village was chosen, Mark ("Marko") Oestreicher and Dan Kimball flew to Minneapolis to meet with Brian McLaren, Tony Jones and Doug Pagitt. During that meeting, Marko, who had just become president of Youth Specialties, formed a partnership with Emergent Village to publish books and hold events. Thus the emergentYS line was developed and the annual Emergent Convention began. Meanwhile, the term *emerging church* continued to be used, says Dan, for churches rethinking what it means to be the church in our emerging culture. Thus Emergent Village, of which Brian, Doug and Tony are the most visible writers and speakers, represents one branch, maybe the most visible, of a large growing movement. So it is wrong, as so many critics do, to reduce the whole movement to one part.

In this book, I will look mostly at authors within the reconstructionist and revisionist camps. These two camps have received the most pushback from the traditional church.[15] (The relevants have the most in common with the traditional church, at least theologically.) Influenced by Anabaptist and Mennonite sources, the reconstructionists' biggest challenge to the traditional church lies in the area of ecclesiology and community. The revisionists' epistemology, influenced by postmodernism, challenges the church's stance toward culture and its proclamation of the good news.

WHY DEFINING THE EMERGING MOVEMENT IS IMPORTANT

Someone in my church once asked me why it is so important to define the movement accurately. What can we learn from this exercise? What difference does it make to us? So, some people are unhappy with the church. What's new? I honestly can't remember my response. But here is what I would say today.

First, the emerging church is passionate about the health of the church. They have serious problems with the traditional church and want to see changes. Since they are our brothers and sisters, we have a responsibility, out of love, to take them seriously, to listen to them and to understand them accurately.

Second, protest can be good for the church. As Protestants we realize the importance of reform, which does not come without protest. We should welcome serious examination from fellow believers.

This does not mean that the emerging commitments are all correct. I think they are seriously amiss in some areas. Their protest is too sweeping. At times it borders on iconoclasm. In wholeheartedly rejecting the evangelical church—some Anabaptists reject the entire church all the way back to the time of Constantine—they sweep many great thinkers under the rug.

For example, a well-known target is Carl F. H. Henry. I may agree with them that Henry's epistemology (theory of how we know reality) was wedded to Enlightenment rationalism, but wholesale rejection misses all his great contributions to evangelicalism, particularly his call for the church to move away from anti-intellectual, world-denying fundamentalism. The evangelical church took great strides under the leadership of Carl Henry and his cohorts. I agree with Rich Mouw, a friend of the emerging church, that this iconoclasm is not fair, and if not tempered it will handicap this reform movement, potentially leading it into a new kind of sectarianism, mimicking some of the same mistakes of the past—anti-intellectualism, anti-tradition and tribalism.

Finally, in order for us to dialogue fairly, we must understand the movement, its protests and its core beliefs. Just as we do not want our views distorted, we must respectfully and fairly represent our dialogue partners' views. We reject setting up a straw man just to knock it down.

I have a bone to pick with how our disagreements take place in the evangelical world. I'll start with the traditional church. It seems that every time someone criticizes the emerging church, they pick the worst-case scenario or the most extreme statements. No traditional church thinker, says a Calvinist, wants his or her theology reduced, for example, to the burning of the heretic Servetus or to the claim that John Calvin was a theocrat and that thus all Reformed churches are sectarian and legalistic. Calvinism can't be defined by one or two unfortunate events. But what is good for the goose is good for the gander. As I read on a blog, "it seems relatively simple to ask that everyone who says, 'we are trying to reach the postmodern, emerging culture, not be saddled with every fault and criticism of every book/talk by McLaren.' "[16]

The emerging conversation is bigger than postmodernism and more expansive than even Brian McLaren. Brian would agree. As Scot McKnight says, we must define our conversation partners in a way that they would recognize. Most definitions of the emerging church would not even be recognized by them. This would include McLaren. It is wrong, cautions McKnight, to narrow emerging to emergent, emergent to Brian McLaren, Brian McLaren to postmodernity and postmodernity to denial of truth. This is a stereotype that is not fair to Brian, who is not a hard postmodernist, and the emerging conversation.[17]

The same bone can be picked with the emerging church. They too need to recognize the vast differences in the traditional church. Linking everyone in the traditional church with the worst case of fundamentalism, sectarianism, foundationalism and irrelevance is simply not fair. Doing this can be just as sectarian and divisive as the worst kind of fundamentalism.

Where does this leave us? Can the two sides come together and learn from each other? I think they can. But before this happens, both sides need to see the importance of unity. In this chapter we have seen that the

emerging church defines itself as a church in mission, pursuing the kingdom of God in the midst of a changing culture. We have also highlighted
their seven major protests of the traditional church and have begun to
illustrate the three main branches of the movement. If one thing is sure,
there are clear differences between the emerging and traditional wings
of the evangelical Protestant church. My goal is to bring out these differences, learn from both sides and forge a third way. Ultimately, my goal is
to restore unity, the kind that Jesus calls the church to in John 13 and
that Paul pleads for when he asks his readers to "stand firm in one spirit,
contending as one man for the faith of the gospel" (Philippians 1:27).

    This command to unity is not an option. It is part of the faith we are to
contend for. Thus before I move on to the seven protests, I need to make
the case that unity is vital to the kingdom and mission of Jesus. Without
it, the church's witness to the world is irreparably handicapped and
harmed. And until we see the importance of unity, we often lack the motivation to listen well and understand what our critics might be saying.

THE QUEST FOR MERE
CHRISTIANITY

Before Roberta Green and her family joined Redeemer Presbyterian Church, she had one final question. Years before, she and her husband had been part of a small Reformed denomination that was very sectarian and inward-focused. It was not a happy experience. She had also grown up in a fundamentalist church and had the scars to show for it. "Is Redeemer ecumenical or sectarian?" she asked. "Because I grew up deep in the fundamentalist world where every kind of church or believer who was not in our denomination was a heretic and needed to be shunned and I don't want to be part of a church like that again."

I had gotten to know Roberta and her family well over the preceding months, so I knew of their wide-ranging contacts with Christians of all traditions and denominations around the world. Although they had differences with these people, what they shared in common was more important, especially in the face of widespread persecution by the Muslim governments of the Middle East and Africa. They rallied around orthodoxy, a belief in the historic creeds and deep passion for Jesus. This family was also passionate about John Calvin, his world- and life-view, and the ancient church fathers like Ambrose, Augustine and Athanasius. They had spent weeks traveling through Egypt and Turkey in search of ancient Christianity and the early church fathers. So when she used the word *ecumenical*, I knew what she meant. It was not the old ecumenism of dying liberalism but the new ecumenism, or what Tom Oden calls the surprising "rebirth of orthodoxy" around the world.[1]

Before responding to her, I asked her a question: "Can Redeemer Church remain faithful to its theological traditions rooted in the history of the early church and Reformation and at the same time remain passionately committed to unity with all genuine believers?" Roberta responded, "Absolutely." "Then," I said, "I think Redeemer will be a good fit for your family." A short while later they became members.

A few months later my wife and I were invited to a dinner party at Roberta's home. It is not uncommon for the Greens to host a party of ten or twelve, usually around a special guest or a wonderful topic. Delicious food and great wine combined with stimulating conversation make for a wonderful evening. Their guests have included people from Cambridge, Copenhagen, Cairo, Charlottesville, Rome, Moscow and Washington, D.C., to name just a few. On this occasion, the honored guest was theologian and prolific author Tom Oden. A few weeks before the dinner I ordered his book *The Rebirth of Orthodoxy*. Having not read any of his books, I wanted to be able to add to the conversation. I did not realize how groundbreaking this book is. It deeply challenged me and opened my eyes to a reality I did not know existed.

In the previous chapter I argue that no real dialogue or learning can take place between the traditional and emerging churches without them listening to and fairly representing each other. What is missing from the dialogue, what would help us move from accusation to mutual learning, from innuendo to honesty, is trust. Trust is confidence that the other person's intentions are good and that we have no reason to be protective or careful around them. When one party feels disrespected or feels that their ideas have been summarily dismissed, trust is broken and communication is disrupted. Both sides are locked in a cycle of distrust and self-protection. Isn't this what has happened between the emerging and traditional sides? And doesn't this harm the witness of the church (John 13:33-35)?

Of course, many traditional churches aren't seeking unity with the emerging church, which, after all, is theologically liberal in their eyes. A serious charge, no doubt. If they are theologically liberal, that is, they reject the rebirth of orthodoxy, then ecclesial unity may be neither possible nor desirable. I hope this is obvious. If someone denies the deity of Christ or the incarnation, for example, unity would not be possible. Nevertheless, on a personal level, love, civility and kindness would still guide us. Dialogue is always a good thing even with those outside the bounds of orthodoxy.[2]

But what if the emerging church is *not* theologically liberal? What if those within it are nonetheless distrusted and made to feel as if they are the enemy? They would feel insecure, on guard and threatened when talking with traditionalists. They might even return the favor by dismissing the traditional church. This makes real dialogue nearly impossible. When each side distrusts the other, we have a divided evangelical church.

UNITY

Is there a way forward? How do we get to the point where both sides can talk about their differences and learn from each other without being accused of heresy? By first agreeing about what binds Christians together. It is that simple. We have to arrive at what John Stott calls the "unity of the gospel." All unity has a doctrinal aspect. No unity is possible without boundaries of thought and belief around something. There is always a limit to what any group can tolerate without being torn apart.

In his book *Evangelical Truth*, Stott argues that the apostle Paul "begs his readers to 'stand firm in one spirit, contending as one man for the faith of the gospel' (Phil 1:27). He goes on to urge them: 'make my joy complete by being like-minded, having the same love, being one in spirit and purpose' (2:2)."[3] Stott argues that Paul is not calling for unity at any price, for example, being willing to compromise fundamental truths in order to maintain relational unity, or splitting from those who are not in total agreement on every theology point and doctrine. "It is rather unity in the gospel, in evangelical essentials, 'stand-ing . . . side by side in the struggle to advance the gospel faith' (Phil 1:27 REB)."[4] This is a commitment to both the purity of biblical teach-ing and the peace of togetherness.

The problem for evangelicals, Stott contends, is that we have a "patho-logical tendency to fragment."[5] We place doctrinal purity over unity, or we stress relational unity over sound doctrine. The reality is that Jesus wants us to be equally committed to both—the peace and purity of the church. When this is not the case, our disunity is a major hindrance to our evangel-ism and witness to the world. We fail at the "final apologetic," our love for one another.[6] If we can agree on the essential matters, the "unity of the gospel," then we have a shot at rebuilding trust and moving forward.

What Stott calls the "unity of the gospel," Tom Oden calls the "new ecumenism." This "new ecumenism is above all committed unapologeti-cally to ancient ecumenical teaching."[7] It is committed to God's Word, "a long-term view of a cumulative, historical consensus, and a classic ecumenical view of God the Father, God the Son, and God the Holy Spirit."[8] It also holds, he continues, "to the classic consensual doctrines of incarnation, atonement and resurrection, and the return of the Lord."[9] As Oden makes clear, "These are fixed boundary stones in the ancient ecumenical tradition—stones that we are commanded not to move or attempt to refashion. In the old ecumenism . . . these classic doctrines were largely submerged under the provocative rhetoric of supposedly radical social transformation."[10]

Oden uses the word *classical* to describe his position. The word is important to what he is calling for and presents something that fur-thers my argument about trust. For Oden, classic Christianity is "most reliably defined textually by the New Testament itself," and "it is most concisely summed up in a primitive baptismal confession that was en-tirely derived from Scripture as salvation history."[11] The core of this doctrine is found in the Apostles' Creed, the Nicene Creed and the so-called Athanasian Creed, all of which have bound Christians together for centuries.

APOSTLES' CREED

I believe in God, the Father Almighty,
>	Maker of heaven and earth,
>	and in Jesus Christ, His only Son, our Lord:

Who was conceived by the Holy Ghost,
>	born of the virgin Mary,
>	suffered under Pontius Pilate,
>	was crucified, dead, and buried;

He descended into hell.

The third day He arose again from the dead;

He ascended into heaven,
>	and sitteth on the right hand of God the Father Almighty;
>	from thence he shall come to judge the quick and the dead.

I believe in the Holy Ghost;
>	the holy catholic church;
>	the communion of saints;
>	the forgiveness of sins;
>	the resurrection of the body;
>	and the life everlasting.

Amen.

NICENE CREED

I believe in one God, the Father Almighty, Maker of heaven and earth, and of all things visible and invisible.

And in one Lord Jesus Christ, the only-begotten Son of God, begotten of the Father before all worlds; God of God, Light of Light, very God of very God; begotten, not made, being of one substance with the Father, by whom all things were made.

Who, for us men and for our salvation, came down from heaven, and was incarnate by the Holy Spirit of the virgin Mary, and was made man; and was crucified also for us under Pontius Pilate; He suffered and was buried; and the third day He rose again, according to the Scriptures; and ascended into heaven, and sits on the right hand of the Father; and He shall come again, with glory, to judge the quick and the dead; whose kingdom shall have no end.

And I believe in the Holy Ghost, the Lord and Giver of Life; who proceeds from the Father and the Son; who with the Father and the Son together is worshipped and glorified; who spoke by the prophets.

And I believe one holy catholic and apostolic Church. I acknowledge one baptism for the remission of sins; and I look for the resurrection of the dead, and the life of the world to come. Amen.

ATHANASIAN CREED

Whoever wants to be saved should above all cling to the catholic faith.

Whoever does not guard it whole and inviolable will doubtless perish eternally.

Now this is the catholic faith: We worship one God in trinity and the Trinity in unity, neither confusing the persons nor dividing the divine being.

For the Father is one person, the Son is another, and the Spirit is still another.

But the deity of the Father, Son, and Holy Spirit is one, equal in glory, coeternal in majesty.

What the Father is, the Son is, and so is the Holy Spirit.

Uncreated is the Father; uncreated is the Son; uncreated is the Spirit.

The Father is infinite; the Son is infinite; the Holy Spirit is infinite.

Eternal is the Father; eternal is the Son; eternal is the Spirit: And yet there are not three eternal beings, but one who is eternal; as there are not three uncreated and unlimited beings, but one who is uncreated and unlimited.

Almighty is the Father; almighty is the Son; almighty is the Spirit: And yet there are not three almighty beings, but one who is almighty.

Thus the Father is God; the Son is God; the Holy Spirit is God: And yet there are not three gods, but one God.

Thus the Father is Lord; the Son is Lord; the Holy Spirit is Lord: And yet there are not three lords, but one Lord.

As Christian truth compels us to acknowledge each distinct person as God and Lord, so catholic religion forbids us to say that there are three gods or lords.

The Father was neither made nor created nor begotten; the Son was neither made nor created, but was alone begotten of the Father; the Spirit was neither made nor created, but is proceeding from the Father and the Son.

Thus there is one Father, not three fathers; one Son, not three sons; one Holy Spirit, not three spirits.

And in this Trinity, no one is before or after, greater or less than the other; but all three persons are in themselves, coeternal and coequal; and so we must worship the Trinity in unity and the one God in three persons.

Whoever wants to be saved should think thus about the Trinity.

It is necessary for eternal salvation that one also faithfully believe that our Lord Jesus Christ became flesh.

For this is the true faith that we believe and confess: That our Lord Jesus Christ, God's Son, is both God and man.

He is God, begotten before all worlds from the being of the Father, and he is man, born in the world from the being of his mother—existing fully as God, and fully as man with a rational soul and a human body; equal to the Father in divinity, subordinate to the Father in humanity.

Although he is God and man, he is not divided, but is one Christ.

He is united because God has taken humanity into himself; he does not transform deity into humanity.

He is completely one in the unity of his person, without confusing his natures.

For as the rational soul and body are one person, so the one Christ is God and man.

He suffered death for our salvation. He descended into hell and rose again from the dead.

He ascended into heaven and is seated at the right hand of the Father.

He will come again to judge the living and the dead.

At his coming all people shall rise bodily to give an account of their own deeds.

Those who have done good will enter eternal life, those who have done evil will enter eternal fire.

This is the catholic faith.

One cannot be saved without believing this firmly and faithfully.

In a nutshell, "Orthodoxy is nothing more or less than the ancient consensual tradition of Spirit-guided discernment of scripture."[12] Tradition is the "faithful handing down from generation to generation of scripture interpretation consensually received worldwide and cross-culturally through two millennia."[13] As patristic scholar Christopher Hall says, "The Holy Spirit has a history."[14] God has sovereignly watched over his church so his message would stand. And we can learn from and be confident in this tradition.[15]

This is where it gets exciting. Oden says that Christians whose traditions have long separated them from each other are now finding their unity in the classical consensus. Trust is being rebuilt! "How do such varied Christians find inspiration and common faith within this joint effort?" "By affirming together," says Oden, "that the texts on which Classic Christianity" rests are ecumenical and catholic in their cultural range.[16] As he concludes, "people of vastly different cultures are recognizing in these witnesses their own unity as the people of God, despite different cultural memories, foods, garments, and habits of piety."[17]

TWO TIERS

During an interview with theologian Michael Horton, I brought up a famous fundamentalist who has been quite vociferous in his attacks on the emerging church, charging it as being nothing more than neo-liberalism. When I asked Mike if he still has contact with this well-known radio personality, he said no. "He won't speak to me," said Mike. Knowing of their long-standing friendship and ongoing dialogue (and commitment to orthodoxy) my face must have registered surprise and shock. Mike responded to my shocked look with, "He accuses me of being a liberal." I broke out laughing. You have to be pretty far to the right to call Mike a liberal.

I guess in the hypercharged world of polemics and rhetoric, we feel we have the right to suspect anyone who does not hold our positions. This is especially true if we occupy a far-right or far-left position. Anyone to the right of a radical liberal or to the left of a radical conservative looks like a heretic. There is no room for even the slightest difference or change.

The two sides become ever more polarized, stuck in their polemics and rhetoric. Is there a way to move beyond this calcification?[18]

Yes, at least in part, if we agree on what binds us together. I have been helped in my thinking on this topic by Robert Greer's *Mapping Postmodernism*.[19] After covering similar ground to Oden and Stott, particularly on the early creeds, Greer posits the need to develop a two-tiered system that divides the essentials of orthodoxy from the particularities of differing traditions within the boundaries of orthodoxy. The top tier matches the creeds of the early church that have historically and universally defined orthodoxy. The bottom tier corresponds to the distinctives of each individual church body.

This two-tiered system has a number of practical benefits. First, it minimizes, says Greer, triumphalism or denominational chauvinism. When the top tier is agreed upon, the various parties mutually trust and respect each other as orthodox. Then discussions that deal with bottom-tier teachings become opportunities to learn and grow, and not tests of orthodoxy. As Greer aptly says:

> A two-tiered system reflects the phenomenon of family resemblances within the Christian faith. The top tier establishes the overall family resemblance. The bottom tier makes room for different looks within the family. This sense of unity *plus* diversity offers the church an opportunity to love one another, as Christ prayed in his high priestly prayer, and thereby be an effective witness to an unbelieving world (John 17:20-23).[20]

As I was working on this chapter I contacted Scot McKnight, who is a professor of religious studies at North Park University in Chicago. Scot, who is in his fifties, has attached himself to the emerging conversation as a supportive older brother. His blog continues to be the most visited blog in the emerging world. As an older brother, he is also not beyond exhorting his younger brothers when they need it, but never as a Pharisee.

"Scot," I said, "I am working on a 'third way' book that learns from both the traditional and emerging voices and yet transcends both sides, providing an alternate choice called the deep church." He was excited, having already committed to a "third way."[21] Scot said, "Whether you agree or not with Brian McLaren's book *A Generous Orthodoxy*, what it proves is that there is a huge contingent of people who are looking for a third way."

"What bothers me," he candidly added, "is that the argument has become so polarized—with the neo-fundamentalists on one side and the neo-liberals on the other. Neither side is talking to the other, save for the snipping that takes place at their respective conferences." And unless we find the common ground, this polarization will get worse. The church as a whole suffers. Our witness is compromised.

Of course, Scot is on target. The level of distrust runs pretty deep. I could not help but think that this is where Greer's two-tiered system is helpful. It identifies the common ground—classic/orthodox Christianity—which is the starting point for unity and discussion. This new consensus not only can begin to rebuild the trust but will also prophetically call those on the extremes to acknowledge this consensus.

For example, many in the traditional church fear that the emerging voices are theologically liberal, that is, they deny the core doctrines of the faith. Well, this may be true of some. McKnight fears that a few in the emerging church are moving in this direction.[22] But how do we know whether they remain orthodox? The two tiers are helpful. Does a particular thinker affirm the classical, orthodox consensus, the top tier? These certainly can be talked about and examined. But they must not be fundamentally tampered with. Any who affirm this are orthodox—even if they hold different views on the bottom tier. However, if they are unwilling to affirm that these core doctrines are based on Scripture and have been and are accepted "everywhere, always, and by all," then they are not part of the new ecumenism.[23]

Just as the traditional church fears the emerging church, the emerging church is put off by the dark side of traditionalism and fundamentalism. At the heart of this dark side is a triumphal belief that it is correct on all matters of doctrine and practice. There are few signs of what Rich Mouw calls "cognitive modesty," the belief that beyond the classical consensus there are widespread differences within orthodoxy that need to be respected. Instead, the legacy of the traditional church is, "If the Bible says it, I believe it, and that settles it." Relationships are then pushed to the side.

From the emerging perspective, the traditional view posits a particular theological conclusion that is absolute, reflecting God's perspective on theology; all competing claims are not only false but possibly heretical. Greer calls this "triumphalism" and says it leads fundamentalists to see themselves as "God's self-appointed police force, guardians of truth who perceive themselves as wearing a 'badge of divinity' upon their own theological systems."[24] And of course this overconfidence so often leads to disagreement and schism within their own theological and ecclesiastical bodies. This is what Stott means when he says evangelical Christians have a "pathological tendency to fragment."[25] The two-tier system would call the traditional church to have great confidence (the proper confidence) in the new ecumenism and deep humility in the bottom tier, what Calvin called "things indifferent."

MERE CHRISTIANITY

Is there a way beyond the present polarization? I believe there is: this new (or should I say old?) ecumenical, classical consensus. In the preface to his *Mere Christianity*, C. S. Lewis, the patron saint of evangelicals, says, "I have thought that the best, perhaps the only, service I could do for my unbelieving neighbors was to explain and defend the belief that has been common to nearly all Christians at all times." In words that remind us of Oden's new ecumenism, Lewis continues:

> I hope no reader will suppose that "mere" Christianity is here put forward as an alternative to the creeds of existing communions as if a man could adopt it in preference to Congregationalism or Greek Orthodoxy or anything else. It is more like a hall out of which doors open into several rooms. If I can bring anyone into that hall I

shall have done what I attempted. But it is in the rooms, not in the hall, that there are fires and chairs and meals.[26]

Of course, the "fires and chairs and meals" are Lewis's description of the second tier, the separate ecclesial traditions. And they are wonderful places to hang out. The main hall is "mere Christianity," the Great Tradition, which is common to all. This view allows Christians to agree on the essentials but cling to their differences, with humility and charity. We can put our foot down on *mere Christianity*, the classic, consensual tradition of the gospel,[27] but at the same time hold to our particular traditions as important but less certain than the first tier.

When we become more humble in our beliefs, we are willing to see that our own denominations or traditions do not have a corner on all truth, and we become more open to dialogue with other traditions. We might find that we are sometimes wrong and the different perspective will correct our error. But even where we are right, the dialogue can improve, sharpen and enliven our perspective and give nuance to our understandings.[28]

As I am writing this section of the book, I am sitting in the Four Seasons Hotel in Istanbul, Turkey, listening in as a group of journalists from around the world discuss the problem of fact and rumor. The majority of the fifty journalists are Christians, many from less economically developed parts of the world. The theme of the conference is "truth and rumor": what it means for a journalist to report the facts, the real story, in a world that is overrun by rumor, urban legend and conspiracy theory. As one Muslim speaker said, the Islamic world is awash in conspiracy theory, mostly condemning Israel and America. Though some of the theories are funny, they are taken seriously in the Middle East.

As he recounted some of the outrageous conspiracy theories, people laughed. But it was a nervous laugh, knowing that terrorist bombs had recently gone off in Turkey and that five former soldiers were watching the door. As we ate dinner that night, I was sitting at a table that included journalists from Uganda, India, Philippines, Slovenia and the United

States. They were Christians from different traditions, ranging from Anglican to Methodist to nondenominational. I was the only Presbyterian. It seemed every journalist had a story of political persecution, struggle for justice and the lack of freedom of the press in their country. They were excited to be together, and the conversation went on for hours.

Two journalists from Slovakia had their own TV show and weekly magazine. We kidded them about being celebrities. We shared the kind of laughter old friends are capable of. But we had just met. There was a bond of Christian fellowship. In the middle of the conversation I mentioned this chapter to them. I asked them, in light of the dangerous world they lived in, whether what we had in common as Christians outweighed our differences. "Without a doubt," one of them said. "On the front lines, all Christians are our brothers and sisters." I reflected on the fact that each morning of the conference this diverse group of journalists gathered for a devotional, including singing and a small sermon. It is amazing to see unity in action.

Here were Christians from around the world, with a myriad of backgrounds and traditions, joining together each morning for worship of God Most High. Differences in traditions and theological perspectives were put aside to worship. It is not that the differences don't matter, but they are not as important as our commonality—the good news of Jesus Christ. This is the rebirth of orthodoxy Tom Oden speaks of. After worshiping our Creator and Redeemer together, we got back to the business of the day, learning how to cover and combat a movement that persecutes Christians and threatens the peace and stability of the world. When it came to worship we put aside our differences. When it came to fighting a common enemy that is killing Christians, we rallied together to look for solutions.[29] There was trust in the room. These journalists clearly had each other's backs. Did it mean that differences were not discussed? No. I had multiple conversations with these journalists about not only what holds us together but also what separates us doctrinally. It was wonderful.

DEEP UNITY AT REDEEMER

These conversations got me thinking. What kind of church do I want Redeemer Church to be? What does the deep church look like in the area of unity? As I pondered this, I was reminded of an e-mail I got from another pastor in my denomination. Someone brought to his attention that our church had ethicist and theologian Vigen Guroian speak on culture and literature.[30] I will never forget the Friday night talk on Pinocchio from a Christian worldview. The audience sat entranced as this master teacher took us through the story, episode by episode, bringing it alive in a way we had never heard. Why had we not learned this in school?

This other pastor who e-mailed me wondered why we would have someone from the Orthodox tradition speak at our church. This was causing confusion in our little corner of the denomination, making it hard for pastors like him, he said, to explain to people what our denomination stands for. In his eyes, our churches don't host Orthodox thinkers who don't hold the same views as we do. By having Guroian speak, we were endorsing, in this pastor's eyes, faulty theology. He described our church as being less than Reformed and Presbyterian.

I didn't respond to the e-mail. But if I had, I would have explained to him that Vigen came to speak on culture, not Eastern Orthodox theology. But even if he had come to enlighten us on Orthodoxy, that would have been fine. We can learn from him. But this topic aside, Redeemer Church stands squarely and proudly on our tradition and heritage. We are not ashamed of our tradition; we embrace it and practice it. But at the same time we desire and promote the broader unity of the church. We hold strongly to the classical consensus, finding our unity with Vigen and others in the "unity of the gospel" as articulated in the creeds of the first four centuries. This allows us to be very open and charitable to fellow believers who hold different bottom-tier views than we do.[31]

How does Redeemer hold faithfully to the tension of plurality and particularity, that is, being deeply rooted in a historic tradition and at the same time open to dialogue with our differences? Let me give some examples. First, we root our congregation each week in historic liturgy that draws from the best of Christian history. Our sermons and our weekly school of discipleship are rooted in a commitment to teach the full counsel of God in a way that is culturally relevant, timely and informed by the Reformed tradition. We teach the Bible. But our understanding of the Bible has been wonderfully shaped by the tradition we are part of.

But we also celebrate our commonality with other Christians. For example, there is no "safe" book list at Redeemer. We allow and encourage our people to read widely from the other traditions of Christianity. Our book table contains—right alongside Luther, Calvin and the Puritan divines—Miroslav Volf, Vigen Guroian, N. T. Wright, Glen Stassen and Dallas Willard. All of them affirm the classical consensus even though our bottom-tier views differ. We train our members to read discerningly, to think for themselves and to be enriched by other traditions even as they dig deep in the soil of their own tradition.

Second, we don't merely *preach* deep church distinctives; we *practice* them. In other words, we spend our time and energy joyfully living in our Christian commitments; we don't spend a lot of time pointing out our differences from other denominations, churches or Christians. We don't want to be defined by what we are against but what we are for.

Third, we watch our attitude. Sinful attitudes divide Christians. As my former professor John Frame says, "Because we want glory for ourselves, we seek to find fault in others. Contentious people are constantly looking for something to argue about, some way to start controversy and disrupt the peace."[32] Though we strive to be discerning, we don't dwell on the faults of other traditions or Christian thinkers. Even when we disagree with others, we try to find their strengths and don't blow their weaknesses out of proportion to make our case. This is divisive. We give others the benefit of the doubt, reading them in the best possible light to preserve unity and foster mutual dialogue in order to learn from and exhort one another. Agreeing with Frame, we eschew harshness, jealousy, snobbery, party spirit, bitterness and lack of openness—all enemies of unity.

Fourth, we watch our assumptions. We reject the temptation to think that nothing can be learned from those outside our tradition. We don't believe that God has only given his wisdom to us, a small segment of the Christian church. This does not mean we lack confidence in our tradition, but we are humble in what we believe and are willing to learn from others. We reject the idea that our tradition's distinctives are more important than the doctrines and practices we share with other traditions. We agree with Frame that the most important things are those that are most broadly confessed across denominational and theological traditions.

Fifth, we have a low bar for membership. We don't require a member to subscribe to anything that is outside the bounds of Nicene Christianity and other evangelical churches. Prospective members don't need to agree with every aspect of our theology. We rally around the unity of the gospel, and tolerate differences, particularly on matters like eschatology, baptism and covenant theology, even as we look to teach, deepen and mature our people, growing them in the Scriptures and in appreciation for our historic creeds and confessions.

Sixth, we recognize that growth takes time. Each believer or new convert comes to us at a different stage of growth. Even church leaders, me included, have some growing to do. Growth is a process; we can't expect members to be spiritually mature from the start. Certainly, God calls us to guard all his truth, "once for all entrusted to the saints" (Jude 3). But there are some areas where the church has to admit it does not know everything. We are not infallible and neither is our tradition. This is why differences remain among Christians. We accept this reality, working together to grow in our understanding and maturity. We need to be patient with people and hope they are patient with us. At Redeemer we try to cultivate patience. This creates a safe environment to learn and grow. And we have seen tremendous growth in knowledge and grace among our people.

My dream is that this kind of unity would take place between the traditional and emerging churches. I hope that both sides would work hard to understand each other, finding agreement on classic orthodoxy and striving to maintain unity even though there are second-tier differences.

In the chapters that follow I will do my best to model this quest for unity, even as differences are discussed and an alternative vision is worked out. Moreover, it is my hope that the deep church I propose will be a road map for unity. Learning from traditional and emerging voices, I believe that deep church moves beyond them to a more excellent way—mere Christianity.

Part 2

PROTEST, REACTION

AND THE DEEP CHURCH

Six months before we launched Redeemer Presbyterian Church, I took part in a local conference on church planting. It was sponsored by The Ooze, an emerging church website led by Spencer Burke.[1] Most of the speakers were successful church planters in the Orange County area. In one of the breakout sessions, we were asked to discuss how we are trying to reach the culture with the gospel and if the postmodern milieu required new methods. Good questions. Contextualization is something that all church planters need to ponder. The leader of the breakout session was the twenty-two-year-old pastor of a fast-growing church plant in Fullerton, California, that was reaching people in their twenties. He began by saying that churches will never reach this generation until they become postmodern. That was new to me, but not because I didn't understand the term. Four years earlier I had completed my Ph.D. dissertation, which included a chapter on postmodernism.[2] I felt like I understood it fairly well.

So I raised my hand and asked this young church planter a question. "Are you saying the church needs to be the kind of church that can reach postmoderns, or that the church needs to become postmodern to reach this generation?" His reply surprised me. We need to *become* postmodern, he said.

This shocked me because I understood postmodernism to be synonymous with relativism.[3] So in my mind this young pastor was saying he wanted to pastor a *relativistic* church, not that he wanted to minister to those who believe in relativism. But as far as I could tell, his church was solidly evangelical and gospel centered, not postmodern. The conversation quickly moved on to other elements of contextualization like music and video. But his response stuck in my head. Had postmodernism been redefined? Had they compromised the gospel? Or was I just getting old?

I set out to understand what the young pastor meant. I discovered right away that the emerging writers were *not* using the term *postmodern* the same way that I was. The pastor must have picked up this new definition while reading a book like Brian McLaren's *The Church on the Other Side* or Tony Jones's *Postmodern Youth Ministry*.[4]

As I read their books, I realized that McLaren and Jones not only had a different understanding of postmodernism than I, but they were also more sweeping in their denunciations of the evangelical church's marriage to the Enlightenment than I was comfortable with. They took no prisoners; even the tradition that I stand in did not survive their criticism. That hurt. But I kept reading. I wanted to understand them. Like them, I too disliked Enlightenment foundationalism (an epistemological term I will define shortly). It has led to so many deformities in our culture and the church. But their solution, postmodernism, seemed to me to be part of the problem. I was intrigued. Was I misunderstanding them, or were they mistaken?

THE WAY IT USED TO BE

When I attended Fuller Seminary in the early 1990s, postmodernism was a relatively new concept. As far as I can remember, there was no class that specifically dealt with it. Even Georgetown University, which is on the cutting edge of trends, did not cover postmodernism in any of the political philosophy classes.

After my two years of course work at Georgetown, I had to choose a topic for my dissertation—a somewhat daunting task. In a panic I called my buddy David Van Heemst, who was working on the same degree at the University of Virginia in Charlottesville.

"David," I complained, "I have no idea where to begin. I need to find a topic that will keep my interest for the next three years. Can you help?"

"Jim," he countered, "after two years of studying the best in the history of political philosophy, what are the burning questions that you are still dying to find an answer for?"

After a pause, I mentioned four or five, including one on epistemology (how we know reality) and one on ethics (how individuals and people build community without killing each other). They're good political philosophy topics and also great questions for ministry and the church.

Without hesitation, he replied, "Postmodern writers are asking the same questions."

That piqued my interest. I wanted to know more.

So, I jumped into my research. I read everything I could get my hands on regarding postmodernism, both secular and Christian. I learned that the vast majority of scholars, secular or Christian, were using the term *postmodern* as synonymous with radical modernity.

DEFINING MODERNISM AND POSTMODERNISM

Let's begin with a definition. Modernism, which was birthed in the seventeenth century, is a worldview that rejects transcendent truth, instead finding meaning in reason and the solitary individual. We don't understand our world from revelation but from reason. But four hundred years after it started, this worldview has led to the breakdown of morality, self and community. Reason alone did not have enough resources to sustain ethics and morality. Once the rational individual was cut off from divine revelation as the source of being and ethics, he or she did not have the resources to sustain a healthy sense of self or participate in community. The individual stood alone, rootless, apart from tradition and community. This has led to the breakdown of community, which requires stable, mature participants who are capable of giving to others. The best description of a twenty-first-century human is a person watching TV alone.[5]

Though modernity is bad, postmodernism is even worse, according to certain critics. In fact, most authors equated the two, calling postmodernism hypermodernism, the flip side of the coin of the Enlightenment. One author calls postmodernism radical modernism.[6] It pushes individualism to the extreme. Each individual, now cut off from the larger tradition and community, invents him- or herself anew each day.[7] Truth becomes whatever brings comfort or helps the person cope with life. Thus all truth is relative to each person. Relativism reigns, community breaks down, and ethics is thrown out the window. Postmodernism is worse than modernism because it pushes modernism to its logical conclusion. From this perspective, no matter how you shape it, postmodernism is not a good thing. As a solution to modernism, postmodernism is a cure that would kill the patient even faster.

HAS POSTMODERNISM CRACKED UP?

Having a negative view of postmodernism, I was not surprised by Chuck Colson's 2002 *BreakPoint* radio commentary "The Postmodern Crackup."[8] I am a huge fan of Colson.[9] I have read most of his books and admire what he has done in Prison Fellowship over the years.[10] I had no trouble agreeing with the broad outline of the points he made about postmodernism, even if I would have phrased it differently. How could anyone find fault with it? Yet it elicited a letter of protest from Brian McLaren.[11] He thought Colson had completely mischaracterized the issue and was unfair to many in the emerging church who appreciate postmodernism and believe it is an ally to Christianity.

What did Colson say that was so controversial to McLaren? Colson defined postmodernism, as I had done in my dissertation, as a continuation of the worst of modernism. He contended that postmodernism has led to the claims that "there is no transcendent truth," that there is "no grand metanarrative that makes sense of reality" and that "all principles are merely personal preferences." Holding these would be devastating to the church and the culture. In the end, without a divine Lawgiver, life boils down to power and who can impose their preferences on others. And in a post-9/11 world, this view is dangerous and does not enable us to make moral judgments about evil.

Is Colson right? What could McLaren possibly find wrong with Colson's analysis?

CONTINUITY VERSUS DISCONTINUITY

When I read Crystal Downing's book *How Postmodernism Serves (My) Faith*, the light went on.[12] I got it. Our view of postmodernism, she observes, depends on whether we think it is a continuation of or a clean break from the Enlightenment. I, along with Colson, saw postmodernism as a radical *continuation* of modernism, but McLaren and others in the emerging church believe it is *discontinuous* with the Enlightenment. And thus they view postmodernism in a more positive light. They see postmodernism as the end of modernism's quest to remake the world in the image of Enlightenment reason, which brought us Marxism, communism, fascism and even capitalism.

This is exactly what we see in McLaren's response to Colson. He makes it clear that he too is against moral relativism and the loss of all boundaries and truth. He too believes in transcendent truth. Unlike Colson, Brian does not see postmodernism as synonymous with Enlightenment relativism but as the solution to it. And this highlights the problem in the debate: the emerging church's understanding of postmodernism is very different from the traditional church's, which has created all kinds of confusion, distrust and animosity. To traditional thinkers *postmodern* means relativism, no truth and no morality. They don't want this philosophy coming into the church. End of story. This is the way I formerly saw it, which is why I reacted as I did to the young church planter at the conference. I could think of nothing worse.[13]

TWO SHIPS PASSING IN THE NIGHT

The more I read, the more I realized that the emerging and traditional churches did not realize how much they differ in their view of postmodernism's relation to modernism. Though they are using the same term, they are not talking about the same thing. They are like two ships passing in the night. And at the same time they are both guilty of generalizations and overexaggerating the faults of their opponents. Both are guilty of setting up a straw man.

Let me illustrate. Emerging voices tend to overstate the traditional church's captivity to the rationalism and individualism of modernism by ignoring the last hundred years of evangelical criticism of Enlightenment rationalism by thinkers such as Abraham Kuyper, C. S. Lewis, Cornelius Van Til, Herman Dooyeweerd and Nicholas Wolterstorff.[14] Long before postmodern thinkers came on the scene, these Christian thinkers have been debunking the church's captivity to science and rationalism. It concerns me that bright scholars like Stanley Grenz and John Franke, two influential thinkers for the emerging church, do not bring this up.[15] It seems the emerging church, for rhetorical purposes, uses sweeping generalizations about the traditional church that are unfair.

But the traditional church is just as guilty. By not taking the time to understand what the emerging church means by *postmodernism*, traditional thinkers jump to the conclusion that the emerging church is abandoning historic Christianity. This is certainly not true of the whole movement. And as Scot McKnight contends, many in the emerging church, including Brian McLaren, reject "hard" postmodernism. Few embrace radical relativism or deep constructivism that rejects all revelation or external authority. Fairness would dictate, contends McKnight, that the traditional writers attempt to define the emerging movement as its adherents do. Until this is done, I am afraid, the two sides will continue to talk past one another, to the detriment of the whole church.

FOUNDATIONALISM AT THE UNIVERSITY OF VIRGINIA

In December 2008, I made a trip to the University of Virginia, which was founded and designed by Thomas Jefferson in the 1820s and is one of the most beautiful universities in America. The grounds, modeled after Greek and Roman architecture, are simply stunning and inspiring. I first went to the Rotunda, which is at the heart of the original grounds, and climbed the big stairwell to the third-floor Dome Room. After admiring the dome, which Jefferson modeled after a Greek temple, I opened the brochure I had picked up at the entrance. It informed me that "Jefferson modeled the Rotunda after the Pantheon in Rome. Strongly influenced by the Enlightenment, Jefferson's guiding principles were the forces of logic and reason." This is why Jefferson placed the library in the center of the Rotunda. Unlike the Puritan-inspired schools like Harvard, Yale and Princeton, no church was at the center of Jefferson's "academical village." For over a hundred years the Rotunda served as the school's library, the center of knowledge, the university's "temple." From reason and knowledge, freedom and liberty would be sustained. This was the Enlightenment dream.

From the Rotunda I headed north. After a ten-minute walk, I arrived at University Circle. In the midst of old mansions that now house fraternities sits a fully restored house that now is the home of the Institute for Advanced Studies in Culture. I was there to interview one of its scholars, retired Yale professor Nicholas Wolterstorff, one of the foremost philosophers in the United States. He is also a committed Christian.[16]

"Was Jefferson a foundationalist?" I asked Nick. His answer surprised me.

"Yes, of course he was. But so are most evangelicals today."

I mentioned that many in the emerging church think the same thing. Foundationalism is at the heart of their protest of the traditional church. Foundationalists, says the emerging church, are held captive to the Enlightenment and modernity.

"Nick, what is foundationalism?" I asked.

He paused, choosing his words. "You know, it is like child abuse. No one wants to be called a foundationalist. It has become a term of derision. Basically it is a quest for certainty. It is an attempt to justify one's beliefs, to build them on a foundation that can't be assailed."

I thought about my days studying the Enlightenment at Georgetown. During the Thirty Years' War (1618-1648) René Descartes published *Discourse on the Method*, in which he attempted, apart from religion, to lay the philosophical foundations that could unify people across na-

tional and ethnic lines, and end the wars that had plagued Europe.
Foundationalism is the view that knowledge can be based on self-
evident truths that don't need any backing from religion or any other
external authority, that is, knowledge that has "invincible certainty."
Emerging thinkers contend that foundationalism has infected the traditional church and shaped its view of preaching, leadership, community
and church structure.

I held up Nick's book *Reason Within the Bounds of Religion*. "This is really
the reason I am here," I said. "I read this book back in graduate school.
And I reread it on the plane ride out. Though you don't name it, you seem
to be coming up with a third way. Is that right?"

"You are right, I don't name it. But it is a third way."[17]

I reminded him of a quote from the book, "on all fronts foundationalism is in bad shape. . . . It seems to me that there is nothing to do but give
it up for mortally ill and learn to live in its absence."[18] "Do you still agree
with this statement?" I asked.

"Yes, that is right," he said. "It is in bad shape."

"Are you a postfoundationalist?" I queried. He nodded his head, and
went on to say that the Enlightenment quest for certainty based on unassailable reason and science is a dead end. It cannot be pulled off. It never
has been done.

"Do you tend to agree with those in the emerging camp that there is
no 'bomb-proof' certainty?"

Nick responded, "I think that is right. Nothing is bomb proof or certain when it comes to what we know. Classical foundationalism built on
self-evident truth is not tenable."

As he said this I looked down at my notes from his book: "Our future
. . . will have to be a non-foundationalist one."[19]

"Well, if it is dead," I asked, lifting my head from my notes, "why do
you say that evangelicals are foundationalists?"

"It is dead," he said, "but even if they don't know it, they still act like
foundationalists."

HOW FOUNDATIONALISM AFFECTS THE
TRADITIONAL CHURCH

I told Nick that the emerging church would agree. They too argue that foundationalism has affected the traditional church, whether they admit it or not. I recounted a conversation I had with Tony Jones of Emergent Village. Tony calls foundationalism "bounded set" thinking. What he means by this is that bounded-set churches—in an attempt to prove the Bible is true—have utilized the tools of Enlightenment reason and science. And this reliance has led to overconfidence and a triumphalistic spirit. It is the kind of overconfidence that can lead to arrogance and a lack of humility in what we know.

I believe Tony is saying that this overconfidence, built on the quest for indubitable or bomb-proof certainty, is what turns off the emerging church the most. To them, foundationalist pastors often come across as mean and arrogant. They don't seem teachable or kind. They have all the right answers; everyone else is wrong. I think many emerging leaders have been stung by this arrogance. It shuts down conversation, learning and growing. Nick agreed this is possible.

How did the traditional church get to this place? Nick continued, "They are rightly committed to realism, that is, that there is a 'ready-made reality.' But here is the problem. They think that this view of metaphysics [theory of reality] means they are committed to a foundationalist view of knowing. It is this that makes them stiff and arrogant, triumphalistic, in the way they argue their case." This spirit has wounded many in the emerging camp, who, like Nick, are postfoundational.

"But," I asked, "does being postfoundational mean we believe that we can't know reality?" Does it commit us to the view that we are responsible for constructing reality? "In short, Nick, does this mean that we believe in 'constructivism all the way down'?"

"No," he said emphatically.

Just because we are not foundational in our theory of knowing (epistemology), does that mean we don't believe in a "ready-made reality"? As he says in *Reason Within the Bounds of Religion*, he is not denying that "there is an objective reality with a nature independent of what we all conceive and believe" or "that you and I can't attain true belief concerning objective reality." Neither is he saying that rejecting foundationalism means accepting the attitude that "anything goes."[20]

But what then about the emerging church? They are postfoundational. They accept the postmodern critique of modernity.

"Postmodernism," Nick responded, "is good when it does its negative work. But not so good when it tries to be positive, that is, find a basis for justice and human dignity."[21]

"Why is this?" I asked, making sure I understood him.

"Because postmodernity is not always committed to a ready-made reality. They often are anti-realists when it comes to the theory of being, that is, what is present, what is real."

"That is interesting," I said. "Is it possible that the emerging church is right to look to postmodernism for its critique of Enlightenment foundationalism, but may have jumped on the bandwagon too early in regard to its positive agenda, creating a theory of being to safeguard justice?"

"I think that is right," Nick said.

JUMPING ON THE POSTMODERN BANDWAGON TOO QUICKLY

Later, as I pondered what Nick said, I thought about Tony Jones. In rejecting foundationalism, which Tony believes has hurt the church with a triumphalistic and arrogant spirit, I wondered if Tony has been too quick to see the similarities between postmodernism and postfoundational Christianity, and has ignored the differences. In other words, has he jumped on board too quickly? And will this have an adverse effect on emerging church ministry?

As I thought about what Nick said, I realized that this could be seen in Tony's first book, *Postmodern Youth Ministry*. Written right out of Fuller Seminary and under the inspiration of professor Nancey Murphy,[22] Tony makes the case that postmodernism is absolutely relevant to youth ministry and the church. Right from the start he contends that postmodernism is a friend to Christianity. Postmodernism has rejected Enlightenment modernism and thus has become a foil to lingering foundationalism in the church. In the course of the book, Tony uses the postfoundational arguments we have already looked at. Recognizing how he defines *post-modernism* and its discontinuity with modernism helps us understand why he says some apparently shocking things in the book. For example, when he says "there is no Truth with a capital 'T,' " he is not saying there is no truth but that there is no truth grounded on Enlightenment foundationalism.[23]

And when Tony says "everything is relative," he is not arguing in favor of individual self-creation of truth but saying that all reality is interpretation.[24] It is shaped by the glasses we are wearing, that is, the beliefs we bring to the table, our presuppositions. Thus, "All things become matters of faith."[25] He goes on to say that "postmodernism is not the evil that some Christian thinkers make it out to be. On the contrary, many postmodern critiques of modernism should be welcomed by the church. No longer are we beholden to the scientific proof model. . . . [E]verything does not need to be explained or rationalized."[26]

When postmodernism is used negatively to critique classical foundationalism, I think Tony is right on. Postmodernism helps us see the importance of interpretation as well as the fallacy and danger of universal, totalizing reason. We have seen its destructive results in rampant individualism in the West and political ideologies like communism in the East. Epistemological certainty is not possible. Nick Wolterstorff would agree.

WHERE POSTMODERNISM FAILS

Postmodernism is not as helpful on the constructive side. Once the Enlightenment is deconstructed, what constructive tools does postmodernism provide? It is one thing to reject classical foundationalism but quite another to explain how we take our varied interpretations and build a way of life out of them. Can postmodernism help Christians not only build a healthy, transforming community but also facilitate constructive cultural contextualization? What does it say about self-identity and the formation of mature individuals? What resources does it provide for securing justice?[27] Here we move from epistemology (the theory of knowing) to metaphysics (the theory of being).

I asked Nick, "Where has the emerging church gone wrong?"

"I think they have made a similar mistake as the traditional church," he responded. "If the traditional church thinks that their theory of being commits them to a foundational epistemology, the emerging church makes the opposite mistake. They think that their postfoundationalism commits them to an anti-realism metaphysics. That we can't know reality apart from what the individual or the community comes up with. But the truth is, reality is there. I see it. You see it."

I agree. Even without divine revelation, non-Christians can see this reality, though it is not as clear for them as it is for believers who have God's Word. We have an outside authority to tell us about this reality. Calvin called this "spectacles," said Nick—glasses that bring into focus the reality that is already there.

The bottom line is that although postmodernism is open to some revelation, it cannot and does not provide an outside authority to guide life in community. Without outside revelation, how do we truly know how to construct or lead the good life? Postmodernism suggests ethics is constructed within community. In fact, Tony Jones calls his position a "relational hermeneutic" for discovering reality (hermeneutics is the theory and methodology of interpretation, especially of the Bible). Truth is discovered in community, together, with the Holy Spirit. This of course is contrasted to the "bounded set" propositionalism of fundamentalism, which is enslaved to foundationalism.

After my conversation with Nick, I realized why some aspects of emerging thought make me nervous. Even though I reject classical foundationalism, I am not comfortable adopting a relational hermeneutic. I believe that God's revelation in the Word tells us what is real and provides the authority for Christian community. We build our metaphysics on divine revelation. It gives us confidence that we substantially know "ready-made reality."

I think many in the emerging church have moved too quickly to embrace postmodernism's "constructivist" epistemology, that is, that knowledge is created and constructed by people living in community. But apart from revelation, there is nothing to hold a particular tradition, community or history accountable. There is no prophetic voice.

Apparently some in the emerging camp don't realize that there are different kinds of postfoundationalism. Some are more in line with and others are antithetical to Christianity, particularly those that are anti-realist. Anti-realism is incompatible with Christianity because it is actually hypermodernism or hard postmodernism. I am *not* saying Tony Jones or others in the emerging church have adopted anti-realism but that they are not always careful to distinguish their enthusiasm for postfoundationalism from anti-realism.

Why is this dangerous to the church? Those Christians who uncritically adopt hard postmodernism open themselves up to what James K. A. Smith calls the "correlationist model."[28] The danger is that the surrounding history, language and community, and not God's revelation, establish their worldview. In other words, faith is correlated to culture. Liberal theology has done this for years. If it is not careful, the emerging church could fall into the same trap. If it happens, says Smith, the gospel will get swallowed by culture. I worry that in their desire to contextualize the gospel to reach out to postmoderns, they will lose the gospel's counter-cultural message. Lesslie Newbigin calls this "syncretism."[29]

BEYOND FOUNDATIONALISM AND HARD POSTMODERNISM: FOUR DECLARATIONS

If it's true that the traditional church's realism is correct but not its foundationalism, and that the emerging church's postfoundational critique is on target but not its metaphysics, what is the alternative? "Splitting the two," says Nick Wolterstorff. The trick is to be neither foundationalist nor anti-realist. We can't meld an incompatible metaphysic and epistemology, which both sides have tended to do. A third way rejects classical foundationalism and hard postmodernism. This is what it means to be the deep church.

I left Nick's office and walked back to the university grounds. My head was spinning with new insights and alternative ways of looking at this debate. I sat on a bench on the north side of the Rotunda and wondered, *What does this third way mean for the deep church? How does it affect the kind of church we are—both inwardly and externally?* I came all the way to Charlottesville to look for the answer, and I think I found it.

First, I have no doubt that the deep church must be postfoundational. Following Nick's insights, I realize there is no unassailable certainty, even for believers. There is no philosophical foundation to uphold our view of knowing. But this does not mean "anything goes." Even though we realize that language always stands between us and reality, that beliefs always shape how we interpret the world, we still believe there is an objective reality outside of us, that we can have some knowledge of it and that everything is not relative to our condition or community. We can transcend our culture.[30] But we don't do it by going back to the Enlightenment and individually or corporately creating our own reality. We do it by living within the biblical story, which teaches and transforms us.

Second, the deep church believes in foundations. But the foundations are built on belief, not reason. I have learned this best from Nick. We believe in order to understand. We walk by faith in the truth of revelation rather than by indubitable foundations. We follow Augustine, the original postfoundationalist, who said, "I believe in order that I might understand." Our pursuit of truth is characterized by the "hermeneutical circle." It neither starts with knowledge that leads to faith nor with faith that leads to knowledge. How do we get into this circle? The starting point lies beyond us, with the Holy Spirit who places us inside the faith-knowledge circle. This means that we are neither objectivists nor subjectivists. We are something different. Thus we do not align the gospel too closely with the culture and become syncretistic. We steer clear of correlationism or radical constructivism, which sees community as the sole source of truth.

Third, we stand firmly in what Newbigin calls "proper confidence." We are chastened, that is, humble in what we know because of who gave this knowledge to us. We realize we are sinners, prone to see reality through our selfishness and conceit; we see clearly it is all grace. This demands humility toward nonbelievers who can't see what we see. Thus we are patient in the public square when politicians are unable to perceive what we know to be true.

Having the "proper confidence" makes us gentle with other believers who have different perspectives on the Bible and truth. Recognizing the influence of sin on us, we realize that we don't always see clearly and that our theological positions may not explain biblical truth in the fullest. We are open to learning from other traditions, believing that their perspective may be helpful to us. Reality is like a multifaceted diamond, and we tend to see only one or two facets. Therefore we need other traditions to show us more of the diamond. The deep church calls this "multiperspectivalism." We see this in the Gospels; all tell the same story from varied angles. Multiperspectivalism reduces pride, making us cognitively modest.

Finally, being postfoundational does not mean we are timid. Our confidence is not in ourselves and our wonderful ability to grasp and see reality, but in knowing that God knows all things and has chosen us to be part of his story. He has revealed the beginning and the end, and asked us to be his loyal representatives in his world. This good news takes the focus off of ourselves and our existential search for meaning—because we know the source of meaning and our identity is secure—and allows us to spend our efforts in boldly serving others for the common good.

WELLS NOT FENCES

As I sat looking up at the Rotunda, my mind drifted back to a two-day conference at Fuller Seminary in 2006 led by Michael Frost and Alan Hirsch, both Aussies who are part of the emerging church.[31] Like Tony Jones, they suggested that traditionalists belong to bounded-set churches animated by foundationalism. These churches are often arrogant and bombastic, confident in being right all the time, and they do not allow space for those who are seeking or might be at a different place on the journey. They operate with an "us versus them" mentality. Skeptics do not feel welcome.

I remember a friend telling me about his frustration with his little church. When a visitor came, which did not happen very often, members would approach the guest not to welcome them but to test their orthodoxy. They wanted to make sure the newcomer would be a good fit and not disrupt their fellowship. So, under the guise of being friendly, they subtly questioned the guest. The vast majority of guests, not surprisingly, never returned. This is a bounded-set church.

Having laid out the bounded-set church, Frost and Hirsch described the centered-set church. The first priority is not to draw a tight border to determine who is in. A centered-set church is defined by its core values, and people are not seen as either in or out but rather by their relationship to the center. In this sense, everyone is potentially part of the community. These churches are Christ-centered, according to Frost and Hirsch. Centered-set churches see the gospel as so refreshing that lovers of Christ will not stray too far from him. And outsiders will be drawn into the community like thirsty pilgrims seeking water. They illustrate this in their book *The Shaping of Things to Come:*

> In some farming communities, the farmers might build fences around their properties to keep their livestock in and the livestock of neighboring farms out. This is a bounded set. But in rural communities where farms or ranches cover an enormous geographic area, fencing the property is out of the question. In our home of Australia, ranches (called stations) are so vast that fences are superfluous. Under these conditions a farmer has to sink a bore and create a well, a precious water supply in the Outback. It is assumed that livestock, though they will stray, will never roam too far from the well, lest they die. That is a centered set. As long as there is a supply of clean water, the livestock will remain close by.[32]

This is a wonderful illustration. For traditional churches that are still wedded to foundationalism, boundaries are the key. Postfoundational centered-set churches, on the other hand, focus on the Well at the center—Christ.

But what about the churches that embrace hard postmodernism? There really are three groups—bounded-set, centered-set and relational-set (my term for those who adopt a relational hermeneutic). The third group is closest to hard postmodernism. Ed Stetzer puts them in the revisionist camp. Tony Jones says the relational hermeneutic churches discern truth in community; that is, the community, guided by the Holy Spirit, discovers truth and what the church should look like in each age and environment.[33] This hermeneutic leads to a church with fewer boundaries than the bounded set or even centered-set church.

It's my contention that the deep church is postfoundational and centered-set. We are not bounded by foundationalism on the one hand or committed to hard postmodernism on the other. We are a third way. What does this church look like in practice?

FROM CRYSTAL METH TO CHRIST

Cheryl, a young woman who is a member of our church, hit rock bottom three years ago.[34] She told me her story over breakfast at the local IHOP. Sitting in a trailer in Caliente, Nevada, three hours north of Las Vegas, strung out on crystal meth, an insidious drug, she cried out to God for help. She had not slept in ten days and was fearful someone wanted to kill her. The combination of drugs and sleep deprivation were driving her crazy, literally. If this went on much longer she would die. "I felt it in my gut," she said, pointing to her stomach. "I knew I was dying."

How did she get to this low point? It began two years earlier after she had dropped out of community college and was working full-time at Pep Boys, an automotive supply store. There, she met a guy and moved in with him. This was the beginning of her downward spiral. Her boyfriend, Sam, had severe anger problems, which caused him to lose one job after another. Each time, they moved a little farther from home, seeking the next pot of gold. Eventually they ended up living in a trailer park in this small town. "It was a dead end," she said.

One afternoon, whiling away the hours with friends, one of them brought out a pack of crystal meth. Not wanting to disappoint them and not having the inner resources to say no, she smoked the drug and was hooked. She now lived for the next high. So here she was: far from home, addicted, lonely and living with a verbally abusive boyfriend who cheated on her. She thought to herself, *How did a girl from Orange County and a good home end up in a trailer park strung out on drugs?*

"Although my mind was messed up on the drugs, I knew in my heart that this was not how it was supposed to be."

"So what did you do?" I asked.

"One day," she continued, "after not sleeping or eating well for ten days, I did something I have never really done. I prayed. I asked God to help me sleep, which would keep me alive. I said to God that if he kept me alive for the night I would leave this place."

Right after she prayed, she lay down and fell asleep for the first time in a week and a half. The next day she was still alive. She could not believe it. So she packed up all her stuff, got into her Jeep and, by the providential hand of God, was able to drum up just enough coherence to find the interstate highway back to Southern California. She left her boyfriend, the drugs and her old life behind. The date was December 7, 2006.

Three weeks later a friend, who had been attending Redeemer Presbyterian Church for a few months, invited her to church. "When I first visited, I looked terrible; the drugs had taken their toll on me physically. But right away, I recognized Redeemer as the place I needed to be. It was hopeful, good, something drew me deeper in," she said. So she came back the next week, and for the next six months! She sat, listened, sang and participated in the liturgy. She was drawn to the Well.

"What about the drugs?" I asked her. "Did you need to go through detox?"

With tears in her eyes, she said, "Redeemer was my detox."

Each week her mind got a little clearer and her heart began to soften toward the gospel. The community at Redeemer opened their arms to her, welcoming Cheryl into the church. It became a safe place for her to think, question and experience the love of God. She was given space. There were no boundaries to keep her out. She was invited in and was not condemned or judged. During that spring my associate, Steven Cooper, and I preached a sermon series on the Ten Commandments called "The Beautiful Life." The Christian life was being presented as the blessed life, the life God has designed us to live. This is the life Cheryl wanted. She was being drawn into the life of God, invited to come to the Well that is Christ.

As part of a centered-set church, the pastors of Redeemer attempt to preach and lead worship in a way that is sensitive to the seekers in our midst. Humbled by our own sin and need for the gospel, we remember what it feels like to not believe. We don't want to be bombastic or arrogant know-it-alls. We don't set up unnecessary boundaries for those who are searching for meaning. But this does not mean we are not confident about the Well in our midst. We are not hard postmoderns. Our confidence is in Christ, not ourselves. When it comes to the gospel, we are confident, even dogmatic, because the message comes from God's revelation. He has spoken to us in his Word and made the message of salvation clear. Thus we confidently proclaim the existence of the Well in our midst. Through our preaching, liturgy, weekly Lord's Supper and a community of believers united in Christ, we want to provide a cup of living water to a dying world. We want to see others drawn to the source of life.

This was Cheryl's experience. Six months after her first visit, Steven Cooper preached a sermon on hope, based on Romans 5. With tears streaming down her face she heard these words:

> Therefore, since we have been justified by faith, we have peace with God through our Lord Jesus Christ. Through him we have also obtained access by faith into this grace in which we stand, and we rejoice in hope of the glory of God. More than that, we rejoice in our sufferings, knowing that suffering produces endurance, and endurance produces character, and character produces hope, and hope does not put us to shame, because God's love has been poured into our hearts through the Holy Spirit who has been given to us.

For while we were still weak, at the right time Christ died for the ungodly. (Romans 5:1-6 ESV)

She had suffered. She had endured. She had developed character. But now through Christ she had hope. Her shame was gone. God had poured his love into her heart because she believed right then that Christ had died for her. With tears streaming down her face, she came forward for Communion, a new believer in Christ. She had found the Well. This is a centered-set church.

◆ ◆ ◆

It was now almost dark in Charlottesville, and I was getting cold. The historic street lamps had come on. I could see the Christmas lights up the hill at the president's mansion. People walked by with shopping bags in hands; undoubtedly some contained Christmas presents. I wrapped my scarf a little tighter around my neck and looked up at the Rotunda. Illuminated in a glorious light, it looked like a church. But it is a temple to reason.

I picked up the visitor brochure one more time. It says that Jefferson wanted the south part of the Lawn to be free of buildings so he could stand on the third floor of the Rotunda and see "forever." Knowledge would create freedom, liberty. It would root our sense of being. But ironically, it led not to stability and good ethics but to such chaos in the early days of the university that a professor was killed in front of the Rotunda by rowdy students. Their attempt to create their own meaning and purpose was a disaster. Foundationalism, like postmodernism, is cut out of whole cloth.

A few years after Jefferson's death, Cabell Hall was built, enclosing the view on the south side of the Lawn. Jefferson would have been deeply sad. But more space was needed for classrooms. The irony is not lost on me. Jefferson's unlimited freedom to discover reality eventually had to find some structure. His epistemology ran up against reality. There is a ready-made reality apart from what we think, what we can discover through knowledge or even community. Jefferson needed a third way. Ironically, it can be found right up the road. I had gotten what I came for. I knew I would never be the same. I was sad to leave but filled with deep hope.

Until my mid-twenties the majority of what I knew about evangelism and community was picked up from Francis Schaeffer, the American missionary to post–World War II Europe. Out of his experience he wrote a number of books on apologetics and spirituality. Over the years I have read most of them to great profit, even when I disagree with him on points. I first read Schaeffer back in college. In fact, I had the honor of hearing him speak just months before he died of cancer in 1984. I will never forget the picture of this man. With thinning hair in a ponytail, a long beard and hiking knickers, he looked like a prophet.

What made him so convincing, besides his presence and his writings, was that he had spent most of his life creating a vibrant, beautiful community, L'Abri, in Huémoz, Switzerland. As an ordained minister, Schaeffer left his successful pastorate to bring the gospel to Europe. I love how Schaeffer modeled his apologetic. Though he had no trouble striking up conversations with strangers on a train or a boat, he came to realize how important it was for people to ask their questions and do their seeking in community. Francis and his wife, Edith, were famous for their hospitality.[1] Edith, in particular, was deft at creating an environment of hospitality that welcomed the stranger.

In their early days in Switzerland the Schaeffers had no thought of starting L'Abri. But when one of their daughters started bringing university friends home to ski for the weekend, they experienced Edith's hospi-

tality and discussed philosophy and religion with Francis late into the
night. Soon these friends brought more friends. Word got out that young
people could not only experience community but also find answers to
questions at the Schaeffer's chalet. Through conversation and community, L'Abri was born. One of my great regrets in life is that I never got a
chance to live at L'Abri when Francis was alive. I am about ten years too
young to have made the pilgrimage in the sixties or seventies. I love hearing the stories, however, of my friend Os Guinness, who lived there for
eight years. He confirms what a unique community it was—a safe place
to seek, ask questions, dialogue, argue and observe what the gospel
looked like in community.

Francis and Edith have continued to inspire me over the years. I remember weeks before we launched our new church I was petrified. I was
worried that the kind of church we were attempting would never get off
the ground. I was so anxious I had trouble sleeping. Would our vision
actually work? Could we create the deep church? Would seekers come?
Would mature disciples find a home alongside those on the journey to
faith? For inspiration, I picked up Edith's book *Tapestry*, in which she
beautifully chronicles the story of L'Abri. I needed to be inspired, my
flagging spirit raised. So each afternoon when the discouragement and
the loneliness of church planting was palpable, I would read a few chapters. It was like being with a good friend. And it helped. Edith's description of L'Abri and God's faithfulness to them empowered me. It gave me
the courage to launch the church. To this day, when I get discouraged I
remember L'Abri.

DRAWN TO THE WELL

I was thinking about the Schaeffers the other day when I interviewed
Jason, a member of our church.[2] He came to Redeemer Church because
he heard it was a safe place to ask questions, to work out what he believed. I asked him to start at the beginning of his journey. His story began in San Francisco with his live-in girlfriend. She worked in the city,
he from home. Because of many hardships, he found solace in drugs.

Though his girlfriend at the time was an unbeliever, she was seeking. But Jason wasn't. He despised Christians and the church. They were too hypocritical.

One day his girlfriend stumbled upon a sermon on the Web by Tim Keller, pastor of Redeemer Presbyterian Church in New York City. She could not believe that a Christian could be thoughtful, intelligent and sincere. She listened to more Keller sermons. She finally convinced Jason to listen. He was intrigued. Here was an intelligent person who believed in Christianity. He was impressed by Keller's honesty about suffering and how the gospel speaks to this. Then one Sunday they visited City Church, a church planted by Keller's church. Immediately, they liked the people. They seemed real, authentic, not what they expected. "They were successful people but gracious at the same time," Jason commented. This shocked him. They also found the pastor's sermons challenging. For two years they attended once or twice a month. They just hung around, observing, listening, learning, asking questions. They were part of the community.

Two years later, Jason and his girlfriend broke up. Some of it was over the guilt of living in sin, he said. God was starting to work on their consciences. He moved back to Orange County. Ironically, his ex-girlfriend challenged him to find a church there. She came across our church website and told Jason he needed to attend. He began coming and was immediately drawn to the community.

"As I got to know them," Jason said, "I realized that some of them were just as messed up as me. But I found a difference. I realized that these people understood the human condition, their struggle with sin and unbelief, and were open about their suffering. They were not trying to cover things up or put a nice wrapper on the ugliness. They were refreshingly authentic." This drew him in.

I asked Jason, "Was it just that our people are a mess that appealed to you? Because I agree with you that we sure are twisted."

He laughed. "It was not just that they were messed up," he continued, "but that as people in the midst of real trouble they were still faithful. Here I was struggling with depression, addiction and loss. Some of these people wrestled with the same things but put their hope in Christ. Every time hard times hit, they were not medicating their pain with drugs and sex like I was." He was beginning to believe. He was coming closer to the Well.

BELONGING BEFORE BELIEVING

Over the past few days I have pondered this conversation and the relationship of community to belief. As we saw in chapter four, Cheryl could specify when she crossed the line into belief. She experienced it in her heart and mind and will. Her first act as a believer was to come forward for the Lord's Supper; later she became a member. But what about Jason? His move to belief seemed slower, less discernible. It happened over a number of years. But something happened nonetheless.

These two conversions reminded me of the emerging church's dialogue on the nature of conversion—how people come to faith. What do people have to believe before they belong? What is the role of doctrine? What is the role of community in bringing people to and nurturing them in the faith?

These questions lead us to the emerging church's second protest against the traditional church. Simply put, the emerging church does not like the traditional church's insistence that belief (adherence to certain doctrines) must precede belonging (being part of the community). In the emerging church's experience in the postmodern environment, people come to faith after first belonging. Thus belonging precedes becoming.

One writer who understands the conversation well is Tim Conder, who pastors Emmaus Way in Durham, North Carolina, which is a "missional Christian community."[3] Tim is a graduate of Gordon-Conwell Theological Seminary and part of the coordinating team for Emergent Village. I think Tim's views on conversion represent most camps in the emerging church.[4] In *The Church in Transition: The Journey of Existing Churches into the Emerging Culture*, Tim writes that traditional churches have placed doctrine as the guardian of the gate. While he isn't against doctrine, he does not think "doctrine and belief [should] play a dominant role in defining who is and who isn't part of our church communities." They "have become the centerpieces of community formation."[5]

Tim holds that we have set up doctrinal fences around our churches, and unless a person can subscribe, he or she is not welcome. In other words, they have reduced "conversion to doctrinal affirmation or the transfer of theological information."[6] He rejects this view because it is not biblical. Conversion can't be reduced to simplistic formulations. In fact, he concludes, the New Testament records many distinct narratives of entry, from the thief on the cross, who experienced conversion in an instant, to the "followers of Jesus [who] experience an arduous and sometimes frustrating journey to faith."[7] "The conversions of the disciples," says Tim, "parallel the typical 'postmodern conversion,' where a person first enters into a community and it's the involvement with that community that ultimately transforms the whole of his or her life."[8]

Tim believes that this bounded-set mentality has adversely affected the church's witness. Using doctrine as the gatekeeper "essentially slams shut the front door of the church in the face of spiritual seekers."[9] He calls the church to realize that in today's emerging culture "persons will join a community before affirming the beliefs of that community. In other words, emerging culture places *belonging* before *believing*."[10]

To illustrate his point Tim recalls his youth-pastor days when half his group was nonbelieving kids. He would take them all on mission trips of various sorts. In the early days of his ministry, the first question on the mission-trip application was, "Why are you a Christian, and how do you know it?" As he comments, "Note the doctrinal entry point!" Eventually, they changed the application to remove the barrier to participation. They committed themselves to full inclusivity—no child was left behind. The goal was to be sensitive to diversity but hold to a "commitment to the values of Christian mission and community." This change "helped transform these [mission] teams into dynamic communities that pursued the Christian path with a vibrant commitment to relationship, honesty, and dialogue." What he realized over the years is that "we weren't just running mission teams; we were developing a model of missional community that has become the basis for our current trajectories in community formation and ministry."[11]

I like much in Tim's description of his movement away from a bounded-set mentality. I have seen how community plays a huge role in conversion. Doctrine is misused to keep seekers out of the church. I understand the importance of creating a safe, welcoming environment for those who are asking questions and looking for answers. For some the journey to belief is a slow process that may take years. But do we ever get to the point where the seeker is challenged to repent and turn his or her life over to Christ and enter into his kingdom? Will we ever know when someone has come to faith? In other words, is there a point when the seeker moves from belonging to belief? And how does this happen?

Furthermore, when someone joins the community, are there certain things they can't do in the community? How long do we allow them to live in a way that is destructive to themselves and to others (e.g., drug use, theft and promiscuity)? What if their lifestyle starts to adversely affect the community? And what if they teach things contrary to the community's accepted standards of truth (e.g., neo-gnosticism or some strange cult)? Would this be OK? Would it be wrong to establish some boundaries to protect the community? What about Jesus' prescription for church discipline (Matthew 18:15-17)? And what role does doctrine play? Should the church preach the tough doctrines of Scripture to mature its disciples, even if it turns off some seekers? I'm not sure that reversing the order of believing and belonging will answer these questions. I am in favor of belonging, but I don't want to shortchange belief.

These are not theoretical questions for me. As a pastor I face these questions daily as I interact and dialogue with people. For example, a young lawyer I'll call Joe has been attending Redeemer for several months. He is in a long-term homosexual relationship. When Joe first visited our church, he recognized it was a safe place. He has come every week since. He was drawn to the teaching and music, and has joined a community group. When I asked Joe why he would want to be part of a church that holds the historic view on homosexuality and the Bible, he said, "Because I sense the presence of God here. It feels anointed with the Spirit." I am thrilled that Joe is attending. I have had fantastic conversations with him over lunch. My desire is that Joe will be continually drawn to the Well each week as he hears the Scriptures preached.

So simply declaring that belonging precedes belief is not always helpful. What should I say to Joe at lunch tomorrow when he asks about membership? Can he officially join the church even if he can't subscribe to our four basic requirements for membership? What about the Lord's Supper? If he can't become a member because of his lifestyle, should he participate in the Lord's Supper? How do I communicate our views? I want him to be increasingly drawn to the Well. But I want to follow my conscience on biblical matters. I struggle with what to say.

THE TRADITIONAL CHURCH PUSHES BACK

The traditional church has begun to weigh in on this discussion. In his book *Becoming Conversant with the Emerging Church*, D. A. Carson confirms that the emerging church embraces belonging before belief. But Carson thinks that the emerging church has swung too far. He does not fault them for rejecting churches who "are mightily concerned to preserve their own comfort zones, to preserve all their prized traditions (whether they are genuinely mandated by Scripture or not)."[12] But in wanting to correct a wrong view of evangelism and community, the emerging church has overlooked some key biblical themes. First, Carson says, the New Testament affirms that Christians constitute a new and distinctive community, which includes boundary markers (1 Corinthians 6:9-11). And New Testament teaching on church discipline presupposes that "in" and "out" are meaningful categories, or else excommunication, the highest sanction, would be meaningless.[13] Carson also points out that "Christians are called to make distinctions on both doctrinal (e.g., 1 John 2:22) and ethical grounds (1 John 3:14-15; Matthew 7:15-20)."[14]

Second, the New Testament emphasizes teaching and doctrine. Therefore Christianity will challenge seekers to conform to Scripture. In making the church environment welcoming and inclusive, Carson believes we tend to water down the depth of biblical teaching. He concludes that "emergent writers commonly so prioritize *belonging* that it is difficult to see how one can honor the precious responsibilities and privileges of those who have actually *become* Christians."[15] Can we stress belonging without stunting the growth of mature Christians who are already part of the community?

IS THERE A THIRD WAY?

In October 2008 Redeemer Church's pastoral team attended the Christian Community Development Association (CCDA) conference in Miami.[16] John Perkins, a son of a sharecropper, started CCDA in 1989 to support those who had moved into urban America to transform the cities.[17] While at the conference my team and I kept up a running dialogue on what it means to belong before believing. On the last night of the conference, we took a cab from our downtown hotel to South Beach for a late-night dinner and some great fellowship. Our former associate pastor, Steven Cooper, who now is a pastor at the multisite Harbor Church in downtown San Diego, came along for dinner.[18] Living and ministering in a very postmodern environment, Steven had been thinking through the same issues we had been. For two years at Redeemer he helped me think through the deep church from a biblical standpoint. I trust his views and his judgment.

I asked Steven to summarize the third way of evangelism and community from a biblical standpoint. He took the challenge and summarized his views in the course of the fifteen-minute cab ride from downtown Miami to South Beach. It was brilliant. The highlights follow.

He made the case that beyond the bounded-set and relational-set views of evangelism, there is a third way. The key, he said, is to look at the life and ministry of Jesus. "What we see," he explained, "is that each of the Synoptic Gospels can be broken up into three main parts. The first part chronicles Jesus' ministry with the disciples in Galilee and the north [Matthew 1:1–16:12; Mark 1:1–8:26; Luke 1:1–9:17]. The second part of his ministry narrates Jesus' travels with his disciples south to Jerusalem [Matthew 16:21–20:34; Mark 9:2–10:52; Luke 9:51–19:10]. And the third and final chapter of Jesus' ministry tells us of his entrance into Jerusalem and his actions there that led to his death and his eventual resurrection [Matthew 21:1 28:20; Mark 11:1–16:8; Luke 19:11–24:53]."

"Why is this relevant?" I asked.

Over the sound of Latin music from the taxi's radio, Steven said, "In the first part of Jesus' ministry, he's training the disciples so they would know exactly *who* he is. Through his teaching, his miracles, his actions, his ministry, Jesus is answering the disciples' questions about Jesus' identity. The authors tell us what he's like, what he does, what the kingdom he's bringing is like. You see all these amazing miracles that are foretastes of the kingdom. It's all designed to draw you in to see Jesus. They want to convince you that he is the Messiah, God's anointed King who can rescue the whole world. In this section Jesus is surrounded by tax collectors and sinners. They are part of his community. Like the disciples, these outsiders belong to the community. In a sense, this is the section that many in the emerging church look to to form their ideas of belonging."

So what is wrong with this? I thought to myself as I stared out the window at urban Miami.

"What is interesting," Steven pointed out with increased intensity as we barreled down the freeway toward the beach, "is that there is a gap between sections one and two of each Synoptic Gospel. Each Gospel relates the same events and conversations, which underscore the reality that these are actually the key to moving from the first section to the section. Said in another way, *Jesus would not embark on his final journey to Jerusalem until after this specific transition took place.*

"What is that transition?" Steven asked us rhetorically. Without waiting for our reply, he said, "Notice that Jesus asks the disciples the ultimate question, 'Who do you say that I am?' He is ensuring that they've figured it out. Then the Gospels specifically state that 'From that time Jesus began to show his disciples . . .' [Matthew 16:21 ESV], 'And he began to teach them . . .' [Mark 8:31 ESV], and 'he strictly charged and commanded them to tell this to no one, saying . . .' [Luke 9:21 ESV]. This major transition occurs once the disciples *finally* understand exactly who Jesus is.

"In the final section of the Gospels," Steven continued, "Jesus unveils to his disciples that he is going to have to go to Jerusalem, be rejected, suffer at the hands of men, be crucified, and then be raised again. Directly following this revelation, Jesus calls his disciples then to take up their cross and follow him. And we find that throughout the second section of these three Gospels Jesus repeats this prediction of his upcoming sufferings, death and resurrection multiple times."

"So what does this mean for a third way?" I asked. I wanted him to finish before we got to the restaurant because we were meeting friends and the conversation would change. I sensed this could be a breakthrough in my thinking. My anticipation was growing.

"The way I see it," he said, "the emerging church wants to invite people into the community, not push them to have a 'decisional conversion.' There are some positives to this. I think it's legitimate to have an unbounded set with no barriers to the church community so that non-Christians can wander in and out. But the bounded-set of the traditional church also has positives—there are reasons for pushing people to make a decision to accept certain truths in order for them to understand that they are being converted from one way of life to another." While they are in the midst of the community, they will either drink from the Well or not!

So who is right? Or is there a different way to look at belonging and believing? Steven returned to the narrative flow of the Gospel. "What we see with Jesus is that thousands of people were invited into the community of Jesus. But once they joined the community, Jesus challenged them to not just be part of the community but to commit themselves to him [John 6:26-29, 43, 53, 66]. For those who followed him because of his teaching and signs about his kingdom, Jesus challenged them to embrace his mission and its application by taking up their cross and following him. And many did. They became his disciples."

Steven drove home the point: "What we really have is *two* circles around Jesus, the Well of living water. The outer circle is the seekers, those hanging around as part of the larger community who are learning about Jesus and his message. We see this in the first part of the Gospel narrative. But at some point, Jesus calls for commitment, for belief. His disciples respond. They move closer to the Well, to the inner circle."

"That's it!" I said. Just before we exited the cab, I asked him, "Would you put this all in an e-mail to me in case I forget some of it?" He said he would be glad to. The day after we arrived home Steven e-mailed me a summary of our conversation. But he also added the story of the rich ruler in Luke 18 to clarify his points. This story helped me understand this idea of two circles. Steven wrote:

> This is an example of Jesus himself challenging someone who has joined the community. The Rich Ruler comes to Jesus, clearly *thinking* that he is in the inner circle (a true believer in Jesus and part of God's covenant family). In the conversation, Jesus demonstrates his love and concern that the Rich Ruler not be deceived about where he stands by challenging him. Jesus calls the Ruler to follow him *so that the Ruler would realize that he's not in the inner circle.*

This demonstrates that though Jesus was in favor of inviting people into the community, he also challenged them to know whether or not they were *truly* following him. This takes the insights of the traditional church (the need for boundaries) and the teaching of the emerging church (the need to belong before believing), and steps beyond them into a third way. Belonging is important. Jesus invited many into his community. This is what got him into so much trouble with the Pharisees (the original bounded-set people?). But at the same time he did not shy from the truth of the gospel and the need for his followers to repent of their idols. They had to believe in his kingdom, his kingship, and his death and resurrection. Yes, belonging is important, but we still have to believe at some point. He calls those in the outer circle to come into the inner circle, to be close to the Well.

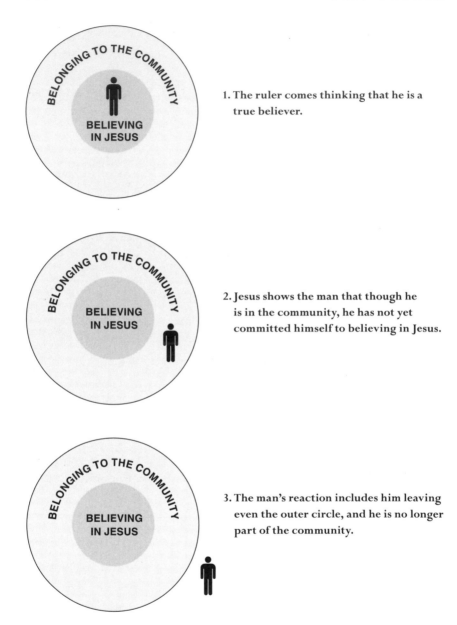

1. The ruler comes thinking that he is a true believer.

2. Jesus shows the man that though he is in the community, he has not yet committed himself to believing in Jesus.

3. The man's reaction includes him leaving even the outer circle, and he is no longer part of the community.

JASON MOVES TO THE WELL

We see this pattern working out in the life of Jason, who I mentioned earlier. For almost three years at two different churches he hung in the outer circle of the centered-set church. He learned about Jesus, his mission, his life, his power to save and the call to be part of the kingdom. He experienced Jesus' love in community with Jesus' authentic followers. As he came into contact with Jesus in the sermons and lives of other believers, he was challenged by the Word and the Spirit to decide who he believed Jesus was. The full gospel was clearly laid out before him each week in the service and small groups. Eventually, Jason stepped into the inner circle. When exactly this happened, I don't know. Neither does he. But at some point he moved from just belonging to believing. And when he did, he became a member. He made promises to the community, and we made promises to him. As he moved deeper into the inner circle, he joined the leadership team and sought training and discipleship.

What is also fascinating to me is that as he got closer to the Well— Christ—it did not keep him from welcoming others into the community. In fact, after about a year at Redeemer, Jason's life began to look different. And his family began to notice. His sister, Jane, even though a nonbeliever, was so amazed that her brother had become a nice person that she just had to check out our church.[19] Six months later she moved from belonging to belief during one of the sermons. Soon after this, Jane invited her best friend Cheryl to church (see chapter four), days after she returned from the Nevada desert. And then, if this is not amazing enough, when Jason and Jane's parents saw the change in their children, they had to come and are now members of Redeemer.

DEEP COMMUNITY

Seconds after writing the last sentence my wife called me and was in tears. Our little fearless two-year-old Meghan had been attacked by a dog. My wife had gone to vote at a polling station and had the girls with her. The dog was tied up outside, and before my wife could stop her, Meghan ran up to the dog, who knocked Meghan down and bit her face. I am still sick to my stomach as I think about it. As we were rushing to the ER, we called a member of our church, Dr. Richard Lee, one of the best plastic surgeons in California. He met us at the Hoag Hospital emergency room and closed four deep cuts on Meghan's face. We pray that the scars heal and fade over the years.

On the way home from the hospital my wife said how blessed we are to have a member of the church care for Meghan: "It was so calming to know that Richard loves Meghan and our family." I could not agree more. It was the best of community in action. My wife's comments brought me back to this chapter, which I had left just hours earlier. I thought of Steven's concentric circles. Richard and his family have been members of Redeemer since the early days. He is a leader in the church, hosts a small group, ushers and is a mature disciple. He is close to the Well.

As I drove, I thought, *I am so glad that we are committed to being a church that not only works hard at welcoming the seeker in our midst, people like Jason and Jane, but at the same time is a church of sufficient depth to disciple and feed those who have made the commitment to travel deeper in.* I am deeply thankful Richard was there to help us. As busy as he is, Richard dropped everything to come to our aid. And he did it for no charge. Why? Because he loves us, and we are part of *his* community. We are in this journey of the kingdom together.

In subsequent chapters we will look at how this depth is created. It is an important part of a centered-set, deep church. But first we will examine how people move from the outer circle to be closer to the Well. Although not all know exactly when the moment occurs, at some point a person moves from seeking to believing, even though it may take years. What engenders belief? What empowers us for discipleship? The key is understanding the gospel of the kingdom in all its fullness. This takes us to the third protest of the emerging church.

I remember the first time I heard the phrase "kingdom of God." It was not a term I grew up with in mainstream evangelicalism. For us, salvation was primarily personal—being saved from our sins and living morally for God. This consisted mostly in doing stuff for God, saving souls, supporting our foreign missions program and having our quiet times. It was about, to borrow Gordon MacDonald's phrase, "ordering your private world," which I am not against.[1] If Christianity does not affect a person on the inside, it's just one more moralistic religion.

The first time I heard that Christianity was bigger than just me and my devotional life was at Gordon College. I was sitting in the introduction to politics class and Dr. Bill Harper was talking about Abraham Kuyper, a new name to me.[2] Kuyper, he told us, was a pastor, journalist, founder of a university and the prime minister of the Netherlands from 1902 to 1905. Kuyper is an example of why Christians should care about politics and the world. When I was in college in the early 1980s, in spite of the Moral Majority and Ronald Reagan's presidency, the belief that Christians have a responsibility to be involved politically was not endorsed by all segments of the evangelical world. So Dr. Harper had to clear some ground and attempt to convince his students that Christians are called to be salt and light, and this included the public square. He told us that for Kuyper all of creation, including politics, belonged to God. In spite of the Fall, God still ruled over all of creation. He had not given up on creation and neither should we. God is in the reclamation business and is calling us to be part of it.

Over the course of the semester, I learned that Kuyper had borrowed his vision from John Calvin, who had worked out a profound understanding of God's sovereignty that affected every area of life. Because God cared about all areas of life, we should too. I had never heard this before. Up to that point in my education, I believed God was in the soul-saving business and everything else was going to burn up in the fire of judgment day. Christians were to save as many souls as possible. But Calvin and Kuyper taught that God cared not only about souls but also about his entire creation. And we were to care as well.[3]

This captured my imagination. I began seeing my college education as not only a time to develop job skills for employment but also a time to develop a Christian worldview, to begin to think about life as God thought about it—in every realm. If I was going to live my faith in the public realm, in the world, I needed to learn as much as I could about the world and how Christianity could transform all aspects of God's creation. I needed to develop the skills to help make new culture. I remember how excited I got about my studies, particularly my politics, sociology and history classes.

This desire to impact the world got a huge boost when I attended the American Studies Program, a semester-long program for Christian college students in Washington, D.C., which combined seminar learning with an internship on Capitol Hill.[4] My internship was with a think tank that focused on Central and Latin America. The seminars, which were held three days a week, were led by three professors, John Bernbaum, Jerry Herbert and Rich Gathro. Living and working on Capitol Hill for four months was thrilling. No one can walk past the lighted Capitol every night and not appreciate U.S. history. It was breathtaking.

At the first weekend retreat on the eastern shore of the Chesapeake Bay, the three professors were talking my language. They too were excited about the sovereignty of God, his kingdom rule and the implications this had for every aspect of our lives. The failure of the modern church, I remember them saying, was that it had forgotten the doctrine of creation. The church focused too much on individual salvation, evangelism and Christianity as a private affair. It's not that individual salvation isn't important. It is. But it must be balanced with Jesus' teaching on the kingdom of God. They taught us that the kingdom was a realm encompassing the area of God's creation that was living under God's reign.

Now in one sense, God reigns over all. His sovereignty is complete. But from another angle, the Bible indicates that a person, institution or part of creation who is not serving God is outside the kingdom, in the realm of darkness. When we become believers we join this reign; our goal is not only to help bring others into God's kingdom but also to help transform culture—the family, politics, the arts, the marketplace, all aspects of creation. For a twenty-one-year-old, this was a heady vision. It was cosmic, big, bold, dramatic. I could not stop talking about it.

I had finally found something big enough to base my life on. I remember returning to the Gordon campus at the end of the semester and starting a kingdom-of-God group to share this exciting news. I even managed to get Dr. Harper to help us by bringing in speakers and suggesting books for us to read. I recall thinking that I couldn't believe that this teaching had not gripped others the way it had me. I was convinced that recovering this biblical teaching would revolutionize the church and change the world. The good news had just gotten bigger for me.

THE EMERGING CHURCH AND THE KINGDOM OF GOD

Over the past ten years the emerging church has discovered this same revolutionary teaching about the kingdom of God. When I read their books I detect the same excitement I experienced twenty years ago. They are learning about God's kingdom and wondering why it is missing in the traditional church.

In fact, Brian McLaren's book *The Secret Message of Jesus* is subtitled *Uncovering the Truth That Could Change Everything*.[5] It is a much longer version of the argument he makes in *The Church on the Other Side* and *A Generous Orthodoxy*. Brian thinks Jesus' message has been lost to the church and needs to be recovered. The kingdom of God, which is critical to the church's missional call, is at the heart of this lost message.

According to Brian and others, the traditional church has emphasized individual salvation, which has led it to neglect God's creation. Thus Christianity is mere "fire insurance." The answer to this privatized faith, they say, is regaining a robust view of the kingdom of God and the church's mandate to mission.

In his writings, Brian takes an approach similar to that of my professors at the American Studies Program. He begins with individualized American Christianity. In his bestselling *Generous Orthodoxy*, Brian describes vividly why he is excited about the kingdom of God.

> Over the years a feeling grew within me, usually vague but sometimes acute, that I was missing something, perhaps something important. Jesus' cross in the past saved me from hell in the future, but it was hard to be clear on what it meant for me in the struggle in the present. And more importantly, did the gospel have anything to say about justice for the many, not just the justification of the individual? Was the gospel intended to give hope for the human cultures and the created order of history?[6]

Like me, Brian grew up in conservative evangelical circles, where the heart of Christianity was centered on individual salvation. There was not a lot of talk about the relevance of salvation for creation. Most of the focus was on the individual's growth and obedience, and mostly in the moral realm.

"The more I study the Bible," he argues, "and reflect on the life and teachings of Jesus, the more I think most of Christianity as practiced today has very little to do with the real Jesus found there." What is this real Jesus? His "wise teachings and his kind deeds."[7]

What "teaching" is Brian thinking about here? The kingdom of God. Instead of focusing on the heart of Jesus' message, some in the traditional church have turned the gospel into "an individualistic theory, an abstraction with personal but not global import."[8] Does this mean Brian does not care about the salvation of individuals? I don't believe so. In fact, he continues:

> I still believe that Jesus is vitally interested in saving me and you by individually judging us, by forgiving us our wrongs, and teaching us to live in a better way. But I fear that for too many Christians, "personal salvation" has become another personal consumer product (like personal computers, a personal journal, personal time, etc.), and Christianity has become its marketing program. If so, salvation is "all about me."[9]

The biggest problem, and I think he is right, is that churches that stress salvation as "fire insurance" (escaping from hell) "tend to become places of self-interest and purveyors of goods and services, constantly shopping and trading up for churches that can 'meet my needs' better." Brian is absolutely right when he says, "No wonder it is hard to convince these churches that they have a mission to the world."[10]

From the time of the Reformation, traditional churches, according to Brian, have so emphasized the doctrines of atonement and justification— the saving of souls from hell to the exclusion of the Bible's teaching on the kingdom of God—that the church has lost its vision for the public realm. In *The Secret Message* Brian credits Anabaptists John Howard Yoder, Stanley Hauerwas and Jim Wallis for helping him see the public side of Christianity. "Although Christianity is personal it is not private, they taught."[11] Because of Jesus' teaching on the kingdom of God, Christianity is political as well as private. "I've been convinced," Brian offers, "that [Jesus' message] has everything to do with public matters in general and politics in particular—including economics and aid, personal empowerment and choice, foreign policy and war." "The fact is," he continues, "Jesus called his message *good news*, itself a public term that evoked the political announcements of the Roman emperors."[12] Through Jesus, God was launching a new world order, a new world, a new creation. Having grown up with a Christianity that was only privately relevant, Brian was starting to see its social implications transcend individual salvation.

Through Yoder, Wallis, Hauerwas and the influence of Anglican N. T. Wright, Brian saw the kingdom of God as Jesus' central message. Jesus came to preach the good news to everyone. This gospel begins with Abraham. God not only blessed Abraham but told him that his family would be a blessing to the whole world.

According to Brian the church stresses God's blessing to Abraham, his salvation, but neglects God's promise to bless the world. The traditional church is missing half of the gospel. Brian wants the church to recover a full-orbed view of the gospel. When Christians start living out the Sermon on the Mount, both individually and in community, they bless the world around them, including nonbelievers. We are then called to rejoice that God cares for the whole world, Brian concludes, and Jesus invites us to be part of this community.

THE TRADITIONAL CHURCH PUSHES BACK

Last week, I took my two boys to see my beloved Red Sox play the Angels in Anaheim. My friend Curt Pringle is the mayor of Anaheim so we were able to sit in the city's corporate box seats, spoiling my boys forever. We took along Johnny, a young man in his twenties who is a graduate student in psychology. He too is a baseball fan. Since I am mentoring him, I wanted to get to know him better. I also wanted to ask him why he loves *The Secret Message of Jesus* so much. Johnny indicated that Brian McLaren gives him the freedom to question, explore and doubt that he didn't have in the traditional church. He said his last church practiced a faith that was highly individualistic and privatized, and did not have a vision for changing the world. Johnny resonates with Brian's description of the kingdom of God and the church's call to be missional.

In other words, for Johnny, Brian has brought balance to the Christian message, one that stresses salvation *and* service. So if I were to suggest to Johnny that the emergent conversation is rushing headlong down the path of classic liberalism, he would probably laugh. No way!

It is hard to understand how someone could disagree with Brian's contention that the church has sold out to individualism and that it needs to recapture Jesus' teaching on the kingdom of God. But then, many in the traditional church believe Brian and others in the emerging church are on a slippery slope to liberalism. They accuse the emerging church of being another brand of the social gospel movement, which has inflicted the mainline denominations over the past eighty years. Brian's concern for the kingdom of God, they contend, does not bring balance to the church but fundamentally changes the Christian message.[13] Instead of hearing a call to make Jesus Lord as well as Savior, traditionalists detect a reduction of the full message of the gospel (i.e., justification, atonement, penal substitution) to the promotion of social justice and righteousness through our own efforts.

Furthermore, traditional critics commonly complain that Brian's stress on the Sermon on the Mount and Jesus' teaching that the "kingdom of God is at hand" diminishes the importance of the cross. Many in the traditional church dismiss Brian because of his political views. This is proof that Brian is moving down the same path as the old mainline church, which toward the end of the nineteenth century began to view missions as nothing more than educational, medical and agricultural endeavors. As Darrell Guder argues, the mainline no longer linked social action to the proclamation of the gospel.[14]

Having fought theological liberalism for three generations, many in the traditional church are convinced that the emerging church's talk of the kingdom of God means it is moving to the theological left. Soon it will drop the cross and atonement altogether, and the gospel will be reduced to social action, obedience, moral living. One member of the traditional church said to me, "We are way past the point of dialogue." He meant that the emerging church has left the fold and it is time to confront their apostasy.

The traditional church doesn't believe Brian is trying to correct a tragic reduction of the gospel; they see in him and the emerging church a wholesale abandonment of the gospel. They contend that once the church loses the hard edges of the cross, which judge as well as forgive, it is a short step to going soft on hell, eternal judgment, homosexuality and other religions. Without the doctrine of atonement at the center of Christianity, the hub of the wheel, it is easy to abandon the King of the kingdom. Then the truncated church merely promotes such benefits of the kingdom as social justice, "the preferential option for the poor" and "liberation theology."[15]

BEYOND REDUCTIONISM

I have to admit that building bridges between the emerging and traditional church is hard work. There are days when I despair that neither side wants to listen to the other.[16] Both claim that they are misunderstood. Yet, ironically, both claim to understand the other side perfectly well, which is why each rejects the other's position. The distrust builds as each side argues past the other and preaches to the choir.

Is the traditional church correct in its assessment of Brian's message? Do traditionalists have a right to claim that the emerging church is nothing more than theological liberalism in new clothing? If this is true, we need to reject what Brian is teaching. If it's not true, the church is sadly mistaken and needs to heed Brian's call to reclaim Jesus' teaching on the kingdom—even if Brian's politics are not their cup of tea.

Can we learn from both sides and maybe even transcend some of each side's weaknesses? I think we can.

The way forward is to realize that each accuses the other of reducing the gospel. The traditional church argues the emerging church has reduced the gospel to social action and the emerging church contends that the traditional church has reduced the message to individual salvation. But according to Darrell Guder's book *The Continuing Conversion of the Church*, all reductions of the gospel are wrong.[17] In his brilliant chapter "The Reduction of Salvation and Mission," Guder points out that "our greatest priority, particularly in our theologies of salvation, should be to join the benefits of salvation with the responsibilities and call to the saved to enter into God's mission in the world."[18] Recognizing this truth is the first step in moving beyond the impasse.

GOSPEL MISGIVINGS

Brian McLaren clearly points out how the overemphasis on individual salvation has created a church of "goods and services." Christian people care only about their own selves, always taking their spiritual temperature, concerned only about their private souls and ignoring the rest of the church community and the world. This is gospel reductionism. But in reacting so forcefully against individualism, he and others in the emerging camp risk making the opposite mistake.

As I have closely read Brian's work, I get the sense that his critique of the traditional church's gospel reductionism has led him to downplay certain doctrines of salvation—the doctrine of atonement and more specifically the teaching of justification and penal substitution. He doesn't deny these teachings but downplays them in an unhealthy way.

As I was wrestling with this important topic in Brian's thinking, a topic that is at the heart of the deep church— being gospel-centered—I traveled to Pasadena to meet with Richard Mouw, president of Fuller Seminary. I began by saying that I appreciated Brian's emphasis on the kingdom of God, but I was also struggling with some misgivings. I thought many in the traditional church had misunderstood Brian and others in the emerging church. Most are not against atonement theories and justification but want to see it balanced with the message of the kingdom of God.[19]

Rich has taught me much about working out a third way. He has also overseen the hiring of a number of Anabaptists and emerging professors at Fuller, to the chagrin of many in his Reformed tradition. He thus surprised me with his response: "I don't think it is about balance in this case. I think it is more about priority, order." And as he so often does, he told a story.

"A few weeks ago," he began, "I was on the East Coast moderating a dialogue between Catholics and evangelicals. One participant said to me, 'I don't even bother with sin and salvation anymore when I present the gospel. I invite them into a movement in which Jesus has destroyed the principalities and powers of the world and in which he is inviting them to become a full participant.' With that story still fresh in my mind, I got into my rental car to drive back to the airport. As is my habit, I found a Christian radio station to listen to. I like to hear what people are teaching. As I listened, a man was describing his conversion. He had been mired in drugs, his wife had left him, and he was suicidal. At his lowest point he heard a preacher on the radio talking about the blood of Jesus and how the cross could wash away his sins, free him from his addictions and save his soul. Old-time gospel religion. With tears streaming down his face, he accepted Christ and was set free. His life has never been the same." Salvation, gospel transformation—but no talk about the kingdom or being invited into it.

Then Rich leaned forward and asked a question, risking the absence of balance to make his point:

> What are we missing when we no longer preach *that* kind of gospel? If we put the stress on the kingdom of God and missional living, as important as they are, will we raise up a generation who, like Wesley, can write great hymns like this?
>
>> Long my imprisoned spirit lay,
>> Fast bound in sin and nature's night;
>> Thine eye diffused a quickening ray—
>> I woke, the dungeon flamed with light;
>> My chains fell off, my heart was free,
>> I rose, went forth, and followed Thee.
>
> Amazing love, how can it be?[20]

He has a point. Something would indeed be lost. Now as Rich and I talked further he made it clear that he was not discounting other theories of atonement (how we are saved). The gospel is indeed many-faceted. And he certainly was not rejecting the need to recover a robust view of the kingdom of God. But he stressed that justification or penal atonement on the cross had to be held as "first among equals." That is not what I expected him to say.

As I walked out of his office that day, I reflected on what Rich had said. I was convinced he was not embracing penal atonement to the exclusion of the other views of the atonement that are laid out in the Bible. Rather, he was saying that penal atonement—that Christ died on the cross for us individually to satisfy the wrath of God toward sin—is the necessary foundation of salvation.[21]

I could not wait to get back to rereading Brian's books. I realized that Rich had put his finger on what had been causing me to have some misgivings about Brian's teaching. I was having what Rich calls "Calvinist misgivings" about the way Brian responds to the classical reductionism of the gospel. As much as I appreciated Brian's stress on the kingdom of God and missional Christianity, I was worried he could not avoid the charge of reductionism if he did not integrate more clearly the blood of Jesus into the gospel. I think I would feel a lot better, more confident that Brian can avoid reductionism, if he had spent more time talking about personal sin, God's displeasure at sin, the need for the blood atonement and what Jesus accomplished for us on the cross. He could still do this, I believe, and not lose the connection to the kingdom of God.[22] After all, the Synoptic Gospel writers lay out the kingdom of God in the first section of each Gospel but eventually get around to Jesus' challenge to his disciples to believe in him and his impending death. Jesus linked the kingdom of God with his atonement.

I was pleased to come across an article titled "McLaren Emerging" by Scot McKnight in which he asks what role the cross plays in the emergent kingdom vision and Brian's view in particular. According to Scot:

> What McLaren has written about the Cross . . . approaches French intellectual René Girard's theory—namely, that by the Cross God identified with the victim and both unmasked and undid evil, systemic violence, and injustice. In *Secret Message*, McLaren says that at the Cross, "God exposed and judged the evil of empire and religion" and that the King "achieves peace not by shedding the blood of rebels but by . . . *shedding his own blood* . . . [The] crucifixion of Christ can in this light be seen as a radical repudiation of the use of violent force."[23]

Well, yes, McKnight says. But this is not enough.

> Yes, I believe this unmasking role of the Cross is not only true, but also vital to a political reworking and revitalizing of the Cross. Given the sociopolitical focus of [his *The Secret Message of Jesus* and *Everything Must Change*], perhaps McLaren didn't think any more needed to be said.
>
> But I feel obliged to ask, "Can we have more?" Emergents believe that penal substitution theories have not led (as they should have) to a kingdom vision. What I have been pondering and writing about for a decade now is how to construct an "emerging" gospel that remains faithful to the fullness of the biblical texts about the Atonement, and lands squarely on the word *kingdom*. Girard said something important about the Cross; so does McLaren. But they aren't enough.[24]

McKnight captures my misgivings about Brian's teaching.

DEEP CHURCH, ATONEMENT AND THE KINGDOM OF GOD

It is often said that the different views of the atonement of Christ are different ways of looking at the same thing. The gospel is like a multifaceted diamond and each theory is one facet of the diamond. I have said this myself on occasion. But Hans Boersma, who has worked out a third way on atonement, says, though charitable, this "isn't quite satisfactory."[25] This discussion is important because it gets to the very heart of what the gospel is and how disciples are made. It also helps us avoid reductionism.

Boersma cites theologian Henri Blocher's perspective "that the penal model forms the foundation for the Christus Victor [Christ's victory over the principalities and powers at the cross] model and that the very victory is gained both through obedience and through penal suffering."[26] That makes sense. How can victory be gained if sin is not first atoned for? How can we start to live in the kingdom unless our sins are first forgiven and we are given new power to live in the service of and obedience to the kingdom?

I was on to something. I kept reading. It was getting clearer. Boersma contends that what Jesus did on the cross is the "how" to his victory, and without it the victory does not happen or make sense. Boersma continues, "On the one hand, it safeguards the penal character of the cross. God's judgment against sin forms in a significant sense the foundation for life in fellowship with God. Legal categories have a place in atonement theology. On the other hand, [this view] does not overemphasize the penal character of the cross. . . . The legal metaphor has its place, but it is restorative in nature. Punishment always looks beyond itself to the restoration and flourishing of the community."[27]

These were new insights to me. Boersma is trying to find a way to safeguard the doctrine of penal atonement while rooting it deeply in the message of the kingdom. The next step in my investigation was to take these insights back to Brian McLaren's writings. I reread *The Secret Message* and *A Generous Orthodoxy* for a third time, carefully looking for these nuances. I discovered I was not wrong to have some Calvinist misgivings. Brian stresses obedient living, Christ's victory over the powers, and the kingdom. What is missing, however, is "how" Jesus accomplishes this through the cross, through the blood of Jesus and forgiveness of our sin. This is the key for how a person moves from the outer circle of community into the inner circle of belief and commitment.

Why is this so important? I got a hint in the section of *A Generous Orthodoxy* where Brian reveals what Anabaptism has taught him. Though Brian does not claim to be an Anabaptist in this book, he does say he strongly appreciates what they teach. And he says his view of the kingdom came first from Anabaptists like Yoder and Hauerwas. So we can learn from his appreciation of Anabaptism. When discussing the weaknesses of Anabaptism he says, "Anabaptists have (for better and for worse) traditionally been weary of too much speculation about . . . atonement theories. . . . Instead they feel their calling is to focus on living out Jesus' teaching about how we are to conduct our daily lives, especially in relation to our neighbors."[28] I sense this same reluctance in Brian. But because of this, he opens himself to the charge of reductionism, even if he is not formally denying penal atonement.

For example, on the blog *Pomomusings* Brian writes,

> The kingdom of God isn't something you simply hope for someday. It is something you come to terms with today. That "coming to terms with" means, for starters, that we repent—we rethink everything in light of this message. And it also means we trust Jesus as the king—so we decide to "take on his yoke," learn his way, and follow him, so we can be like him. . . .
>
> For Jesus, the kingdom wasn't something we build or advance or expand. It was something we see and enter and receive. To see it, we need to repent and acknowledge how blind we have been, becoming teachable and "young" again, like children. To enter it, we need to become a part of it, and to receive it, we let it become a part of us.[29]

This is a wonderful description of the kingdom and our invitation to embrace its reign. But I worry about what is missing in the description. It is curious to me that nowhere does he mention or link the kingdom of God to the doctrines of atonement, justification, union with Christ or our need to be forgiven. I realize Brian is not denying these doctrines, but by not mentioning them he may be allowing them to eventually die of neglect. And besides, without them the definition is not correct. This is, I am afraid, gospel reductionism.

WHY THIS IS SO IMPORTANT

As I have made clear, I appreciate Brian's stress on kingdom living, but his description leaves us powerless to enter the kingdom and to live it out. How could we possibly live up to these lofty goals unless we are first sure of our membership in the kingdom; that is, how are we brought into it? And how is it possible to live it without daily renewal by forgiveness, grace and reconciliation? Just reminding us of the story of what God is doing to create a new heaven and new earth, and our calling to participate in the kingdom, is not enough. Without the daily renewing grace of God, which comes from the cross and is applied to my life by the Holy Spirit, I simply can't pull it off.

Ironically, Brian's view of the kingdom, which is supposed to be so liberating, tends toward legalism. Without God's atoning grace, the message of the kingdom sounds like law. And this is, I believe, why so many of my college friends dropped out of Christianity. They could not pull it off.

This point was clearly brought home to me in Brian's discussion of Matthew 5:21-22 in *The Secret Message*. Brian correctly sees that Jesus was condemning the Pharisees for stressing external obedience and was calling instead for an internal change of heart. Nevertheless, Brian's description of this internal change comes awfully close to being self-induced. "We must deal with greed and lust, arrogance and prejudice in the heart."[30] We learn to do this by developing correct habits that lead to a changed heart. This is often called "virtue ethics."

I understand that a certain cooperation of the will is required for Spirit-led Christians to develop godly habits. This is part of working out our "salvation with fear and trembling" (Philippians 2:12). But if this is not balanced, perhaps superseded, by the doctrine of transforming grace, what I call "grace ethics" (God's grace in our lives is what gives us the power to change and live the kingdom life), we will produce two types of people—(1) those who are burned out and cynical because they could not live this way, or (2) those who have become proud or arrogant because they think they pulled it off on their own. Ironically, once the latter figure out they can pull this virtue ethic off on their own, they will start thinking they can change the world through their own efforts, and we move right into social gospel reductionism.

SAFEGUARDING THE DEEP GOSPEL

In 2006 Redeemer Presbyterian Church celebrated its fifth year. What started as a dream, a vision for the deep church, was starting to be a reality. I met a lot of people in the year before we began the church who said it could not be done. No one would want this kind of church, especially in Orange County, where seeker-driven churches were pioneered. I remember the night before we held our first Sunday morning worship service. I was scared no one would show up. Thankfully, they did, and God has graciously built an amazing church. Many of our goals have been accomplished. We have much to be grateful for. But we have so much further to go.

A number of months before our fifth anniversary, our leadership began talking about the next five years. What is God calling us to do? How can we be part of what he is doing in the world, right here in Orange County? We decided to reassess our original vision, core commitments and strategy. Much of it was still vibrant. But we wanted to freshen it up, reaffirm who we are and prayerfully plan for where God might be taking us over the next five years.

As we looked at our seven core commitments that had marked our church over the past five years and would do so for the future, we realized we could simplify them, make them easier to understand. We settled on four words: *gospel, community, mission* and *shalom*.

The one that we struggled with the most was gospel. We had spent five years translating or contextualizing the gospel to the Orange County setting, and we wanted to be sure we had not reduced it in any way. As we wrote about our gospel commitment, we wanted to stress the atonement as well as the kingdom of God. We wanted to make it clear that Christ's cross, which paid for our sins and took away our guilt, is the foundation for Christ's victory over evil and oppression, and allows us to join God's family and his kingdom reign. It was the key to belief, moving deeper into the community of his faithful. Thus we wrote:

> The gospel is at the center of all we do. The "gospel" is the good news that through Jesus, the Messiah, the power of God's kingdom has entered history to renew the whole world. Through the Savior God has established his reign. When we believe and rely on Jesus' work and record (rather than ours) for our relationship to God,

that kingdom power comes upon us and begins to work through us. We witness this radical new way of living by our renewed lives, beautiful community, social justice, and cultural transformation. This good news brings new life. The gospel motivates, guides, and empowers every aspect of our living and worship.

Three years later, I think it holds up well. If I were writing it today, I might add a word here or a phrase there, but overall it captures the deep church. It makes it clear that we are about the gospel, but one that avoids the historic reductionism of the past. It links the atonement to the kingdom of God, revealing that they are part of the same glorious news and making it clear that the power of the gospel transforms us and empowers us to live differently and change the world.

For the deep church, the gospel is at the center of all we do—our worship, discipleship, community groups, mercy ministry and cultural renewal (seeking the shalom of the city). It moves us from belonging to belief. It matures us individually and corporately. To make this clear our four core commitments are presented like this:

Gospel—Community—Mission—Shalom

The order is important. As we are affected by the gospel, we are empowered to move into community to care for one another. And as we care for one another, we begin to reach outside of our community with acts of mercy—mission. And as we move into our community with acts of service and mercy, we begin to look for ways to make and renew culture and its institutions so that they honor God's original design for creation. This is shalom. The more we live in community, are merciful and transform culture, the more we need the gospel to empower and transform us, and the circle starts over again—gospel, community, mission and shalom.

One of the great tragedies of church history is how often different movements in the church have been guilty of reductionism and lost the gospel. At Redeemer we are aware of this tendency and want to guard against it. Frequently, we pray at our elder meetings that God will keep us faithful to what we have been entrusted with. We want to be missional, to be agents of mercy, to connect and to transform culture. But in doing all these things, we don't want to be guilty of gospel reductionism. Without the gospel, Christianity is just one more system of morality or man-made religion.

I have grown up in the midst of the worship wars in the evangelical church. According to Robert Webber, until 1970 evangelicals mainly used traditional forms of worship: "There was little pressure to change until the music revolution of the fifties, the rise of the hippie movement in the sixties, and the emergence of the Jesus Movement in the seventies." The Jesus movement "introduced music-driven casual worship, and the church has been in an uproar ever since."[1] For the next twenty years or more the church battled over which is more biblical and which style reaches people more effectively.

I witnessed this struggle firsthand at our church in Pasadena in the early 1990s. For over one hundred years the church's worship was traditional—choir, organ, hymns, sermon and an order of service with little liturgy and infrequent Lord's Suppers. With close to five thousand members there seemed no reason to change. But in the early nineties, when a new senior pastor came on board, the leadership decided to start a Saturday night contemporary worship service. Though it was ultimately well-attended by over eight hundred people, the battle to stop it was fierce and the church was injured. Many left the church. Those who stayed fumed over the service for years.

Those of us who have grown up with this battle have been left confused. Webber captures the sentiment of many in my generation: "I find that younger evangelicals feel somewhat 'dizzy' over all the changes and the shouting matches going on between traditionalists on the one hand and those who demand a regular plate of contemporary worship on the other hand."[2]

Though each side at the church made their case by marshaling their best biblical arguments, I realized they were really arguing for their preference, the style of music they grew up with. They wanted worship to represent *their* tradition—that is, what they liked or were used to.[3]

As the battle raged around me and as I was struggling to lead the small-church-sized Twenty-Something Fellowship (the name given to our group after moving from the house to the church property), I went in search of resources. I wanted to know how to best define worship and how to lead in the most biblical way possible. I believe that worship should be more than an emotional high. But more than this, I had to admit that the options—traditional and contemporary—left me cold.

I longed for the experience of God's presence and desired the restoration of liturgical elements of worship. I had grown weary of the thinness of contemporary worship, which seemed so lifeless and often done by rote. But I didn't want to return to the traditional style I grew up with, which seemed devoid of the real presence of God and focused on the passing on of information.

So while everyone was jousting over whether the church should be traditional or contemporary, I began to realize that I wanted neither. They both have flaws. I knew there must be some alternative. I was anxious to move beyond this limbo. I desired a third way: worship that embodied a genuine encounter with God, had depth and substance, included more frequent and meaningful Communion, was participatory, read more Scripture in worship, creatively used the senses, provided more time for contemplation, and focused on the transcendence and otherness of God. This vision eventually was embodied in Redeemer Church's worship. It is our attempt at a third way—deep worship.

THE EMERGING CHURCH'S WORSHIP PROTEST

By 2004 I recognized that I was not the only one of my generation who was attempting to find a third way. In fact, for the past ten years, there has been a groundswell of those in their twenties and thirties who, in the words of Chris Armstrong, "are uneasy and alienated in mall-like church environments; high-energy, entertainment-oriented worship; and boomer-era ministry strategies and structures modeled on the business world."[4]

One pastor and author who has shared this uneasiness is Dan Kimball of Vintage Faith Church in Santa Cruz, California.[5] His book *Emerging Worship* has been a handbook for the emerging church as they attempt to move beyond boomer-oriented, entertainment-driven worship.[6] Dan, like me, has grown tired of the contemporary format (a few songs, announcements, sermon, closing song) but has no desire to go back to traditional worship either. Dan says that emerging worship is not just about singing; it is more than getting our felt needs met, it is more than an information dump, and it transcends a reliance on the traditions of the recent past. In short, church is more than just a few songs and a sermon.

Dan is calling for "new wineskins" in our formal times of gathering for worship. These, he offers, "are needed in response to our postmodern culture." What is required is a "multisensory approach comprised of many dimensions and expressions of worship."[7] According to Dan, this means:

> We now see art being brought into worship, the use of visuals, the practice of ancient disciplines, the design of the gathering being more participatory than passive-spectator. Instead of the pulpit and sermon being the central focus of worship gatherings, . . . we now see Jesus as the central focus through a variety of creative worship expressions. . . . What I mean here is that teaching and learning in the emerging church happen in various ways; it's no longer only one person standing on a stage preaching to everyone else.[8]

As I first read the words *multisensory worship* I was intrigued. I had heard theologian R. C. Sproul say something similar, and that since the time of the Reformation the church has succumbed to a sort of intellectualism in its worship. So I decided to experience Vintage Faith for myself. One Sunday, after leading worship and preaching, I dragged myself to the airport to catch a flight so I could attend the 7 p.m. service in Santa Cruz. When I arrived, I discovered a church under construction—literally. Vintage Faith had merged with a dying church with a very large, sprawling facility that was in disrepair. They have poured thousands of dollars into rehabbing it—redoing offices and classrooms, establishing a coffeehouse, and beginning work on the three-hundred-seat sanctuary with stained glass. They have done a great job retaining the old and combining it with the new. Their offices reminded me of a hip architect's office with track lighting, art on the walls and the original hardwood floors. I tried not to covet (and did find out that most of the materials and labor were donated).

The sanctuary is a work in progress. Half of the pews have been replaced with chairs. And in the back corner a prayer room was constructed out of pipes and drapery. It has several prayer stations; some had kneelers with an open Bible and a map of the world in front. I guessed that they might be praying for the world at that night's service. As I walked around the sanctuary, I noticed the old stained-glass windows were a work in progress too.

I grabbed a seat close to the front but off to the side (I wanted to be able to turn around and see how many people were actually singing!), and a young woman named Lauren greeted me. She was the fifth person to greet me in the thirty minutes I had been on their campus. This is unusual for most churches. And even more shocking, she didn't just greet me but actually asked me questions. This takes depth. I realized that they take outreach seriously. They are aware of the stranger in their midst. This makes sense because Dan has such a heart for evangelism, and it has rubbed off on his people. That is probably why they have seen so many conversions over the years. I wish all churches had this passion.

The service began with a high-energy song by a very talented band led by Pastor Josh Fox. I had trouble focusing on the words at first because Josh was so interesting to watch. I also noticed the band was off to the side. My guess is they did not want to be the center of attention, to be a show. Josh exhorted us to focus our attention on Jesus. I did my best.

When the band began the second song, I turned to observe a very young group, almost all under twenty-five. A few were singing, but most were taking it in and mouthing the chorus. I turned back around and noticed the lyrics were projected on two screens with still and moving images behind the words. Some might think it distracting, but it did not bother me. An artist worked on the other side of the stage, creating what looked like hands coming down from heaven. The front of the church was visually interesting—candles, draped cloth, a large metal cross, a big Bible, artwork. It reminded me of an artist friend's loft in Pasadena. Vintage Faith had worked hard at making it visual, warm and spiritual. So whether through candles, crosses, artwork, the Communion table, the baptismal, projected visuals, stained glass, Dan writes, "the room invokes a sense that this is a spiritual gathering happening here and that Christianity is not just a modern religion, but an ancient one."[9]

Dan writes frequently about sacred space and multisensory worship in his books. He contends that most contemporary worship churches have stripped the sacred out of their worship centers. Emerging churches are making their worship space feel sacred again. Since the emerging generation craves a sense of mystery and the wonder of God, they design their worship space to reflect this. "Multisensory worship involves seeing, hearing, tasting, smelling, touching, and experiencing."[10]

I did not see or experience all of these on my visit. Since Vintage Faith Church serves the Lord's Supper once every five weeks, there was no tasting or touching. Nor did I experience any liturgy. Dan told me afterward that it did not really fit their community, except at Advent and Easter. But there is a strong desire to embrace ancient forms of worship at Vintage and other emerging churches. Some emerging churches focus on the Christian calendar of Advent, Christmas, Epiphany, Lent, Holy Week, Easter and Pentecost. Along with the calendar, there is movement into the ancient forms rooted in Judaism, he told me. Most emerging churches include a Passover Seder as part of their worship year. Time is spent teaching the Jewish perspective of the Bible. This desire for the ancient has led to a revival in hymn singing in some emerging churches.

After the second song, there was a mutual greeting time. The congregation then read a portion of Scripture. This was the closest they came to liturgy. Then Dan preached. Using projected visuals, he taught for forty-five minutes on the question, Does God judge those who have not heard of Jesus? Dan is aware that non-Christians are present and that Santa Cruz is religiously pluralistic, so he worked hard to be guest-friendly, especially in claiming that Jesus is the only way to God and salvation (John 14:6).

Dan's sermon was filled with Scripture, making the point of Jesus' exclusivity in the face of different religions. The traditional church might be shocked at how conservative Dan's teaching is. He spent a full twenty minutes of the sermon expositing Romans 1. Following his sermon, he interviewed a Chinese American, who is a Ph.D. student and a former Buddhist. I recalled Dan's point that emerging worship is not speaker-focused but community-centered. So speaking is shared as much as possible to avoid dependency on one person.

Dan wrapped up the teaching time with a summary of what Vintage Church is all about—reaching out to those who don't know Christ Jesus because their very eternity is at stake. I could sense Dan's passion for evangelism and desire to reach the lost.

Before he finished, Dan gave directions for the prayer room. I was correct about the maps. Each person was to put a small sticker on a country and pray that the people there would be bold in their witness. When he finished the directions, the band began to play, more softly this time. About 20 percent of the congregation left their seats to make their way to the prayer room. Dan frequently speaks about the need for freedom of movement in worship, which comes into play in this part of the service. The goal is participation, not spectatorship. As people moved about, the band played the old hymn "Great Is Thy Faithfulness." The people sang heartily. The old hymns have great depth and encourage full congregational participation.

As people filed back to their seats, the band picked up the tempo, adding the drum kit back into the mix. I could sense the end of the service might be at hand. People sang out louder yet, and some raised their hands. Finally, announcements were made and we were exhorted to give on the way out as special music was played. After the last "closing song" this seemed a little anticlimactic. When the service was over, people streamed out toward the church's coffeehouse next door.

While not everything in the service suited my style or my preferences, I felt like Dan and Josh worked hard to make the service God-focused and Christ-centered. It was solidly evangelical. I had been ministered to. Overall I would say Vintage Faith Church works diligently at multisensory worship. The way the sanctuary was adorned, the dynamic music and the preaching were visually and acoustically appealing. But Vintage also stressed holistic experience, not only through the singing and the sense of sacred space throughout the sanctuary but also through the prayer room, which included all the senses. After the service, Dan gave me a copy of a book he cowrote with Lilly Lewin titled *Sacred Space*, a handbook for creating multisensory worship. The book is a step-by-step guide for designing prayer rooms to reinforce the message of the sermon.

After the service, Dan and I went out for dinner to talk. I asked Dan if my hunch was correct that he and Vintage would fit into the "relevant" part of the emerging camp.[11] He agreed, though he wanted to make it clear it was not being hip or cool that made them relevant. He is well aware that the traditional side has accused him of merely offering a different kind of entertainment worship. After all, isn't what he is offering just meeting the demands of the consumer? How is it any different than the myriad devices used in large seeker churches? He is sensitive to this charge and worries that we can easily adopt "new worship tricks and cool innovative things in our worship gatherings."

As he says in *Emerging Worship*:

We can try to impress and please those who sit and watch what we do. . . .

In the emerging church, there is great danger if the focus of our worship gatherings subtly shifts to our video backgrounds, prayer stations, ancient creeds, candles, artwork, etc. If that happens, we'll begin teaching people (without saying it) that the worship service is a service we provide for people.[12]

That is, it is just one more form of entertainment. Dan is right. They need to guard against this kind of consumerism or the emerging church will fall into the same mistake of some megachurches.[13]

THE TRADITIONAL CHURCH REACTS

What has the response been to emerging worship? Not always positive. A number of traditional critics point to the 2004 Emergent Conference as proof that emerging worship is off-target. Some of these critics have mentioned Andy Crouch's article "The Emergent Mystique" in *Christianity Today* to buttress their case. As dispassionately as he can, Crouch describes the worship at the Emergent Conference:

> During one particularly experimental worship session, featuring a well-known British dj (hair: spiked) whose pulsating techno music (complete lyrics: "It's just you and God") builds to a climax that would have played well in pagan Corinth, I find Brian McLaren outside the convention hall. "I hate it," he says ruefully of the worship music. Another Emergent leader tells a seminar, "The general sessions are a betrayal of everything Emergent stands for."[14]

As Crouch concludes, "The truth is that the convention makes it difficult to tell what Emergent does stand for." He goes on to say that "even the invited guests seem bewildered." He quotes plenary speaker Robert Webber as saying, "They claim to be rejecting the last 30 years of evangelicalism—and they're repeating the last 30 years of evangelicalism." And bestselling author Lauren Winner, who was dismayed by the video loops playing constantly behind her during her talk, ruefully commented: "I feel so alienated from my generation."[15]

Juicy quotes like this are pounced on by the traditional church. Traditional critics, most by their own admission, have never visited an emerging church. Yet they have picked up Crouch's description and have used it to make their case that emerging worship is just one more form of experiential, entertainment worship. In fact, critic Ron Gleason argues the irony is that McLaren and Webber (who were critical of their own movement) are to blame, for "they were instrumental in opening this Pandora's Box. So why are they saddened or surprised when people take their teaching to their logical conclusions?"[16]

Ron argues that the emerging church at its core is anti-authority, anti-tradition and individualistic. They are more concerned about their own felt needs, what suits them and their own experience, than they are about worshiping biblically. In this sense, he claims, they are not unlike the contemporary, boomer megachurch movement that they criticize so much. They are just a more contextualized version of the same thing. And just as the megachurch is losing the next generation, the emerging church will have to continue to find new ways to entertain and stay ahead of the game. If they don't keep finding new ways to entertain, continues Ron, people will move on to the newest attraction. If you pander to the consumer, he says, you will eventually get burned. Once they get bored they will move on. The harshest criticism leveled at the emerging worship is that it really is not any different than the megachurch worship they eschew. Both groups, says Gleason, are self-focused; it's about me and my felt needs.[17]

The traditional critics charge that both the emerging churches and megachurches have no way to stand apart from the consumer culture around them. Even though Dan Kimball and others in the emerging church work hard to avoid this, they have not been able to. In fact, Ron Gleason accuses them of syncretism. In their attempt to reach the culture, to be more contextualized than the traditional church, they have become like the culture, mirroring it in its music, art, technology and worldview.[18] Ironically, they have reached their own form of irrelevancy, not able to live differently than the world around them, say the critics.

ACHILLES' HEEL

Are Ron Gleason and other traditional critics right? Is emerging worship just about experience? About entertainment? Is it really no different than the megachurch worship, just maybe more contextualized to the newest generations?[19] Is emerging worship's use of the ancient traditions of the church faddish? Does it merely skim the surface of all traditions rather than getting to know any of them well? Are emerging churches spending so much time with trendy elements that they have edged out the Word?

I think that Vintage, with its commitment to ancient church practices and disciplines, is a huge step beyond most low-church evangelicalism, whether contemporary or traditional. Most traditional churches are heirs of the low-church movement of the sixteenth and seventeenth centuries, in which independents reacted against the traditions of the ancient church. The fact that their progeny are called traditionalists is ironic. The independent movement would never have wanted this appellation attached to their worship. Biblical, yes; contextual, maybe; traditional, no. "No creed but Christ" was the rallying cry. Today, low-church worship has its own tradition. So do seeker services. Contemporary churches have their own type of liturgy, or order of service, which seldom varies. They are no longer spontaneous.

So Dan and Vintage Faith Church hope to move beyond this antitraditionalism built into most of evangelicalism. This is good. But can they pull it off? Have they moved beyond low-church worship? Or are they creating (by using parts of the past) one more contemporary style that does not provide the strong medicine needed to reform evangelicalism? Are they willing to adopt the tradition that the sixteenth-century Protestants and today's evangelicals deem as extrabiblical?

After talking with Dan, I am not sure he can fully accept the ancient tradition. There is much in it he welcomes. But there are parts that make him nervous. He is afraid to be locked in to anything but the Bible. I appreciate his fear. Yet, the irony is that both the emerging church and traditional church are committed to the same low-church worship. So I wonder, how different are they at their core?

Put another way, I suggested to Dan that the emerging and traditional churches have the same Achilles' heel—a faulty view of tradition. Both are committed to the low-church view of church tradition. This has locked them into a model of worship that is dated and severely influenced by the Enlightenment. They are handcuffed by a style of worship contextualized during the Reformation that no longer connects with postmodern people. The goal is not to simply contextualize or become more like the surrounding culture, but to first adopt church tradition that would give them the resources to connect with the culture without becoming syncretistic.

Even though emerging church views allow them to adopt some ancient practices, this is done in a way that is cut off from the Great Tradition that birthed them. It is as if the emerging churches want the fruit but not the roots from which it came. So in their attempt to be culturally relevant (which they are doing very well), their traditions are not strong enough, I fear, to resist being absorbed by the surrounding culture. There simply is not enough depth in the rituals, disciplines and practices that are adopted.

BEYOND EMERGING AND TRADITIONAL WORSHIP

Is there a way forward? Does the deep church go beyond emerging and traditional worship? In thinking about this question, no book has been more helpful to me in understanding the weakness of free-church evangelical worship, whether emerging or traditional, than D. H. Williams's *Retrieving the Tradition and Renewing Evangelicalism: A Primer for Suspicious Protestants*. Williams, a Baptist minister, realizes that evangelicals have been raised to be suspicious of Christian tradition. I know I was.

Williams comments that believers whose (unacknowledged) tradition is that the Bible is their only guide for faith and that there is no reliable Christian tradition must come to terms with how they got this view before they are willing to adopt the early church tradition as their own. In trying to help evangelicals be more aware of their views, Williams reveals how much of evangelical "tradition" is connected to the independent movement of the sixteenth and seventeenth centuries that reacted against the Roman Catholic Church view of Scripture and tradition. When he calls evangelicals back to tradition he is not calling them to a tradition that would undermine the sufficiency of Scripture. This is key. Williams says, "[The] Tradition indicates the core teaching and preaching of the early church which has bequeathed to us the fundamentals of what it is to think and believe Christianly. The Tradition of the Christian faith is that fundamental Christian identity for every believer no matter which of the traditions—protestant, Roman Catholic or Orthodox—he or she may profess."[20]

The "Tradition" Williams speaks of is what C. S. Lewis called "mere Christianity." At Redeemer Presbyterian Church we discovered that if this foundation is not present, we are not capable of maintaining worship that avoids syncretism or irrelevance. Only the living tradition of the fourth and fifth centuries, passed on through the ages, what Oden calls classical orthodoxy, can help us contextualize the gospel in our worship without it becoming syncretistic or ossified over time.

Admittedly, the emerging church would say they have this tradition.[21] The problem, however, is that there is often no sustained explanation and consistent use of the Great Tradition. For example, Dan Kimball talks about "sampling" the tradition, but not adopting it along with Scripture as the church's foundation.

The deep church has attempted to root ourselves in tradition to avoid faddishness. We want to avoid the kind of situation that Williams describes in the low-church tradition: "All they possess now are fragments: a knowledge of past experiments detached from the context which gave them significance, parts of theories unrelated to other bits and pieces of theories, a few instruments which no one knows how to use, half chapters from books or single pages from articles."[22] This picking and choosing of ancient practices and traditions is just a new faddishness, says Williams. Fruit without the roots does not nourish, sustain or remain.

But many in the emerging church would say they want the same thing. So, what's new about my proposal? The differences may not seem large but they are nonetheless profound. In *Alternate Worship* Jonny Baker captures well the emerging view of tradition and how it differs from what I am getting at. Here is his reaction to discovering the treasure trove of ancient liturgy: "Post-modern cultural savvy, combined with an evangelical tendency not to defer to high church regulation, led alt worshipers to treat this treasure chest as a kind of dressing-up box."[23]

In fact, he continues,

> the interest in tradition was one of the factors in alt worship being labeled "post-modern," because of the way it combines the use of advanced mixed-media technology with an eclectic use of the worship traditions of the church. One way of understanding this is through the metaphor of "sampling" from music technology.[24]

In this sampling, he writes, a piece of music is "extracted from its original setting" and "inserted into a new musical context," forming a new whole. Thus the emerging church is extracting samples from the old traditions to help them form new meaning. "The practice of sampling feeds into the post-modern emphasis on continuous and shifting processes of constructing meanings. . . . You have to make your own meanings."[25]

This constructing of meanings is what I worry about. This is different than just updating the past and practicing for the present. In this sense, the ancient practice would still retain its meaning; it would just be presented differently. Baker seems to be calling for new meanings. Yet, if all we are doing is taking bits and pieces of tradition to form our own meaning, we are just as modern as those locked into modernism. We are still creating meaning for ourselves. In the end we can't avoid the problem of how far we should accommodate the Christian message to the surrounding culture without losing Christian identity.[26]

We have decided at Redeemer that to be the deep church, tradition is not something we can take or leave. If we are serious about reclaiming the Great Tradition, we must look beyond our own experience to the formative eras (apostolic and patristic) of the faith and not just for the

practices. These are, says Williams, "the joint anchor of responsible biblical interpretation, theological imagination, and spiritual growth," and, I
would add, worship as well.

CONTINUITY AND DISCONTINUITY

But I can hear some objections. Does this mean we are to swallow church
tradition whole? Even the bad parts? Is it all continuity and no discontinuity? Is the ancient church the golden era we need to get back to? No.
There is no golden time to return to, whether the pre-Constantinian era
or the time of the great ecumenical councils and creeds. Golden-age
thinking makes the mistake of the Enlightenment all over again. There
are no universal principles to apply lock, stock and barrel to today.

Robert Webber, who has encouraged the movement back to the ancient church, warns evangelicals about the danger of "primitivism" (the
belief that we can return to a golden age of the church). There is no return to the pristine church, no true historic form; it never existed. And
it does not mean converting to Roman Catholicism or Eastern Orthodoxy. The early church fathers, the tradition, belong to the whole church.
As Tom Oden says, all of the traditions

> have an equal right to appeal to the early history of Christian exe-
> gesis. . . . Protestants have a right to the Fathers. Athanasius is not
> owned by the Copts, nor is Augustine owned by North Africans.
> These minds are common possession of the whole church. The Or-
> thodox do not have exclusive rights over Basil, nor do the Romans
> over Gregory the Great. Christians everywhere have equal claim to
> these riches and are discovering them and glimpsing their unity in
> the body of Christ.[27]

How do we apply the lessons of the past? How is the Great Tradition
helpful? Chris Armstrong makes a good point: "Having learned the lessons of anti-foundationalism," he says, and thus moving "beyond the
'golden age' approach," we must begin to "mix critique with appreciation
and even reverence" as we return to the historical sources. Furthermore,

he contends "it will take a great deal of wisdom to learn the strengths and the limits of each phase of the history" in which we seek answers. We cannot just accept the past in toto. (The emerging church would agree.) This is the wrong understanding of tradition. Even as it is being integrated into our present, we must continually challenge it. Armstrong is right on target.

DEEP WORSHIP AT REDEEMER CHURCH

What does worship look like for the deep church? And what guides us as we plan our worship events? It all starts with how we frame it. At Redeemer Church we attempt to hold the Bible, the tradition and our cultural context in tension, allowing them to inform every part of our worship.[28] Since the Bible does not give us enough information to construct a worship service, we must fill in the blanks. We are told in the Bible to sing songs, but we are not given the tunes, or told what kind of lyrics the songs should have or how emotionally intense the experience should be. When we are commanded to pray we are not told whether to use written prayers or extemporaneous prayers.

In order to be faithful we must draw on not only Scripture but tradition as well. But we also draw on our cultural sensitivities and our desire to "worship before the nations," making sure that our worship is accessible to an outsider. Keeping all three—Bible, tradition and culture—in mind, we are able to craft a worship gathering that is neither irrelevant nor syncretistic. If any one of the triad is missing, we risk falling into one of these two extremes. Keeping them in tension we are able to maintain a powerful worship service that is simultaneously countercultural and culturally relevant. As Tim Keller says so well, "I believe the solution to the problem of the 'worship wars' is neither to reject nor to enshrine historic tradition but to forge new forms of corporate worship that take seriously both our histories and contemporary realities, all within a framework of biblical theology."[29]

The following points reveal how Redeemer Church has attempted to accomplish deep worship.

1. Ancient and new. Deep worship is rooted in two thousand years of the church and the historic flow of worship. The order of the service, the liturgy, should be both old and new. The goal is to take the best of the tradition and breathe new life into it for the twenty-first century. Some of the hymns and songs are ancient and others are recently written. Older hymns with profound depth that have fallen out of use can be rescued with updated tunes.[30] Deep worship uses both set prayers from the history of the church and new extemporaneous prayers.[31] Deep worship in sum combines the best of the free church—moving extemporaneous prayers, longer sermons and room for the Spirit—with the ancient church's commitment to set prayers and a liturgy of Word and Table. The combination of ancient and contemporary speaks deeply to the postmodern desire for ancient roots and a common history.

2. Biblical drama. As one of our musicians says, "We in the Reformed tradition talk about the drama of salvation a lot. And we know a lot about salvation. The problem is that we know nothing of the *drama* of it. There is *no* drama." He exaggerates a little to make his point, but not by much. The goal is to make the drama come alive with rich liturgy and music with content and depth. Worship can be grouped into five acts—calling, cleansing, constitution, communion and commission.[32] God calls us to worship, we recognize our need for cleansing, we hear him speak in his Word and sacrament, and then we are sent out to love God and serve others. Each act is dramatized by powerful singing and meaningful prayer. It should be a drama that rivals the best storytelling in Hollywood.

3. Joy and reverence. Our mantra each week is that we want our worship to balance the twin commitments of reverence and joy. Churches tend to be one or the other: pep rally or funeral. But we are called to both joy and reverence. As we approach God in all his holiness we are solemn. No flippancy allowed. Music should be at times reverent, majestic and awe-inspiring. But God is also the source of joy, laughter and happiness. He is the God of the resurrection and new life. How can we not be excited, filled with joy, ready to praise him? For this we need songs and prayers with energy. We embrace deep theological content in our music that balances reverence and joy. Each worship service should take the congregation through the full gamut of emotions that are fitting for the weekly participation in the drama of salvation.

4. Priesthood of all believers. Deep worship is interactive because God calls everyone, not just the people up front, to participate in worship. This is not a lecture or a concert. As priests, we are all required to be involved. There are no spectators. Thus the liturgy (order of the worship) should be as interactive as possible. It is a dialogue between the people and God. God speaks to us through his Word and we respond. Throughout the service, God engages us in the call to worship, multiple Scripture readings, the sermon and the words of blessing, and each time we respond in prayer, song or action (e.g., taking the Lord's Supper or giving an offering). It is dynamic, action-packed, thrilling.

5. Profound but accessible sermons. The pastors of Redeemer preach sermons rooted in the Bible—both the drama of salvation from each of the Testaments and the wonderful doctrines of Christianity. Whatever part of the Scriptures the church finds itself in at the time, the goal is to preach Christ in a way that is both edifying for the long-time believer and yet accessible to the newcomer or nonbeliever. Timothy Keller's sermons at Redeemer Presbyterian Church of New York City provide wonderful examples. Nonbelievers and mature saints fill his church every week.[33]

6. Weekly Communion. Deep worship participates weekly in the Lord's Supper (Communion or Eucharist).[34] Having confessed our sin in act two of the service, Communion is now a time of celebration, not long faces. God's grace is real and is experienced powerfully in the Lord's Supper. While God's holiness was held up in the first half of the service, God's amazing and gentle grace is now on display. God is sovereign but he also suffers along with us.

This appeals to the postmodern people because they crave transcendence and experience at the same time. They want awe and wonder, and more. They desire emotion but not the emotional hype of so many churches. They want transcendence but not the kind that strips God's joy from the service. The bread is the body of Christ, the bread of heaven and our most profound hope. The cup is the cup of salvation to quench our deep spiritual thirst. Even though people come forward as individuals, it is done as a community—a covenant-family meal. There is something powerful in the imagery here. Communion is about unity; even though it speaks of individually being united to Christ, by taking it together we are saying that we are together, unified in Christ.

7. *Guest friendly—doxological evangelism.* Though the service is primarily for believers, we worship before the nations (Psalm 47:1; 105:1; Isaiah 2:1-4; 56:6-8). We call this doxological evangelism. Nonbelievers should find our worship understandable (Acts 2:11; 1 Corinthians 14:23-24). We lead our worship with the assumption that nonbelievers are present. And we have seen many come to Christ right in the middle of a worship service. We address our guests and nonbelievers at several points during the service: (1) the welcome time before the service, (2) announcement time, (3) the Lord's Supper as they are invited to believe in Christ, and (4) as the gospel message is related to their fears, concerns and hopes. We remember what it means to not believe. The goal is to be respectful, intelligible and always welcoming. We want to draw them to the Well that is Christ.

Have we accomplished all seven suggestions? Are we the perfect worshiping church? Not by a long shot. We are still a work in progress. In many ways, these suggestions represent the ideal more than the reality. But they guide us and spur us on to make deep worship a reality each week.

♦ ♦ ♦

As I left Santa Cruz that cool December day and drove back to the airport, I reflected on how much I had learned about worship in my journey since that Gen X 2.0 conference years before. I had learned much from the emerging church—from people like Dan Kimball—and also from the traditional church I grew up in. I am still learning. Learning to worship is like sanctification; it takes time and is often a long, slow, messy journey. But I take comfort in what Paul says in Ephesians 2:10, that "we are his workmanship, created in Christ Jesus for good works, which God prepared beforehand, that we should walk in them" (ESV). God is at work teaching us to worship and making our worship acceptable to him.

Effective preaching is important to me. Preaching and teaching are a major part of my calling to the church. I work hard each week to be biblical and effective in relaying God's Word in a powerful and life-changing way. My goal is not just to pass on information each week, although my sermons are informational, but transformation of individuals and the community. To do this the best I can, I have become a student of effective communication. Over the years I have read dozens of books on the theology and method of preaching, and listened to and observed thousands of sermons.

Growing up in church, I was dissatisfied with the preaching I heard, even if I did not know why exactly. For the most part I heard solid preaching, but it did not hold my attention or inspire me. Today, I recognize that my needs are not the most important thing; preaching is not just entertainment. But that does not mean it should not be gripping and engaging. God's Word and the drama of salvation deserve nothing less. I was not looking to be entertained, just inspired, caught up in something bigger than my hurts and frustrations. I wanted preaching that was biblical but at the same time connected to my life—that pulled me into a life-changing drama. "Go big or go home" is the marketing slogan. That is what I wanted to hear.

What we tended to get every week was pretty common in churches—three points and a poem, someone once said. What bothered me was that it always felt like three different sermons tacked together. There may have been movement in each point but not between the points. By the time my pastor reached the end of the first point, doing so with great emotion and energy, I felt like he was done, only to have him move on to the next point and what felt like another sermon. By the end of the third point I was exhausted. The sermon lacked unity and dramatic movement. It left me uninspired.

But the problems ran deeper than just lack of dramatic movement. We were exhorted to love Jesus more, live more faithfully, avoid the world and serve obediently in the church. This kind of preaching tended to be moralistic and legalistic. We were told what to do but not where the power comes from to do it. The call to obedience was positive and negative—flee the world and serve God. I remember someone summing up the message of this kind of preaching with, "You suck, try harder." Growing up I got a steady dose of this. I could never seem to pull it off. The harder I tried, the more I failed. I wanted to love Jesus and serve him, like my pastors asked, but I kept falling so short. I bounced from being "on fire" for Jesus to being totally indifferent and demoralized. Every winter at church ski camp I recommitted myself to Jesus only to return from the mountain-top experience and break this commitment the next day. The guilt tore me up inside. I was a mess and I knew it. But I did not know what to do. I just kept going to church where I was told to try harder.

But nothing seemed to work. And it did not work for my friends. Within a few years after attending a Christian college, many of my friends, who like me had grown up with this kind of moralistic preaching, had walked away from the faith. They just could not get their life to measure up to the ideal that preaching presented. No matter how much knowledge they accumulated about the Bible, it did not help. They gave up in frustration. I don't blame them.

I discovered this type of preaching produced two kinds of people: (1) Pharisees, who were proud that they were pulling off the Christian life, or (2) dispirited dropouts, who simply gave up because they could not live up to the high expectations. Often, however, people kept living the way they wanted but kept attending church because it made them feel better about themselves—at least for that day. The preaching, though, was not leading to real transformation. So my deep concern over the state of preaching in America led me on a journey—to discover what powerful, life-changing biblical preaching looks like. I hungered to see lives really changed. I am still on this journey of exploration. I realize I still have a long way to go.

THE EMERGING CHURCH'S PROTESTS ON PREACHING

I have to admit that when I started reading the emerging church's criticisms of the state of preaching I was sympathetic. I shared much of their frustration. They too are disenchanted with traditional preaching that is legalistic, moralistic and rationalistic. They particularly react against the judgmental tone, which comes across as arrogant and preachy.[1]

Though there have been a few articles and chapters written on preaching from the emerging perspective, the only full-length book I have found is Doug Pagitt's *Preaching Re-Imagined: The Role of the Sermon in Communities of Faith*. Doug is part of Emergent Village and would fit best in the revisionist camp of the emerging movement. He is a graduate of Bethel Seminary and served on the staff of an evangelical megachurch for many years before starting Solomon's Porch, an emerging church in Minneapolis.[2] This church has become a model for many church planters in the emerging church. After reading his book, I decided I should visit Doug's church and witness his preaching in person. When I heard that my friend and author John Armstrong had already set up a meeting with Doug and Tony Jones, the coordinator of Emergent Village and a member of Solomon's Porch, I asked John if I could join him.

So in October of 2007, I flew to Minneapolis and took a cab from my downtown hotel to Solomon's Porch, which meets in a residential section of the city. They have rented a traditional church building that probably would seat three hundred people if it had pews. But Solomon's Porch has removed the pews, putting in their place couches and comfortable chairs, arranged in a circle, with teaching stools in the middle. The walls were painted golden yellow and adorned with artwork. It's spiritual but not overly religious. The lighting and candles were just right—not as dark as I would have expected.

As the service began it reminded me more of a young adults' gathering than a formal service. There was a welcome and then some music by a band. It was not your typical rock band, blasting music too loud to hear yourself sing. It was more like an indie band led by acoustic guitars. Though the music was catchy, I did not notice too many people singing. Most just listened; some tapped their feet. A number of people milled about. It reminded me of people sitting at home with friends, listening to cool music, just happy to be together. You could tell these folks enjoyed hanging out as a family. They did not seem to be in any hurry.

After about a half hour of music and an interview about a member's particular mission, the teaching portion began. Doug sat in the middle, along with another member of the congregation. They both taught, in a tag-team fashion. Aside from some interaction between the two teachers, I did not notice too much that was different about the style of preaching from other traditional churches. Following their teaching, the meeting was opened up for questions and comments. A number of people asked questions or chimed in with comments.

As John Armstrong and I left that night, he commented to me how "unradical" the whole night seemed to him. He wasn't being critical. He was just surprised, expecting something much more unconventional. After all, what was all the fuss about? Why the pushback from the traditional church?

"What were you expecting?" I asked.

"I am not sure," he said. "Something really different; something emerging. This reminded me," he said, "of a sixties Jesus-people gathering or something I have seen in the Brethren tradition. It just does not strike me as that out-of-the-box or different." I agreed.

The next morning John and I met Doug and Tony at a famous pancake restaurant. I explained to Doug and Tony that I was writing a book that would dialogue with the emerging church on seven different issues, preaching being one of them. I mentioned that I had read Doug's book and was interested in progressive dialogue. In grad school, I told them, one of my political philosophy professors, Father James Schall, used the Socratic method to teach. I used a modified version of it in my early ministry days.

But right then, Doug stopped me. "This is not about technique," he said. "My book on preaching is not about adopting progressive preaching as just one more method to reinvigorate the pulpit. The problem with Socratic teaching is that the teacher knows the outcome and is just steering his students in that direction." He explained to me that what they are talking about is not a new method but a different hermeneutic.

"OK, can you explain more?" I asked.

At that point Tony jumped in. He explained that there are three views of preaching that predominate in American evangelicalism: bounded-set, centered-set and those with a "relational hermeneutic" (see page 37). Solomon's Porch is an example of a relational hermeneutic. This means, Doug suggested, that they have a hermeneutic of community where nothing is privileged, not even the Bible, over the community in discovering and living out truth. The Bible is just one of the conversation partners, according to Doug. Progressive dialogue then comes out of this hermeneutic. If we don't understand this point, he said, we won't understand what it means to reimagine preaching.

I asked them whether the majority of leaders in the emerging camp are centered-set or relational-set. They replied without hesitation that they are centered-set. But the problem, Tony countered, is that if you push a centered-set person into a corner on issues like inerrancy, they come out fighting like a bounded-set fundamentalist. In other words, scratch a centered-set person and underneath is a bounded-set person who retreats right back into the foundationalism of the traditional church. So in one sense, for Tony and Doug, there are only two groups—bounded-set and relational-set.

On the way back to the airport, John and I processed what we had heard. We agreed with them that the view they were espousing, a relational hermeneutic, put them at odds with not only the traditional church (bounded-set) but also the majority of the emerging church, who largely hold a centered-set hermeneutic.[3] John and I concluded that they seemed to reject any commitment to the classical orthodoxy of the Great Tradition. In the quest for truth, nothing can be privileged over the community—and certainly not a theology that had been worked out in the fourth and fifth centuries.

I asked John, "If we are understanding them correctly, does this view put them outside of evangelical bounds as so many of their critics have been saying? And if it does, does this invalidate Doug's method of progressional preaching as a legitimate third way for the church?" We talked about these questions for hours as we awaited our delayed flights. No doubt, Doug and Tony had stimulated our thinking on this topic, and they had become our friends.

Not wanting to dismiss Doug's views on preaching because of one brief breakfast conversation, I decided when I got home to read his book for a third time, keeping in mind his call for a relational-set hermeneutic as the key that unlocks this new style of preaching. I wanted to see how much this hermeneutic permeated his writings. What I discovered, as I read with new eyes, is that it affects his views throughout.

Moving beyond speaching. According to Doug, his view of hermeneutics can't be understood without first understanding what he is rejecting. In *Preaching Re-Imagined* he calls traditional preaching "speaching," a word he coined. He calls it speaching because it is a one-way monologue. It is the creation of the Enlightenment and depends on foundationalism—overconfidence in our ability to know truth that is universal and transcends perspectives and context. Over many chapters in the book, he makes the case that speaching tends to be arrogant, manipulates emotions and controls outcomes of belief, dehumanizes people and makes them passive, hurts the development of healthy community, and removes the pastor from the congregation in his preparation and sets him up as the only expert.[4] This is a sweeping indictment.

What is the alternative to speaching, and how does it depend on a relational-set hermeneutic? As Doug says, the alternative to speaching is progressional dialogue that "involves the intentional interplay of multiple viewpoints that leads to unexpected and unforeseen ideas. The message will change depending on who is present and who says what. This kind of preaching is dynamic in the sense that the outcome is determined on the spot by the participants."[5] On face value, this could mean simply that the sermon looks different in how it explicates the truth the pastor wants to communicate. In other words, the examples, illustrations and applications may change as people interact with the sermon, but in the end the first-tier content will come through clearly because the pastor makes sure of it.

Before my breakfast with Doug and Tony, I might have read his book this way. But now I realize this is *not* what Doug is saying. If the outcome of truth is controlled then it is not progressional dialogue but just one more form of bounded-set preaching using a cool method of interaction. Doug is not calling for a new technique to energize traditional preaching. He is calling for a new method that is intimately connected to his relational-set hermeneutic. The two cannot be separated. He is not just reacting against fundamentalist preaching, a reaction I share in part, but is advocating a new hermeneutic, one that worries me. As I read, I found myself saying amen to his critique of the Enlightenment and the lack of humility in fundamentalist preaching. But almost in the same breath, I was thinking, *Hey now, wait a minute. You are going too far in the other direction.* I kept repeating this refrain throughout the book.

Discovering truth. Why was I worried? It all comes down to how truth and reality are known. For Doug, progressional preaching, relying on a relational-set hermeneutic, privileges the community in discovering truth. The preacher or main teacher is just one of many voices of the community. "The pastor's voice is not the only one people will hear on important issues of faith," he writes.[6] He calls for the full participation of every member to be the "priesthood of believers" and use their gifts in the church.[7] "The people of God, in communion with the Bible and the Holy Spirit, have the truth of God within them," he argues.[8] In sum, truth is determined by an interaction of the people of God, the Bible and the guidance of the Holy Spirit.

But as much as I agree with him about the priesthood of all believers, the need for all to use their gifts in the body of Christ and the impact each member can have on others—producing profound community—I am left with this troubling question: If the community is the ultimate authority and the Bible just one member of the community, what prevents the community from plummeting into heresy? Moreover, does progressional preaching make every worship service a free-for-all? Doug mentions this concern in his book. He quotes one critic: "I agree that people in our churches have a lot more to say than we give them credit for. But when I hear you talk like this, the only thing I can imagine is a bad version of a Brethren meeting."[9] How does Doug respond? Unless progressional teaching is understood properly, he contends, it could become this.

Doug wants to guard the right of individuals to challenge the church. To keep it honest. To renew it so it does not get stuck in the past. I get his point. But does this mean he rejects what the people of God have held in common throughout the centuries? He says it does not. "I suggest holding to all the church has held to throughout its history."[10]

His reference to the history of the church piqued my interest. Does this mean he is adopting the Great Tradition as a standard to protect the community against heresy? Does he allow the church fathers, who worked out the "rule of faith" or "classical orthodoxy," to be a plumb line in areas of theology and doctrinal faithfulness? Do the Apostles' and Nicene Creeds mark the boundary or first tier of what it means to be a mere Christian? I don't think so. My hope for a common ground on this was soon dashed.

At the same time I was rereading *Preaching* I picked up Doug's essay "The Emerging Church and Embodied Theology," in which he says something helpful about the Great Tradition. He contends that creeds and confessions are too contextually limited. They were helpful for the church at that time and in that context. We live in a different environment that asks different questions. Because of this limitation, "we are called to be communities that are cauldrons of theological imagination, not 'authorized re-staters' of past ideas."[11] We are to forge our own theology, not borrow from the past. This is what makes listening to one another so important. "Community," not tradition or the Scriptures, "is the place where God dwells. . . . In this way, Christian community serves as a hermeneutic of the gospel."[12]

In the margin of the book I wrote:

Community (the people of God and the Bible) + Holy Spirit = theology (preaching)

In summary then, Doug is saying that "Christians have never been intended to be a people only of a book, but a people who are led by the ever-present God, active in our lives, communities and the world."[13] What we need is a "more contextual understanding of what God is saying to us in our day in order to live into it."[14] And we discover this "contextual understanding" in community, guided by the Holy Spirit, using the method of progressional dialogue. It can't come from outside; truth resides within each particular community and must be worked out there.

I concluded after carefully rereading Doug's writings that his message matches what he told me at our breakfast. He is not calling for a new technique but a new hermeneutic, which gives rise to a new method of teaching and the discovery of truth. John Armstrong and I had understood Doug and Tony well at our breakfast. Having come to this conclusion, I was now curious to discover what the traditional church had to say about progressional preaching.

THE TRADITIONAL CHURCH PUSHES BACK

Why We're Not Emergent: By Two Guys Who Should Be by Kevin DeYoung and Ted Kluck presents the most in-depth analysis of emergent theology to date.[15] DeYoung is a pastor in Michigan and Kluck is a sports journalist/writer and a member of DeYoung's church. Though they use the terms *emerging* and *emergent* interchangeably, the vast majority of their examples come from the emergent wing of the movement. It is not surprising then, that they are unhappy with Doug Pagitt's views on preaching and the relational-set hermeneutic.

The need for boundaries. In a section on Doug's preaching, Kevin rejects the view that the Bible is just one of many authorities in the believing community that helps us learn about God and live for him. When the Bible is downgraded this way, he says, its authority and specialness is eroded over time. They "can wax eloquent about the beauty of the story and how the Scriptures read us, but unless people are convinced that the Bible is authoritative, true, inspired, and the very words of God, over time they will read it less frequently, know it less fully, and trust it less surely."[16]

What is most important for the emergents is not the authority of the Bible but how God speaks to the community, sometimes using the Bible and sometimes not. The Bible is one of many voices in a community. It is not privileged; it does not stand above the community. Clearly, Kevin rejects this view: "We end up with functional authority for the Bible that is dependent upon the community rather than intrinsic authority that is based on God having spoken."[17] This means that the community is the ultimate authority in what we think about God and how we act. The emergents have lost confidence in God's Word. For Kevin the Bible must be our foundation, not the community.

Christians need boundaries, says Kevin, that are not at the mercy of community whim. Christianity can't exist without boundaries. "Being a Christian in any biblical sense requires that we not only say yes to many things, but that we also are willing to say no to a number of beliefs and behaviors." He goes on to ask "whether the emerging church has the ability to correct its own abuses and challenge the massive theological errors coming from fellow conversation partners."[18]

Even more important, continues Kevin, does the emergent church even have "the category of theological error"? "Are there no doctrinal beliefs (besides believing in statements of faith) or ethical behaviors (besides undefined lovelessness) that put one outside the camp? . . . What about Mormons? Arians? Hardcore Pelagians? Those who disbelieve the resurrection? Those who love Jesus while also worshiping Krishna, Shiva, and Vishnu?"[19]

The grave problem is that as long as the only standard is trying to "live out justice as Jesus modeled and love in community as Jesus taught, . . . if the emerging church refuses to stand for more than this, it will quickly lose any semblance of being evangelical, and semblance of being historically orthodox, and eventually any sense of being decidedly Christian."[20] This is a serious charge. Are emergents, the revisionists, outside of orthodoxy? And if they are, does this mean Doug's progressive preaching is not a helpful model? Kevin would answer affirmatively.

At its heart, much of the emergent movement's dislike of preaching, he argues, is really "an uneasiness about authority and control." He concludes that this uneasiness is really a loss of confidence in God's Word and the resistance to sitting under its authority.[21] In this resistance to authority, Kevin calls emergent "the new modern."[22] For all their talk about being postmodern, they really are "thoroughly modern." In a strong indictment of emergents, he concludes that "many of the leading books display a familiar combination of social gospel liberalism, a neo-orthodox view of Scripture, a post-Enlightenment disdain for hell, the wrath of God, propositional revelation, propitiation, and anything more than a vague moralistic, warmhearted, adoctrinal Christianity."[23]

Has Doug Pagitt been misunderstood? Unquestionably, Kevin's pushback is strong. Is he on target? Does someone who rejects first-tier beliefs, the kind enshrined in the Great Tradition, find themselves outside of mere Christianity? Are the critics of the emergent church on target? Traditionalists certainly think so. But are they right? Are they the only ones who have problems with Doug's views?

These questions were on my mind one afternoon as I sat at my two sons' tae kwon do class. While I should have been watching them, I reread sections of *Listening to the Beliefs of Emerging Churches*. I was particularly interested in the response to Doug's article by the other four participants, Dan Kimball, Mark Driscoll, John Burke and Karen Ward.

What became clear is that, though all four are associated in some way with the emerging church, Dan, Mark and John are critical of Pagitt's hermeneutic and how it shapes the teaching ministry of the church. This surprised me. All three clearly wanted to distance themselves from Pagitt and the emergent movement. It really brought home to me again the diversity in the larger emerging camp.

The most interesting response came from Dan Kimball, a longtime friend of Doug's. He begins by saying how much he appreciates Doug's analogy that theology is like dancing, that there are times when we need to try out new partners and dance to new songs. Dan too loves exploring new "dances." But the problem, says Dan, is that Doug is not clear about the need for a floor to dance on, and without it Doug is in trouble. We need a floor, a constant, a foundation on which to dance. "But I just keep coming back to the floor," Dan writes, "which would be the core doctrines of historic orthodox Christianity, such as the Nicene Creed. Don't we need some constant foundational floorboards to dance on? Otherwise there would be only falling down, not dancing."[24]

At that point I realized that I had never read or heard Dan articulate this point before, and it kind of shocked me.[25] I think it surprised Doug as well because in his response he writes that Dan's need for a "floor" is enlightening; it tells us something about their differences. "Dan holds to an authority in the Bible that I believe is better placed in the Holy Spirit," says Doug.[26] He continues, "I am not trying to say the Bible is not an important part of our faith and following, but Dan comes from a tradition that places near total authority on the Bible. So for Dan to include the creeds in his authority structure is a true sign of movement and change."[27] This sentence intrigued me. It did appear that Dan had shifted in his thinking or at least was articulating something that he had not before.

So it seems clear from Dan and Doug's interaction that DeYoung and others in the traditional camp may be on target. They are not overstating their case here. When they find fault with Doug's relational-set hermeneutic, they are not alone; many in the emerging camp (centered-set) are critical as well. They have real concerns when Doug places the community (led by the Holy Spirit) over Scripture as the hermeneutical key, and when he rejects the Great Tradition of Nicene Christianity, holding instead that each community of believers, guided by the Holy Spirit, must discover its own first-tier beliefs.

Tradition as plumb line for preaching. I have to admit I appreciate Dan's focus on the Nicene tradition. It backs up what I have been saying throughout this book on the need to reclaim the Great Tradition as a bulwark against theological and ecclesiastical wavering. All along, I have been making the case that we need tradition to help us interpret Scripture faithfully. The Great Tradition is a plumb line, a "rule of faith" the church has used for two millennia to understand the faith, live it out faithfully and pass it on to the next generation. Without this plumb line, we don't have the theological tools to remain faithful to Scripture.[28]

Why is reclaiming Nicene Christianity so vital for the emerging church's views on preaching? Much of faithful preaching is making the text practical to listeners. This requires contextualization, so the listeners can hear it in their culture. But when preachers contextualize the Bible to culture without the wisdom handed down through the ages, we too easily allow culture to shape our theology. Slowly but surely our message looks more like the culture around us. We are molded by the world (Romans 12:2) and aren't even aware of it. Without tradition as an outside marker, we have no way to know how far we have moved from biblical fidelity.[29]

CENTERED-SET PREACHING

Since I can't adopt Doug's progressional preaching because of his hermeneutic, what are my options? Is there an alternative to the kind of preaching I grew up with—three points and a poem? Is there a way of preaching that is biblical, culturally relevant and in line with the Great Tradition? Is there a way to preach and teach that engages hearers, involves them in the cominstry of discipleship, and transforms them without the shortcomings of bounded-set or relational-set preaching? I believe there is: centered-set preaching.

One of my first breakthroughs in understanding centered-set preaching came during my first year at Georgetown. I was struggling in a new city, far from my community, and I was depressed. I picked up a book called *Spiritual Depression* by Martyn Lloyd-Jones, the famous London preacher. A chapter in the book changed my life. In "The True Foundation" he says that so much of our difficulties in the Christian life (including some types of depression) come from our confusion of justification and sanctification. Once we become Christians we ignore our justification—that we are saved by grace, through faith, on account of Christ—and focus on obedience, sanctification. We stop preaching the gospel to ourselves and keep trying to live the Christian life. But we can't live up to the ideal and get discouraged, maybe even depressed. I certainly was.

The solution to this problem is to put our justification before our sanctification every day. Only when we preach the gospel to ourselves—our justification, our adoption, our union with Christ, our participation in the kingdom of God—will we have the power and motivation to obey. We need grace to be saved, and we need grace to obey. Reading this was revolutionary to my life. I had discovered the solution to the roller coaster of the Christian life—commitment, failure, depression, recommitment, failure and depression. I found the answer to security, joy, peace and steadiness. Forget about regaining "my first love." I found a way to never lose it in the first place. I remember calling my buddies who, like me, struggled with feeling close to God. Our failures always dampened our enthusiasm for the faith. What I had found changed everything. And I knew it had ramifications for preaching and teaching.

I soon discovered that this view of justification and sanctification has been called the indicative and imperative.[30] The indicative indicates who we are in Christ through his saving grace. The imperative of the gospel impels or empowers us to obey God's commands as an act of gratitude for the new life that we have. I came to realize that the Bible was filled with this pattern of teaching and preaching—the indicative of new life, followed by a life of service in God's kingdom, the imperative.

> I appeal to you therefore, brothers, by the mercies of God, to present your bodies as a living sacrifice, holy and acceptable to God, which is your spiritual worship. Do not be conformed to this world, but be transformed by the renewal of your mind, that by testing you may discern what is the will of God, what is good and acceptable and perfect. (Romans 12:1-2 ESV)

The mercies of God Paul speaks of are explained in the first eleven chapters of Romans—justification, adoption, perseverance and union with Christ. Because of these mercies it is reasonable to present our lives to him in obedience. The imperatives, that is, the laws, commands and instructions, come out of a transformed life.

This biblical balance is what I was missing growing up. Its absence causes the Christian life to tumble into works of righteousness that engender two types of people mentioned earlier—those who think they are pulling it off in their own strength, and those who despair of reaching this lofty ideal. This insight launched me into the teaching ministry in the church, and I could not wait to share it with other burdened Christians like me. And in the early days of Twenty-Something Fellowship I saw lives transformed by this message.

In addition to the indicative and the imperative, one other insight changed the way I think about preaching. In my early days of ministry I came across Eugene Lowry's *The Homiletical Plot*.[31] According to Lowry, traditional preaching tends to be deductive; that is, it makes three points and sets out to prove them using logical arguments, illustrations and application. But this takes all the drama out of the sermon. It is like revealing the climax before seeing the movie. Once you know the conclusion, all the tension, the myriad twists and turns, and the surprising reversals of fortune are missed. The sermon lacks homiletical drama. That's it. That is exactly what I felt sitting through so many sermons.

Lowry proposes sermons that follow the natural flow of a dramatic story—problem to solution. In every text of Scripture the author is addressing a problem—whether it be sin, idolatry, suffering or the seeming absence of God. Then the author hits us with the solution, be it forgiveness, union with Christ, the kingdom or the providential care of our heavenly Father. Like a good story, the Bible dramatically presents the problem, slowly demonstrates its power to undo the main characters and then takes our breath away with the sudden turn of events that shocks us with unexpected grace.

Lowry calls this the "aha" moment in the sermon. Along with the biblical characters', our lives are suddenly and dramatically turned upside down by the surprising grace of God. Once transformed by this grace, we are free and empowered to live differently. The indicative leads to the imperative. The Heidelberg Catechism saw this movement as "guilt, grace, and grateful living." These steps are the key to a good story, central to the Bible and at the heart of great preaching, which is relevant, gripping, gospel-centered and inspiring. This pulls an audience in as full participants, like the best novel or movie does.

Over the years I have discovered that this method is vital to centered-set preaching. Whereas traditional preaching (deductive, legalistic, imperative-driven) appeals to bounded-set evangelicalism, and progressional preaching (inductive, open-ended, experiential) appeals to relational-set emergents—the homiletical plot attracts the centered-set deep church.

In some ways this method of preaching combines the strengths of traditional and emergent preaching. Like relational-set preaching it is inductive—setting up the problem, asking the questions, analyzing the situation and then moving to the solution together. But then it lays out the solution's ramifications in a deductive manner, similar to bounded-set preaching. The big difference is that unlike bounded- and relational-set preaching, centered-set preaching always includes a linchpin, the aha moment, the life-changing, transforming power of God's surprising grace through Jesus—his kingdom, his gospel, his salvation and the new life he brings. Neither traditional nor emergent preaching consistently provides this in its sermons—and thus it is hard to avoid legalism.

A Christ-centered homiletical plot is centered-set preaching. Our goal is not to set up boundary markers to keep Christians safe or to keep those who don't agree with us out. Rather, we preach Christ in every text, laying out and analyzing the human condition through Scriptures and experience, and exposing the radical, shocking grace of God that enters our situation, transforms us and empowers us to live differently. Thus we do not spend much time preaching against the world—we have enough worldliness inside of us for sermon material. We don't exhaust our energies preaching the need to try harder, live better and be more holy without first exposing our inability to do so apart from the transforming power of the cross and the resurrection in our lives. Anything less is legalism—which ends in pride or discouragement.

DRAWN TO THE WELL

Remember Hirsch and Frost's story of the need for a deep well in the Australian Outback? "It is assumed that livestock, though they will stray, will never roam too far from the well, lest they die. That is a centered set. As long as there is a supply of clean water, the livestock will remain close by."[32] As I see it, the well is the gospel—the continual preaching of it through Word and sacrament, the announcement of Jesus' kingdom, and a grace-transformed community witnessing the power of this new life in the world. Centered-set preaching does this. It emphasizes the gospel, not boundaries. It doesn't major in the minors. (Though minor doctrinal points are important, they are not as vital as sinking the well deep week in and week out.)

Thus centered-set preaching brings new focus to our homiletics. But it also dictates our hermeneutic. Our preaching—based on the indicative-imperative typology and the insights of the homiletical plot with Christ as the aha—places its confidence in the first-tier doctrines of the Great Tradition. Because the Scriptures are so clear here, we speak with great confidence and dogmatic boldness in the area of the gospel. As Dan Kimball says, "we can hold bold confidence about essential core doctrines. In fact, I believe emerging generations are looking for something to believe in. I believe they are looking for 'truth' and when we do have something we know is true, we should clearly and boldly say it."[33]

This is a well sunk deep. We keep coming back for the life-giving water. But as Dan continues, "I have heard such stinky, stinky attitudes from people who nail down their theological beliefs with such certainty that there is an 'everyone else is wrong but us' attitude."[34] What is missing is cognitive humility, admitting that the church throughout history has not spoken in one voice on some of the second-tier issues; we need to be modest toward others in the doctrines we hold. This does not mean that we don't study these second-tier doctrines, preach and teach them, inspire our congregation to be different because of them, but we don't use them to divide us from other Christians.

Let me provide an example. To become a member of Redeemer Church you must be a Nicene Christian, committed to "living as becomes a follower of Christ" and be willing to submit to the community. What about views on baptism? The Lord's Supper? Politics? The end times? The anti-Christ? Although important and although we hold views on each of them, holding different views on these topics will not keep you from the Well of Redeemer and belonging to our church.

Our preaching and teaching attempts to model this centered-set hermeneutic. My goal is to offer the congregation the life-giving power of living water via the redemptive drama that runs from Genesis to Revelation. Using the homiletical plot, I attempt to draw them into the text with in-depth analysis of the problem in their lives, be it unbelief, discouragement, idols, temptation or heart rebellion, exposing these idols and preparing their hearts to hear Christ and how his redemptive benefits supply our every need.

The more I do this, the more people see this drama in the Bible for themselves and are able to recognize the categories of creation, Fall, redemption and the kingdom running through every story, chapter and epistle of the Bible. It is an empowering way to preach and teach that takes the priesthood of all believers seriously, freeing them from a wrong and unhealthy dependence on the preacher as the keeper of insights. They are able to read Scripture and interpret it themselves. As they are built up in the Word, they are able to minister to each other and to me.

Realizing and trusting that Redeemer's members can faithfully interpret the Scriptures and can take these insights and apply them to each other's lives, we have put dialogue and sermon discussion at the heart of our small groups, which we call "community groups." Through dramatic preaching of the homiletical plot, we are giving them the tools to grow deep and disciple each other. Each week we provide their community groups with discussion questions (they can also create their own) that center on experiencing the power of the gospel and living it out in community, in their friendships, family and on the job. Our goal is neither disseminating information nor achieving a certain spiritual experience, but transformation. This happens in centered-set preaching, in community groups and in individual lives as we live out the gospel with boldness, conviction and humility.

My first experience on a church staff was being part of a seventeen-member pastoral team, which was responsible for the shepherding of over five thousand people. And I recall one staff meeting well. After talking with the leaders of the many adult Sunday school classes, which had a total weekly attendance of over one thousand, the pastor in charge of adult ministry told us that the members did not feel shepherded by the pastoral staff. In fact, they complained about the total lack of pastoral care on all levels of the church. The countenances of the pastors fell dramatically. One pastor commented on how discouraging this was to hear. After all, he was already putting sixty hours a week into his ministry. Others too were putting in long hours. What did these people mean that there is no shepherding? How could they say this? Don't they realize how hard we work to "shepherd" them?

But after everyone got over feeling hurt, we began to analyze the situation. We discovered that over 60 percent of our week was taken up by meetings, committees, paperwork and other institutional chores. A large percentage of the remaining time was spent working on sermons or leading events. There was not much time left for face-to-face shepherding or leading our people in mission. I remember at the time thinking that institutionalism was killing our church.

A short time later, I was reading a book by Eugene Peterson, who, along with being the translator of *The Message*, has written many books to encourage pastors.[1] I remember reading somewhere in one of his books that when he was a young Presbyterian pastor, he learned a valuable lesson about bureaucracy. Early on he discovered that the monthly reports he was required to send into the denomination were not being read. Well, at least not entirely. They were being looked at to see how he was doing in increasing attendance, giving and building the institution. When these numbers slipped, he got a call. But they never seemed concerned with how he was doing spiritually or whether the church was growing in biblical knowledge, discipleship and outreach. So just to test his theory, he began writing his monthly reports in a rather shocking manner, describing his doubts about the faith, his struggles with sin and his uncertainties about being called to the pastorate. He kept this up for a number of months. The response? Nothing. He was stunned and saddened. The bureaucrats were not even reading them, save for the numbers. He realized that institutions care most about their survival, even over the spiritual growth of the people and their pastor.

So a few years later when we were starting Redeemer Presbyterian Church, I knew I wanted to do things differently. I wanted our church to be less institutional, more organic, more concerned with the spiritual needs of the church. My convictions on this were strengthened during the first year of the church when I read John Miller's *Outgrowing the Ingrown Church*.[2] Miller was a pastor and a professor at Westminster Seminary in Philadelphia for many years, and has been a big influence on Tim Keller and other church planters. In his book he diagnoses how churches over time become ingrown, focused on institutional survival and maintenance.

Miller says a church slowly becomes a "religious cushion," where people come to hear a message and be reassured that their doctrine is correct and other churches are wrong. Church members are no longer interested in missional Christianity, that is, being sent out into the world to be salt and light. They want safety, not challenge; security, not risk. For a time, Miller, who was a pastor, dropped out of church ministry to sort things out. He came back after much soul searching. What he discovered in his time away was that God's vision for the church is one of thrilling mission, not one of ingrown tribalism. He set out to introduce this exciting vision to his church, and his book is the road map. Reading his book, I had one of those aha moments. This was the kind of community I wanted to start and lead—one that was rooted deeply in the gospel of forgiveness and compelled by God's mercies to become a people of compassion to those outside the church.

For the first few years of Redeemer, it seemed to work well. Because we were small, I could keep the structure to a minimum. I wanted it to be organic, team-led and deeply spiritual. I did not want institutionalism to encroach on what we were doing. One of my first sermon series was on revival and moving away from dead religion. I know I was reacting against my past experience, but I did not want to lose this early spiritual vigor and succumb to dead institutionalism. Because we were so new, we needed and depended on the entire church to use their gifts and get involved. And they did.

But as we grew, an interesting thing happened. We found that people were getting frustrated with the lack of structure. It may have been organic, but the church seemed too loose, a little too sloppy. When a meeting got canceled for a good reason I thought we were being fluid and flexible. When the church service was not micromanaged, I thought it showed we were spiritual and were trusting God. But some thought otherwise. And the lack of organization made it difficult for newcomers to know how to get involved.

Because of these concerns and all the new growth, we began to initiate more structure. We put together a flow chart of all the different teams, who was leading them and how they related to one another. We had monthly meetings and other planning times. We called our new desire to organize "functional structures." The church continued to grow. New leaders were coming on board. Like any growing community, the church was energized by the increase in attendance.

Some of our people loved the new structure. But others hated it. They saw it as my attempt to consolidate my control over the vision and direction of the church. The more leaders I tapped, the more some thought I was just bringing in "yes" people. Others thought the structure was put in place to eliminate their input. I felt I couldn't win. What was the right way to organize a church? Should it be organic or institutional? Or both? What role do structures and authority play? What is the most biblical ecclesiology? With so much on the line, I was determined to find out. As is my custom when I get into trouble or need an answer, I began to read and ask questions.

LIQUID CHURCH

I realized right away that the emerging church was asking some of the same questions. Many of them were as frustrated with institutionalism as I was and were doing some hard thinking on the subject. Their thinking was being fueled by their passion for mission and their conviction, which I share, that the church is sent into the world. But the institutionalization of the church kept getting in the way. So if the church was to return to its original calling, to be missional, it had to rethink its ecclesiology. As I read emerging literature, I was intrigued by their call for the organic church.[3] I found it refreshing, particularly their passion for evangelism.

I came across Pete Ward's *Liquid Church*,[4] which Fuller Seminary uses in some of their classes. Ward's book does not represent the entire emerging movement, which holds a spectrum of views on ecclesiology.[5] In some ways, his views might fit best in the reconstructionist part of the emerging church; not everything he says will resonate with others in the emerging camp.[6] Nonetheless, I believe his thinking captures the thoughts of a large segment of the emerging church and continues to drive the conversation in many parts of the emerging world. To take seriously the call to a more organic ecclesiology to counter institutionalism, I needed to interact with Ward's book.

Pete Ward teaches at King's College in London and attends an Anglican church. He writes in the introduction that "liquid church does not exist yet," nor has he "set up and run a successful, thriving liquid church." His book "is an attempt to imagine rather than describe a different way of being church." What is the liquid church? It's a shift from seeing the church as a congregation that meets in one place at one time to "a notion of a church as a series of relationships and communications."[7] Two or three people in a coffee shop talking about God is the church. Church is more a network or a web rather than an assembly of people. He contrasts these networks with the "solid" churches, which are characterized by structures, institutions and meetings. Church is no longer something we attend but "the communication of Christ through informal fellowship" that "creates connections, groupings, and relationships." Liquid church is something we are part of all the time.

Ward writes that the greatest reason for changing our view of church is because the institutional church is no longer effective in reaching those outside the church. So the motivation is mission.[8] He continues by stressing that the early church in one city did not meet in one place but in house churches scattered throughout the city. Only once in a while did it come together for a large meeting. This gives us the freedom, he posits, to see the church as more of a network of small groups who stay connected via communication. He sees this move to house churches and small groups as another vital reformation.[9]

What has caused this need for renewal? The failure of the institutional, "solid" church. With the shift in culture from solid modernity to liquid (post)modernity, the solid church can no longer effectively reach the population. He argues that the church has internalized some of the core values of modernity. "The importance of attendance at church services, the emphasis on planting more churches, the one-size-fits-all worship and the development of church life as a kind of club all indicate the extent to which church has internalized solid modernity."[10] Many in my tradition would agree.

OK, good enough, I thought. Nothing too shocking here. But what is the way forward for the church? How can it overcome the dead institutionalism of solid church and effectively and confidently move into the future? According to Ward, the church must become liquid.

Ward mentions that his lectures on being liquid engender much criticism. I can see why. It is one thing to be critical of institutional*ism* and another thing to want to throw out the institution altogether. At least this is what it sounds like he is proposing. Ward's critics see his view of liquid church as an attack on the corporate nature of Christianity. They contend that it will lead to more individualism. But he pushes back, saying he is not abandoning the church as community in favor of fragmented individualism. Rather, he wants us to see that there are many different cultural expressions of what this corporate body of Christ might look like; the Bible gives us tremendous freedom in the area of structure.

What would the liquid church look like? According to Ward, it would be characterized by no regular meetings, constant communication, limited or no formal structure, and no ordained ministry or offices. He stresses that the liquid church is about relationships, being connected in a myriad of groupings, activities and events. The goal is to live together every day. Meetings would be varied, with lots of variety in worship, prayer, study and activity. When the group gathers, there would be no ordained clergy; everyone will have a chance to participate. Does this mean that there is no structure, that the groups are leaderless? I don't think so. He seems to be in favor of small doses of structure to water the seed of the organism. He is open to house churches or other relational groups.

THE MISSION HOUSE CHURCH

A friend told me about a house church in Orange, California, about twenty minutes from my house. When I looked it up at OCHouseChurch.com, there were only two or three house churches listed in Orange County, an area with three million people. (Surely there are more.) I contacted the leader, Keith Giles, and we met for coffee at a local Starbucks. Keith, who is married with two boys, works as a writer for a large tech company. He is an ordained Southern Baptist minister who had pastored at different churches around Orange County before taking his present job.

"Do you miss pastoring at traditional churches?" I asked.

"No," he said. "Not at all. What I love most about my job is being in daily contact with nonbelievers. It gives me a chance to be missional."

Three years ago, he and his wife decided to start a house church called The Mission. Their website informs us:

OUR VISION: To be a community that models the life and love of Jesus to our world and to one another. OUR MISSION: We are a community in love with Jesus. We are the Church. We have a mission to be Jesus to our friends, neighbors and our world. WHO WE ARE: We are an outward focused Christian community with an inward commitment to love and disciple others to Jesus' way of life.[11]

Who can argue with that?

I asked Keith if he had read Frank Viola's *Reimagining Church* or Viola and Barna's *Pagan Christianity?*—both of which are popular in house-church circles. He said he had.

"Do you agree with the main thesis?"

"Yes, by and large," he said. "Although I see the danger of them being purely reactive. I mean," he said, "look at the name 'Pagan Christianity?' That is a pretty judgmental title."

I had to agree.

But although he does not like the title, he has come to many of the same conclusions. This is why he left the institutional church to start a house church. He thinks the traditional church has gotten off-track.

"What do you mean?" I asked.

"Well, as I look at the Bible," Keith observed, "I don't see God residing in a temple anymore. We are the temple of God, each one of us. This means every one of us is to act as a priest, this is what the priesthood of all believers means."

"Does this mean that you are no longer in favor of the ordained ministry?" I asked, realizing that he is still ordained.

"Yes, that is right. What I want to see is everyone using their gifts, ministering to one another. I am not in favor of offices or officers, because they get in the way of people doing the work of the ministry. If people think someone is being paid or is ordained to be the pastor, then why should they serve? And they won't. I try to get out of the way as much as possible so others will step up and use their gifts. Sometimes the best house-church meetings are the ones when I am not even there. That way they don't look to me as their leader. They don't over-rely on me to do the shepherding," he concluded.

That night I attended The Mission House Church at Keith's home. When I arrived, the ten adults and six children were eating take-out Chinese food. It looked like a big family gathering. Keith introduced me to everyone. They were very friendly and knew I was there to observe. I felt right at home. After dinner, they gathered in the living room to start their meeting. Keith sat on the floor with a guitar and four song sheets. As he began, everyone, including the children, joined in. Clearly they knew the songs. No overhead or song sheets were provided for me. Luckily I knew a few of the contemporary praise choruses. *But what about a guest or a nonbeliever?* I thought to myself. They would feel excluded. Keith had told me earlier that their house church was mainly for Christians. They were not attempting to be evangelistic in their meetings as some in the organic church are. Evangelism was for the rest of the week. As they sang, the children took turns playing along on two bongos, which were not in tune. But they enjoyed it, and I did not find it distracting. I could tell that having the children present and involved was important for them. I smiled as I thought of my own four children learning to worship.

Following the singing, Keith explained that because they were out of juice, they would not be taking Communion, something they do every time they gather. Normally, they have Communion right after the singing, different from the historic tradition, which places Communion after the preaching of the Word. So instead of the Lord's Supper, they went right into their share time. Keith had explained to me earlier that they had no formal teaching time. He did not preach or teach at either their Sunday-morning gathering or the Thursday-night meeting. Instead they had this time when anybody can read Scripture and explain why it is important to them.

One of Keith's sons began. He asked everyone to turn to Daniel 3, the story of the fiery furnace. After reading the passage, he shared how important it was to fear God and obey him at all costs. Others jumped in, echoing his thoughts. A single woman said, "Would I be like that? I am not sure I would." One of the children asked to share another passage. After her brief comments, the adults added more commentary. And that was the pattern: the children volunteered a passage and the adults responded to it. What struck me is how eager the kids were to share a passage and talk about it. They really loved this part of the meeting. One mom talked about how anxious her son and daughter were to get to house church tonight. They were excited to share their passages. I was also struck by how seriously the adults took the kids' participation and opinions. They valued, listened to and affirmed them.

Finally, I was impressed with the biblical maturity of the adults and their comments on the Scripture. Clearly, these are folks who have been around the church for many years and have heard lots of solid evangelical sermons. After about an hour of share time, they spend about ten minutes in prayer for one another. One little boy was already asleep in his dad's arms. It was time to go. As I walked out the door after saying my goodbyes, I thought about how impressed I was that 100 percent of their offerings go to feed the poor. They spend significant time each month at a local poor hotel, meeting with residents and playing with the children who live there. They are taking their name and their vision statement seriously. I wished more churches would be so committed.

THE TRADITIONAL CHURCH PUSHES BACK

As excited as I was about aspects of organic Christianity, like their passion for evangelism and community, I wanted to see what the traditional church critics would say. Would they be open to the idea of liquid church and organic Christianity? Or would they reject it outright? I found an article on the Web called "An Ecclesiological Assessment of the Emerging Church Movement" by Professor John Hammett of Southeastern Baptist Theological Seminary.[12] *Perfect,* I thought, especially since Keith was ordained in the Southern Baptist denomination. The irony was not lost on me.

I could tell immediately that the traditional church was suspicious of what the emerging church was teaching on ecclesiology. This sentence stuck out: "The more emerging churches target the postmodern generation, the more they risk becoming what they oppose, a religious reflection of our consumer culture." Hammett notes that the "church always faces the twin dangers of cultural captivity and cultural irrelevance."[13] Or as I say so often in my sermons, the dangers of tribalism and assimilation.[14]

Hammett continues by saying that the emerging church is correct in charging evangelicalism as being "captive to modern culture and irrelevant to postmodern culture." Yet the problem is that "the emerging church itself runs the risk of being captive to culture, only to postmodern culture." What is needed is not this type of accommodation but for the church to take the posture of "Christ against culture."[15]

Hammett is saying that the emerging church has succumbed to syncretism in its ecclesiology. A very strong charge. The desire to reach postmodern culture has allowed the culture to overwhelm its ecclesiology, the way it structures and organizes its church. In its attempt to be relevant it has adopted forms and structures that mirror the trends in the culture—leaderless groups, the demise of office, no hierarchy, fluid structures and limited accountability. These are trends of the new business model, and they don't bode well for the church. They open up the church, claims Hammett, to succumbing to the consumer model that they criticize so much in the traditional church.[16]

Keith would agree that they have no hierarchy, offices and fluid structures. But he would disagree that there is no accountability. When I asked him about discipline, he said it is done through the relationships that are built in the house church. He mentioned a few times that he has had to confront the wrong choices people have made.

"But what about when the leader is a lot younger and not as theologically trained? Would they be able to do the same? Or would they just let it go?" I asked.

"If they are not going to listen to me, when I love them," he said, "why would they listen to someone above me in a hierarchy?"

I would have to agree. Maybe. Unless they have made membership promises to do so and had the theological conviction that their leaders watched over their souls (Hebrews 13:17).

But the traditional church's criticism does not stop with the charge of syncretism. As I read more, I found more arguments against the organic view of the church. Other critics were deeply suspicious of its leadership model. They admit that structure and leadership can be and have been abused in the past, and that leaders must allow their authority to be shaped by love. But they are quick to point out that the new business model, which is enamored with leaderless groups and shared authority and decision making, can backfire and lead to abuse of power. Tyrannical leaders work just as well in chaos as they do in tightly controlled authoritarian structures. Maybe even better.[17]

But even more dangerous is the fact that millions in the emerging church are now given an excuse to pursue their faith outside of the institutional church in these loose networks of association. This is deeply troubling for the traditional church critics. In an age of rampant individualism that eschews accountability, discipline and authority because it may cramp total freedom, these people are avoiding some of the very things they need to grow and be sustained in their Christian walks. They need the traditional view of the church to grow in their faith and avoid total enculturation.

STANDSTILL

So here is the problem. The traditional church thinks that Pete Ward, Keith Giles and others are not as biblical as they need to be. They are too enamored with the world's way of doing things and thus have put the church in jeopardy with their ecclesiology. But Ward and Giles would say they have worked out a biblical view of ecclesiology. In fact the emerging church counters that the traditional church is not as biblical as it should be. It is too compromised by the modernism of the Enlightenment.

Both camps, the traditional and emerging, claim to have a biblical view of church. But they reach different conclusions. Same biblical texts, different conclusions. Telling the emerging church that they need a more biblical ecclesiology just won't do it. They believe they have a scriptural view and that the traditionalists need a more biblical view of mission, which should shape the structures of the church to be effective in reaching the world.[18]

So who is right? What will end this standoff? And how can this dialogue help me as a church planter build a biblical, healthy and outwardly focused church?

A NEW WAY TO FRAME THE DEBATE

As I pondered this standoff I found myself deeply appreciative of the organic-church arguments for a new way of doing church. But I also found myself agreeing when the traditional church pointed out the dangers of this networked view of the church. The liquid church inspires me with their passion for mission and the traditional church moves me with their calls for returning the institution to full health. But as much as I liked both arguments, revolution *and* reformation, I also sensed that something is missing in the dialogue.

As I mentally tried to mediate between the two sides, I could not get around the fact that without the Great Tradition being part of this equation, something was not right. So after much thought, here is what I came up with: *Without the Great Tradition teaching us about the inherited forms of church structure and government, we will continue to talk past one another. There is no other way to move beyond this standoff and find a common ground.*

The traditional church accuses the emerging camp of syncretism, of selling out to worldliness. The emerging church accuses the traditional church of irrelevance, of becoming tribal and uncaring to those around it. Each side claims to be biblical. And on it goes. I could not get around Miroslav Volf's contention that we are in danger of sidestepping the deep thinking necessary about the nature of the church, how salvation and growth may or may not be mediated through it, and the place of officers in the church. I was stuck by the irony that Southern Baptists Hammett and Giles, both claiming to be thoroughly biblical, are coming up with wildly different ecclesiologies. Could this be because neither one has the resource of the Great Tradition?

As Volf says, both sides pick what they want out of the Bible to back up their views. And because of this, neither wrestles with the history of the church and what the past two thousand years can teach us about the nature of ecclesiology. I think he is dead on. So with this preliminary hypothesis in hand and with a desperate desire to find unity in the church, I set out to formulate a third way—a vision that could help me build the deep church. I came up with

Bible + Tradition + Mission = Deep Ecclesiology

Instead of seeing only the Bible and its emphasis on mission as the foundation for our ecclesiology (liquid and organic model) or the Bible and second-tier traditions (traditional church model), I add an important third component—the Great Tradition. This three-pronged view allows the deep church to take much of what is good about the organic and traditional views and move beyond them.

We not only take the Bible and mission seriously in our ecclesiology but the "inherited forms" of the church as well. Why? Because without this tradition we lack the individual and corporate wisdom to correctly interpret what the Bible says about the church and how it should be organized. In the crucible of day to day life together, it is too easy to think we are being biblical when we either let the traditions and preferences of the recent past dictate our ecclesiology or let the surrounding culture mold our views of church structure.

The traditional church (especially those with a free-church background) has been influenced as much by the corporate model of modernity of the past 150 years as by the Bible. Traditionalists may think this model is biblical, but without the long view of history and tradition it is hard to tell. On the other hand the emerging church has opened itself up to the cultural reshaping of the Bible's teaching of church offices and discipline. In the end, by not looking to the Great Tradition for insight, neither camp may have the resources to resist cultural accommodation.

I have come to the conclusion the hard way—in the trenches of parish ministry. It is my conviction that tradition and history act as checks on our views of the Bible and the world. If we neglect this vital history of the church and God's faithful working in it, we are bound to repeat the mistakes of the past. Instead, we need to learn from the mistakes, be recalibrated by the wisdom of the past, and work out what it means to be the church today in light of the Bible, mission and tradition.[19] This has been our goal at Redeemer.

DEEP ECCLESIOLOGY

How has Redeemer Church put this triad of Bible, tradition and mission into practice? Tentatively and humbly, yet with confidence. The following outlines five practical ways these are worked out in the deep church.

1. Balance. First, we have concluded that the tradition (and the best of the inherited forms of the church) teaches that the body of Christ is called to be both institution and organism. Having been brought into the faith by the saving work of God through Christ, tradition calls us to take our place in this community.

This past Sunday we had the honor of hearing six-year-old Annika Bahnsen give her profession of faith to the whole church, which in part (she was baptized into God's covenant family as an infant) makes her eligible to participate in Communion. Seeing her profess her faith and make promises to the congregation and to the leadership was amazing. I had a huge smile on my face.

For the deep church, membership is important for all ages. We take our membership promises seriously. Part of being a member of Redeemer Presbyterian Church is submitting—for the love of others—to certain laws, structures and leaders. All healthy communities, even families, have laws, structure and leaders. We have not been afraid to embrace the church as institution. Our life together requires love, and love demands certain laws, whether informal or formal, to be adopted to bless the community. Although most of these laws are not vital to our salvation, they are necessary to maintain the love and unity of the community. Thus they are adopted voluntarily by all members for the benefit of the community. Our four core commitments, our church government and other informal rules of behavior help us to serve the cause of love. We don't shy away from talking about them because we realize they are necessary for the health of the community.

But the church is also an organism. We once were not a people of mercy, but now we are a people of mercy (1 Peter 2:10). God's mercy and his call upon his people to help renew his good creation lead to an outward stance toward the world. We are not only a people called into something—the institution—but we are called in order to be sent out on mission to renew the world. The history of the church calls us back to this important balance. When we don't keep these two aspects of the church—institution and organism—in perspective, our ecclesiology gets out of shape and we enter unhealthy territory.

In short, at Redeemer we realize that the question is not whether the church is an institution, for it certainly is and cannot avoid being so, but what that institution looks like and what its goals are.

2. God calls leaders. Deep ecclesiology learns from the Great Tradition that officers—elders and deacons—have been an essential part of the church from the start (Acts 14:23).[20] As enticing as the idea of leaderless groups and home churches are, it is hard to get around the biblical teaching of official elders and deacons. Yes, we want to be organic and missional, and we want the priesthood of believers to be a reality. But at the same time we realize that no local church can survive long and stay true to its calling without explicitly recognized leaders and, I would say, offices. The long history of the church bears this out.[21]

Recently, in the middle of a worship service, we ordained our newest elder. I got to stand in front of the congregation and explain to them what the office of elder is all about. I am thankful that the Great Tradition (and our particular tradition) has wonderful resources on the importance of ordination and the divinely given authority of the offices. I was able to share with the congregation how elders are called primarily to do four things: (1) guard the integrity of the Word and sacraments and their gospel message, (2) protect the unique, God-given vision of this particular local church, (3) train people to be coministers, and (4) exercise godly discipline when needed.

After making vows to the congregation "faithfully to perform all the duties [of an elder] and to endeavor by the grace of God to adorn the profession of the gospel in your life, and to set a worthy example before the Church of which God has made you an officer," the candidate knelt down. As all the elders laid hands on him, I prayed over him that God would use his life and ministry to strengthen and protect the church and to lead us into mission to the world. I prayed that God would help him not only to be an amazing leader but at the same time raise up others to lead and serve. I was so thankful to be able to draw from the tradition that provides great material for working out the biblical tension between seeing all people as ministers with gifts and certain people being called to lead the church by preaching the Word and administering the sacraments.[22] This is missional leadership in action.[23]

The Great Tradition also teaches us that the ordained office of elder/pastor is charged with godly discipline. According to the Heidelberg Catechism, "The preaching of the holy gospel and Christian discipline" are the means by which the kingdom of heaven is opened and shut (§83). We realize this is not popular these days and has often been abused. But a church can't stay healthy and missional for long without discipline. My greatest concern about house churches like Keith Giles's is that there is no formal structure for discipline. When I asked him who would mediate a struggle between him and another member or leader, particularly if this person was out of line, he really did not know. He would try, he said, to convince that person based on the strength of their relationship. But I have seen firsthand that this is not always enough. Sometimes a higher court, like an elder board or a denomination, is needed.

While the vast majority of discipline in the deep church comes through the discipleship process (e.g., carefully teaching the Scriptures, small group accountability and informal exhortation), there are times when more formal discipline is needed—talking to the elders, suspension from the Lord's Supper or from a leadership post, or even excommunication.

As I ponder how important discipline is for the health of the church, I wonder if the liquid church is so popular, in part, because leaders want to avoid certain challenges to the people they are trying to reach.[24] As a pastor I realize how hard it is to confront someone in habitual sin. But I am called to the task, usually with tears. People today don't want to be held accountable. And they certainly don't want to be disciplined when they do something wrong. But for the good of their souls and the community, we have to embrace the challenge of godly discipline, both informal and formal. The inherited structures of the past teach us this.

3. Worship as a means of grace. Along with what it teaches us about the offices of the church, tradition reveals that the church is not just a voluntary society but an actual means of grace. The ancient church tells us that although worship occurs seven days a week, there is something special about the weekly gathering on Sunday. What is it? Enabling grace for our growth in the Christian life. As we consistently remind our people, the public reading and preaching of the Word play a special role in feeding, empowering, correcting and inspiring them. The sacrament, as an ordinance for the whole community, conveys the real presence of Christ and powerfully speaks of unity. The Lord's Supper is the visible expression of the Word, which is to feed us, energizing us like spiritual fuel for the long journey ahead.

We take this so seriously that we encourage our folks to attend worship with another body of believers when they are away for the weekend on business or pleasure. In fact, some of our members take great pride in bringing back the bulletin and a greeting from the congregation they visited.

4. Cultivate tradition. Moreover, the Great Tradition helps us think about how biblically and missionally informed institutions pass on the best traditions (1 Corinthians 11:2). I think about this often in regard to my four children. I want to pass on to them the best of tradition, to breathe new life into it so that it roots, nourishes and inspires them for the future. They are growing up in an environment where they are, hopefully, learning and imbibing the best of historic tradition: Word and sacrament, hymns and songs, community, godly shepherds, powerful communal witness and deeds of mercy, and the call of God to be salt and light—all mediated through institution, structure and offices of the church. Good tradition feeds our souls. It reminds us that Christianity is greater than the individual, that our salvation is more than therapeutic, that the church is, as Calvin said, literally "the mother of salvation." The Christian life, which so desperately needs the depth of tradition, is impoverished without the institutions to guard it and carry it on. As D. G. Hart says, "if, as evangelicals believe, the most important aspect of Christianity is a personal friendship with God through private Bible reading and prayer, then who needs the ministry of the visible church?"[25] The deep church embraces the visible church.

5. *Tradition is profoundly relevant.* Finally, we learn from tradition that to be ancient is to be profoundly relevant. There is a depth in the ancient church that is very up to date. The deeper we sink our roots in tradition—the entire Great Tradition, including the parts that challenge our idols—the more resources we have for life today. I think of my friend Tom Oden, the editor of the Ancient Christian Commentary on Scripture series, who for years sought relevance by being trendy, chasing the newest fads of the spiritual climate of the day. But only when he sunk his roots deep into the tradition did he become relevant, authentic and in touch with the deepest yearnings of today.[26] One of my friends who has known Tom for years calls Tom a modern-day saint. I believe this depth, his profound authenticity, comes from his drinking of the well of tradition. If the deep church is going to capture this kind of relevance, the kind that really makes a powerful impact on people and culture, we need to rediscover the resources of the Great Tradition for forming our ecclesiology. The deep church is biblical, missional and embraces the best of tradition.

♦ ♦ ♦

As I said earlier, as Redeemer grew larger on Sunday mornings and increased the number of community groups, we had to add more structure. Structure supported our mission. But as the church increased in numbers and more leaders came on board to help, the tension grew among the first generation of the church. I found myself being pressed by these early leaders in ways that had never come up before. All of a sudden there was an increasing resistance to the original vision of the church. A few men began to criticize the direction of the church, its philosophy of ministry, its attempt to face outward and its desire for unity within the larger church. This was not how Presbyterians were supposed to act, I guess.[27] Two different visions of the church were colliding. In most independent churches, this certainly would mean a church split.

I was angry and scared at the same time. So much of our hard work to establish this unique church was about to go up in flames. Being told by other veteran church planters that this type of power struggle is normal when new churches hit the three-year mark was not much comfort. And it certainly did not help when they told me that many new churches don't survive the struggle.

As tensions increased, five men in the church asked me for a private meeting. When I arrived, they presented me with a nine-page petition. I was shocked. After reading just the first page I knew this would mean the destruction of the church. Though I was upset that our church's dirty laundry was going to be aired in the local presbyter, I knew deep down that the presbytery level was the correct and proper place for it to be heard. After all, we did not yet have an elder board, and these men needed a court of higher appeal. I felt I was right, and because I was being falsely accused, I needed the help of the presbytery.

At that moment, as painful as it was to have my leadership and integrity questioned, I was glad I am a Presbyterian. I am thankful for the denomination. I appreciate that we have a book of church order to settle these kinds of disputes. I am thankful for the biblical heritage of discipline. And I am happy that we had godly, ordained leaders who could bring their wisdom to bear on this potentially church-splitting crisis. I was greatly relieved that this is not an independent church. If it were, the consequences would have been catastrophic.

What happened? After forming a commission to look into and hear the charges and mete out discipline where needed, the members of the presbytery commission initiated a four-month peacemaking program, attempting to bring the two sides together. However, when the commission of ordained elders began to challenge the petitioners' recalcitrant spirit, the petitioners quit the church. They were warned to stop disturbing the peace of the church, and when they would not submit to the godly discipline of the commission, they bolted, taking their families and a number of others with them. This deeply grieved me. But happily, they were not able to split the church. Was this a failure? In some ways, yes. Any time we can't keep the unity, we have failed on some level. But on another level it was a success. There are times when discipline has to be exercised for the protection and health of the church. This was one of those times. I am thankful that the inherited forms of the church support the ordained offices in order to protect, strengthen and build up the church.

In the end, the process was the most painful time in my many years of ministry. It took a huge emotional toll on my family and me. It was also painful for the church. But as I look back, I see it as part of God's fatherly discipline. I learned much about my weaknesses in leadership, my need to repent, how to lead out of my own personal brokenness and how to balance the organic nature of the church with the need for biblical structures. I am deeply grateful for the tradition, for the beauty of shared authority with other godly elders, and for the wise oversight of a denomination that is able to protect the congregation from me and me from members of the congregation when either of us have our priorities wrong.

While this chapter mostly looked at the institutional side of the church, our ecclesiology would not be complete until we grapple with the church as organism. This leads us to the final protest of the emerging church.

My first year of church planting and of being part of the Presbyterian Church in America (PCA) was 2001. That year a battle was raging over subscription to the Westminster Confession of Faith, a confessional document that all our churches and pastors must assent to. It's what makes us a confessional church. The debate was over how much of the Confession a minister *cannot* believe and still be ordained. The strict subscriptionists believe that every part of the Confession must be agreed to. The system subscriptionists, on the other hand, believe fidelity to the system of the Confession is more important than holding to every proposition. The battle over agreement tears at the unity of the PCA and has split churches. Strict subscriptionists believe that we can't be faithful believers, build healthy churches and glorify God until we all subscribe completely. System proponents believe this tactic only brings more wrangling, division and wasted time—energy that could be better spent starting more churches.[1]

At the height of this controversy, Tim Keller, one of the most successful church planters in our denomination, addressed our yearly General Assembly. He wanted to bring some relief to the standoff. He said that the problem transcends differences over the Confession and the Bible. It has much more to do with culture and the way the two sides look at the world and with the challenge to contextualize the gospel message to our culture. He argued that the system subscriptionists, of whom he is one,

could sign a document today stating that they now believe in strict subscription, but it would not end the debate. For, although it would tempo-
rarily unify the two sides, by tomorrow, the two camps would be at odds
with one another. Why? Because this debate is not solely about doctrine
and subscription; it is much more about the different ways of looking at
the world. The two sides hold radically opposing views of culture and the
way the church is supposed to address it.

In short, the fundamental difference in the PCA, Keller is saying, is
not over theology or the Confession, it is over culture. The two camps
simply look at the world differently. Thus the breach is not going to be
healed by agreement to the Confession, which does not deal with the
question of culture. It was not even a question being addressed in the
1640s in England, where a Christian culture was taken for granted. We
live in a time and place where the population and culture are no longer
primarily Christian.

I left the General Assembly meeting and headed to lunch feeling that
Keller's talk was a major breakthrough. What else could explain the tension in the PCA between sides that agree on so much? I could not wait to
talk to other pastors about it. When I got to lunch, I sat with a bunch of
young pastors from California that I had recently met. When I brought
up Keller's talk, their response shocked me. They replied that Keller is
dead wrong and believed all the problems in the PCA could be settled
with strict subscription.

"Did you even hear anything he said?" I asked.

"Yes we heard it, but we think he is missing the point altogether. This
battle is about subscription. Culture has nothing to do with it."

Recognizing that things had gotten tense, one of them said, "You had
no idea when you sat down here that you were sitting with so many TRs."
Everyone laughed, including me. "TR" stands for Truly Reformed, those
who believe they are more consistently Reformed than others in the Reformed camp.

I shot back, with a smile on my face, "You mean fundamentalists." It
was their turn to laugh. But after that we just changed the subject.

If this gulf over culture is big between strict and system subscriptionists in the PCA, you can imagine how large the divide is in the evangelical world. In fact, this may be the single biggest cause of division in the dialogue between the emerging and traditional voices. One emerging author notes:

> Gospel and culture lie at the core of the emerging church. Nearly every time I talk about the emerging church or alternative forms of worship, at some point I am asked if we are watering down the gospel. The question grows out of a concern that when the church engages culture, culture will take over. It asks us to make a choice: the gospel or culture.[2]

This captures the distrust well. The Christian community is divided over culture. I like what T. M. Moore says: "No united front for responding to the contemporary cultural situation with viable Christian alternatives" presently exists.[3] I would add that a unified witness to the world around us also does not exist.

Both sides are guilty of this lack of unity. The lines have been drawn. The new emerging voices, often reacting against their culturally narrow fundamentalist upbringing, blame the traditional church for being sectarian, having no desire to reach people in postmodern culture, being uninterested in the biblical call to be creative in the arts and having sold out to Christendom (the church-state political alignment). The desire for power at the heart of Christendom has led, the emerging authors say, to abuse, particularly in the area of politics.[4] Because the church has aligned itself with the state, it has a terrible reputation in society. It is seen as judgmental, hypocritical, power-hungry and unconcerned for the poor. In short, the traditional church has become irrelevant to the cause of Christ in the world.

The traditional church fires back that the emerging church has succumbed to the worst forms of syncretism, becoming indistinguishable from the postmodern world they say they want to reach. They have assimilated, become worldly and lost their ability to be salt. The world has squeezed the emerging church into its mold.

And the claims and counterclaims of the emerging and traditional churches go on and on. The standoff breeds more distrust. There is no common front, no unity, presented to the outside world, which not only damages our witness but our effectiveness. We need to find common ground. We have much more in common than we admit.

We need a third way—a new consensus on which to build agreement about culture. I believe it can be done. I am not naive enough to think that both groups will agree at every point on every method or strategy, but we can dare to hope. As Moore contends, "Parameters can be articulated and a variety of forums created to enable significant members of believers from all communions of the faithful to realize a common voice and stance toward the making and use of culture in all its forms."[5] My goal is to present a third way that ends the standoff and leads to a real consensus on culture. Here we will take a deep look at the seventh and final protest of the emerging church.

THE EMERGING CHURCH PROTEST ON CULTURE

The emerging church is thinking deeply about how postmodernism and the gospel of the kingdom are to interact, and how Christians can create and transform culture. I appreciate what they are doing. And I find some of their thoughts extremely stimulating.

One book on culture that I find provocative is Steve Taylor's *The Out of Bounds Church?* It is clear from the title that the problem with the traditional church is that it has been too bounded, enclosed behind safe walls and thus ineffective in creating community in the postmodern culture.

Taylor mentions an interview with a local radio host that captures well the direction of his book. The radio host was intrigued by Taylor's upcoming church service that would reflect on the spirituality of the musician Moby, who has a reputation for being very worldly. As Taylor says, "try as he might, the host couldn't pigeonhole us. He expected us to fit his biased view that all Christians are close-minded isolationists who want nothing to do with popular culture."[6] And of course Taylor's church was trying to break this mold and this stereotype, which is more often true than not.

Emerging churches, contends Taylor, are trying to break with the dualism that posits a sacred realm (church) and secular realm (world and culture). This is a good goal. I appreciate that he rejects the sacred-secular dualism, which cordons off the world (evil) from the church (spiritual). This has led the church to be isolationist, inhospitable to postmodern seekers, arrogant and judgmental. In effect, the church is irrelevant to postmodern culture.

Is Taylor being unfair? Many critics think so. However a new book, titled *unChristian*, by Gabe Lyons and David Kinnaman of The Barna Group backs up Taylor's assessment.[7] Kinnaman's extensive research has found that among eighteen- to forty-year-olds, the buster and millennial generations, Christianity is seen as hypocritical, sheltered, too political and judgmental. They received this impression primarily from the church, which uses the wrong methods to address the culture around it. I think Taylor would agree. But along with methods, Taylor would add a faulty theology of creation and culture. The dualism that is latent in certain forms of evangelical fundamentalism is patently unbiblical, he argues.

In fact, Taylor contends that the traditional church's view of God's creation and the world has led them to confuse the world with worldliness. Though the Bible rejects worldliness, it does not condemn the world, which, of course, includes God's creation.[8] As my friend, poet and rock 'n' roll biographer Steve Turner, says, "confusing these two usages can lead to disaster. Some strict fundamentalists in the traditional church show disdain toward creation and culture, and yet in doing so become proud, arrogant and uncaring." What is ironic, continues Turner, is that they "become worldly in the very way the Bible condemns and yet are not worldly enough in the way the Bible commands. We are told to be in the world but not of it. People like this are often of the world but not in it."[9] Well said.

What is the solution? Regaining a more biblical view of creation. Taylor correctly calls the church to recapture a biblical view of the world which allows us to engage culture in a way that honors God's calling on our lives—to be missional, or what Jesus calls "salt and light." Creation, although marred by the Fall, is still good and worthy of redemption. Since God has not given up on his good creation, neither should we.

In his most inspiring chapter, "Creativity Downloaded," Taylor lays out the biblical description of God as a musician, composer, designer, garment maker, architect, builder, crafter and artisan. Because God is all of these, Christians are called to also be creators of culture. As he comments, "the mission of the emerging church starts in cooperation with . . . God. . . . It calls for a willingness to live out the creative *imago Dei* [image of God] in ways that touch the culture in which we live."[10] We are able to do this, he continues, because the "Christian theology of creation and incarnation affirm the goodness of matter, and thus by implication human creativity and human appreciation of such creativity."[11]

I am thrilled Taylor and other emerging writers are rediscovering the doctrine of creation, which allows them to discover the good that is still in creation, even in a postmodern culture. I am encouraged that Taylor is calling the church to create a community of faith, as Taylor's subtitle says, in the midst of a culture of change. The goal is to create a community of believers who are open and hospitable to the artists and culture around them, not only welcoming artists and musicians as people but affirming their art and music as wonderful contributions to the family of faith. He also wants Christians to create culture themselves. Churches like the one Taylor pastors have become warm, hospitable places for artists and their works. Taylor believes that art and culture, because it is part of God's good creation, should be a part of our lives and worship on a regular basis.

THE TRADITIONAL CHURCH PUSHES BACK

The negative reaction of the traditional church to the emerging church's call to appreciate aspects of postmodern culture and art has been swift. One traditional pastor, John MacArthur, writes: "The Emerging Church movement has unleashed an unprecedented flood of vulgarity and worldliness on Christian booksellers' shelves. Obscenity is one of the main trademarks of the Emerging style." Providing just one example to build his case, he writes that "most authors in the movement make extravagant use of filthy language, sexual innuendo, uncritical references to the most lowbrow elements of postmodern culture, often indicating inappropriate approval for ungodly aspects of secular culture."[12]

The problem, MacArthur contends, is that entire churches have deliberately immersed themselves in "the culture," which means to him "whatever the world loves at the moment." He calls these pastors "worldly preachers" who pander to every worldly theme, trend and fashion "that captures the fickly fancy of the postmodern, secular mind."[13]

Wow, MacArthur is not pulling any punches. In brief, he charges that under the guise of "connecting with the culture," the emerging church has become worldly. "They have sold out to the world," he argues. "They want to fit right in with the world, and they seem to be making themselves quite comfortable there."[14] They have sold their soul to be popular. Their biggest problem is their refusal to shun the world. They labor under the false impression that in order to win the world for Christ, they have to gain its favor. The church has to make the message, the gospel, nonthreatening to outsiders "to tantalize non-Christians rather than confront their unbelief; to make friends with the world rather than standing apart."[15] This is spiritual adultery. "Biblical Christians have always understood that they must shun the world."[16] And to make friends with the world is to make God an enemy. The bottom line is that the emerging church, for many traditionalists, is guilty of accommodating the world. They are syncretistic.

The irony of the critique is that many in the traditional church are accusing the emerging church of the same thing they are accused of—pandering to the cultural despisers of the day. The emerging church accuses the traditional church of kowtowing to the sacred-secular, public-private split picked up in the eighteenth century, which has led to the reality chronicled in *unChristian*.[17]

TRANSCENDING WEAKNESSES

Although I am thrilled that Steve Taylor has a well-worked-out view of creation, one that regains a positive view of God's good creation, I have some misgivings. As I read much of the emerging literature on culture, I got the sense that their view of creation is still too narrow, mostly focused on the private sphere that touches music, art and film. In other words, they don't recover enough of creation. They do not carry their view of creation into the political, social and economic realms.[18]

I have pondered why this is the case. What I have come up with is that many in the emerging church have been influenced by the Anabaptist tradition, which still plays a healthy role in the evangelical world. Though the emerging church leaders are not as sweepingly negative about culture as historic Anabaptism is, some negativity lingers in certain spheres of life.[19] For example, I sense a general distrust of the state and politics. Though they believe a common consensus in art, poetry and music can exist (and thus they affirm these areas), they don't see this same possibility in the spheres of politics and economics, which they see as much more affected by the Fall and principalities and powers. So the church's influence in the political realm is accomplished not by direct involvement but by being "resident aliens."[20] That is, the church models to the world how to live together. Although there is truth to this contention, it is only part of what the church is called to do. I see this view as handicapping the emerging church and reducing the influence it could have in the culture.

But the traditional church has its faults too. It mostly condemns culture, holding a negative view of creation, which causes it to be tribal, defensive, and uninterested in creating culture or affirming good art wherever it can be found. The traditional church, particularly those of the free-church tradition, tends to be culturally pacifist, in part because of a faulty view of the biblical word for *world* and also because of an unbiblical fear of contamination. But the Bible calls us to be in the world but not of it (John 17:6-19). There is a place for critiquing culture, but we are called to also create it. And we are called to affirm good culture when it is created by nonbelievers. The traditional church struggles with this, not wanting to affirm culture outside of the church. By only stressing a negative view of culture, it forces Christians to retreat more and more into their own enclaves. Ironically, as Christians are discouraged from creating culture on their own, they lose their ability to discern what is good and bad in the world around them, and they succumb to consuming culture uncritically. In the end, they look no different from the world.

So when criticizing the emerging church for getting too close to the world, the traditionalists are sending the wrong message: retreat and become more tribal, more sectarian. This is exactly what the secularists want—no Christians in the public sphere. Christians need to be in the public square but in the right way. This calls for a third way.

TOWARD A CHRISTIAN CULTURAL CONSENSUS

Twenty years ago I was a student in the American Studies Program in Washington, D.C. The goal was to teach us how to relate our faith to the political world. We learned a great deal about the importance of worldviews and the different views of Christ and culture. Three perspectives were laid out: the Reformed, the Anabaptist and the Christian Right. On every public-policy issue the professors brought up, we were challenged to formulate what each of the three traditions would think. It was a very healthy exercise and taught me much about the divisions in the evangelical world over culture. I also think that part of the goal was to build a consensus around the biblical teaching of the kingdom of God. It was exciting. We were enthusiastic about incorporating our views of the kingdom into our internships on Capitol Hill.

Yet our enthusiasm was curbed immediately once we attempted it, because few of the non-Christian staffers on Capitol Hill that we came in contact with had any idea what we were talking about and had no interest in the kingdom of God. The problem was, and the professors figured this out eventually, we students had no common language with which to dialogue with nonbelievers. We did not know how to translate our views on the kingdom of God into language a Capitol Hill staffer could understand. So we tended to remain quiet and acquiesce to the public-private split of the public square, regardless of what faith tradition we came out of.

The professors did not provide students with a common-grace view of communicating biblical truth in the civic realm. Kingdom of God language would not work. Nonbelievers don't understand it and they don't accept the authority of the Bible from which it comes. Common-grace language is needed. But if we adopt the resident-alien view, we don't need a common language in the public realm (because none exists). Then the only language available to the church is the theological language of the Bible.

The inability to come up with a common consensus on moral issues hinders both the traditional and the emerging church. On the one hand, it leads the emerging church (with the exception of Brian McLaren and a few others) to avoid entanglement in politics and the state and to focus on the private aspects of the church and culture. On the other hand, this lack of common-grace consensus causes the traditional church to ignore the realm of culture. In summary, the traditional church is pacifist in the area of culture but not in the realm of politics, and the emerging church is pacifist in the realm of politics but not in the realm of culture. Both sides suffer from the lack of a comprehensive view of Christ and culture that treats the private and public realms in a consistent manner.

RECOVERING A COMPREHENSIVE CHRISTIAN WORLDVIEW

A few years ago Mary Beth Molnar, who has attended Redeemer Presbyterian Church almost from the start, decided it was time to begin living out her faith in all areas of life. First she and her husband, Tim, joined the Symphony 100, a fundraising group for the Pacific Symphony that supports music and culture in Orange County. From this endeavor, their confidence grew. Mary Beth then joined with a group of music lovers and donors to not just support culture but to make it. They came up with an idea to commission an original symphony to be performed at the Orange County Performing Arts Center. The goal was to create something beautiful. So they and some donors hired an accomplished composer and rented out the hall, and the entire Pacific Symphony and Chorale dazzled the audience with a haunting performance of the story of Job. It was breathtaking. *Christians can create culture!* I said to myself that night.

But this concert had a dual purpose. It was not just to show that Christians can create fabulous culture, which they did. It was also to demonstrate that beauty is not just for the rich. The poor too need beauty to inspire and bless their lives. So the "Concert for Hope," as it was called, teamed up with the Orange County Rescue Mission to bring beauty to the poor. Opening night was not at the posh Segerstrom Hall; rather it was in the small chapel of the Village of Hope, a two-year live-in program that performs miracles with down-and-out people. The residents were deeply moved by the beautiful concert. They were honored that the symphony and chorale would perform for them in their own "home"!

But the poor were not only blessed with music; the Concert for Hope was also able to raise awareness for the Village of Hope. Through a preconcert dinner it connected hundreds of wealthy donors to the vision of wiping out homelessness in Orange County. This is what it means to live out our worldview in a comprehensive manner. But for this to happen on a more widespread basis, we need to build a third way in the cultural realm.

INSTITUTION AND ORGANISM

One of the best insights I have come across in building a third way in the cultural realm comes from Abraham Kuyper. I learned from him that the church is both an *institution* and an *organism*. Kuyper says that the church as institution is called to preach the Word, administer the sacraments, discipline and disciple its members, build community, elect elders and deacons, form presbyteries and synods, reach out to the world in mercy, and celebrate Christ. The church as institution realizes that only people radically transformed by the grace of God can live differently. In this sense, the church presents a radical alternative community to the world. We are to stand apart from the world and its idols, but at the same time welcome the stranger into our midst through acts of hospitality. The church lives by this grace ethic. The institutional church is to remain in its specific sphere and must not be directly involved in politics but must remain faithful to its own spiritual purpose.[21]

This seems pretty standard. But James Bolt says that Kuyper goes "beyond the church as institution to insist that the organic character of the Christian life must come to expression in the form of organized Christian communal activity in areas other than the institutional church."[22] The church as *organism* means Christians are called not to hide behind the walls of their distinct community but to take their new hearts, minds and perspectives into the surrounding communities as salt and light. As Kuyper contends, the believing community, gathered around Word and sacrament, must radiate "beams of faith's light into the realm of common grace" into education, art, science, politics, business, economics and the marketplace. The concrete expression of this life of Christian discipleship, organically growing out of changed lives in the church, is "manifested through the rich voluntary associational life of a nation's citizens."[23]

This means that Christians are called to create public educational institutions, build businesses, organize neighborhood groups, create charities, be artists and musicians and writers, and start political action groups. We are to make culture. As Jeremiah exhorted the newly exiled Jews living in Babylon:

> Build houses and live in them; plant gardens and eat their produce. Take wives and have sons and daughters; take wives for your sons, and give your daughters in marriage, that they may bear sons and daughters; multiply there, and do not decrease. But seek the welfare of the city where I have sent you into exile, and pray to the LORD on its behalf, for in its welfare you will find your welfare. (Jeremiah 29:5-7 ESV)

In fact, for Kuyper, this kind of associational life was a mandate of the organic unity of the body of Christ.

Common-grace language. Kuyper saw the institutional church as the place to educate its people to be shalom makers. Christians learn not only to live as servants to the world but also to speak the language that enables them to communicate, work together and build a city of shalom with those outside the church.

Kuyper used a number of terms to describe this language, but the most frequent and helpful term is *common grace*. He defined common grace as the universal bestowal by the Spirit of natural, moral and artistic gifts to believer and nonbeliever alike. Public and natural conscience, natural pity, some religious knowledge and a universal God-consciousness are parts of common grace.[24] This perspective contends that all humans share a consensus on what is just or moral, that they are not enclosed in their prison house of language.[25]

This is the Kuyperian view of common-grace knowledge. It provides just enough insight into reality, just enough conscience and natural pity, to work with others for justice and shalom. The church's goal is to train believers in the language of common grace so that they can work with nonbelievers for the shalom of the city in every area of life.

Common-grace language with those who don't believe. During the time I was working on my doctoral dissertation, which covered, in part, Calvin's view of common grace, I was offered the opportunity to teach an introduction to politics class at California State University at Northridge. There were no Christians in my class, and the vast majority held political views very different from mine. I certainly could not teach about how the kingdom of God gives direction to politics. What could I do, especially if I wanted to teach distinctly as a Christian who rejects the sacred-secular divide? I needed to find a common-grace language that the students would not reject out of hand. I began by appealing to their desire for community, a sense of belonging. We talked about what a good community looked like and what hindered people from getting along. We discussed what was needed to maintain it and cause it to flourish. We looked at our political system for resources to make this a reality.

Eventually the students decided, through reading *The Federalist Papers,* that good community needed to balance freedom of the individual and his or her obligation to the group. They understood that "ordered liberty" was important to the maintenance of strong community and a vibrant nation. Then I had them read selections of Alexis de Tocqueville's *Democracy in America*, and they became convinced that rampant individualism and relativism were tearing community apart in America. They realized that freedom was outstripping order and disrupting community. Once they were convinced that ordered liberty was the standard, we were able to assess all kinds of political platforms in light of their new views on justice, views that I strongly believe cohere with the biblical view of a healthy community.

But without a view of common grace—the understanding that my students held some aspects of natural conscience, pity, common sense and right reason *(sensus divinitatus)* and thus could recognize the "biblical truth" in *The Federalist Papers* and *Democracy in America*—little communication would occur. We would have been stuck in our prison house of language.

From my experience teaching at Cal State Northridge, I came to understand that a Christian worldview which included the church as *institution* and *organism* would help the church become consistent in its interaction with public life. It allowed us to remain distinct but at the same time provided the language to work in the public and social realms, creating culture alongside nonbelievers, sometimes together but often alone. For the first time I understood what it means to be a "resident alien." It's not being tribal or standoffish. Nor does it mean merely modeling community to the world, as important as this is. Instead, as members of the institutional church we see ourselves as cultural "aliens," modeling a radical, alternate way of life. But as part of the organic church, we are "residents" who live in the world, creating culture and working with others through common grace to bring shalom to this world. When held in balance and maintained, this duality has a powerful effect on the church and culture.

DEEP CHURCH: THE NEW CULTURAL CONSENSUS?

Having laid out this third way of cultural engagement and how it helps us transcend some of the weaknesses of the emerging and traditional churches, we now need to see what it looks like in practice. What does it mean for the life of the church? Sociologist Christian Smith argues that evangelicalism best thrives when it is simultaneously *distinct from* and *engaged with* the wider society.[26] According to Smith, this distinction and engagement is the most effective way to remain vital as a church. This is exactly what Kuyper was describing when he said the church is both institution and organism.

This is our goal at Redeemer Presbyterian Church. We believe we are to be a distinctive counterculture and should live an alternate way. At times we need to be critical toward the surrounding culture. But this countercultural attitude must not calcify. A posture of negativity can lead us to be insular and tribal. Critique—though necessary to keep us from being pushed into the world's mold—is secondary to our posture of culture makers.[27] We should be known as those who create culture for the common good, for all people and not just fellow believers, culture that makes life better, whole, for the entire city. While we are distinct from the surrounding culture, we also engage it. Add to this the mandate to seek the welfare of the city, and we get a powerful recipe for cultural transformation.

Church as institution. How does Redeemer Church balance being in the world but not of it? We keep the two aspects of the church, *institution* and *organism,* at the forefront of our thinking. We recognize that we will have no impact on the culture if the institution is not strong. This means preaching the Word and administering the sacraments faithfully and consistently. It means taking discipleship—what Dallas Willard calls *the great omission*—seriously.[28] We have regular discipleship classes on the foundations of the faith. We teach, exhort and organize for community in our weekly community groups that discuss the sermon, pray for one another and carry one another's burdens. We strive to be a church of mercy to our community through a myriad of avenues. And all of these wonderful core commitments are undergirded by a mature, mission-oriented elder board and deaconate. These institutional priorities go a long way in engendering a distinct people who think, act and live differently from our surrounding culture, but at the same time remain deeply hospitable to the stranger in their midst.

Church as organism: Training secret agents. But along with all of these noble things, we also realize that the institutional church is responsible for training its members to seek the shalom of the city—to be culture makers and transformers. At Redeemer we call this core commitment *shalom* to remind us what we are supposed to be: shalom makers during the week.

Lesslie Newbigin once said the church should not talk about politics or economics on Sunday morning. The institutional church was not to be partisan. He did not mean that the pulpit could never address issues of public life. Newbigin contended that the pulpit should be mainly about the gospel witness and the doctrines of grace.[29]

Does this mean the church should ignore the world outside its walls? Absolutely not. But if we don't address these issues in the sanctuary on Sunday, when and where is this focus to take place? In the "basement," away from the public, said Newbigin. The church, he said, must train countercultural "secret agents," teaching them how to think and act Christianly about their vocations, public life, economics and associational life. I like that image. We go about our business without calling unnecessary attention to ourselves. So if the Sunday-morning sanctuary is mainly about the church as *institution*, the weekday "basement" is about the church as *organism:* training its members to be secret agents in the world, creating and renewing culture for the glory of God.

We have taken this mandate seriously at Redeemer. Each year we teach a semester-long worldview class, which addresses what it means to make culture.[30] We have a yearly marketplace ministry banquet to challenge business people to think Christianly. We hold invitation-only salons for the cultural gatekeepers of Orange County to influence the way they think and create. We sponsor lectures, hold debates and conduct dialogues on culture to educate our people and to pique the interest of the nonbeliever.

Inspired by this noble call to be shalom makers, members of our church have begun to take seriously their charge to be the organic church, secret agents in the world.

SECRET AGENT IN ANAHEIM

Mayor Curt Pringle of Anaheim is a member of our church. He was just voted by *Red County* magazine as the most influential public servant in Orange County.[31] One time when we chatted he had just gotten back from the White House, where he had met President Bush. It had been his third time at the White House in four months. I asked Curt how someone gets invited to the White House so many times, and pulled out of him the fact that he had become one of the Bush Administration's top mayoral contacts. When the White House needed to run something up the flagpole that would affect local mayors, he explained to me, they called him. Now that is influence.

A couple of years ago, I asked Curt why he chose Redeemer Presbyterian Church. He said, "The first Sunday I was here you preached on the need for Christians to be 'salt and light' in the world and affirmed the legitimacy of political life for Christians. And you did not bash politics as evil. Right then I knew I had found our church. It was the first church I had been to that maintained the proper balance between being 'salt and light,' that is, 'to be in the world but not of it.' I have come ever since." I remember that sermon. Along with exhorting my flock to be "salt and light" I had encouraged them to fill God's creation with godly culture. I was humbled by Curt's kind words.

Curt is being salt and light in the political sphere. More than any previous mayor, he has put his mark on the city of Anaheim. Using the principles of the free market, he convinced the city to rezone the light-industrial area around Angel Stadium to create a city center filled with apartments, shops, boulevards, cafés and offices. Anaheim, like many suburbs in California in the 1960s and 1970s, wiped out its historic downtown, replacing it with strip malls and parking lots. The city and its community have suffered ever since. Not only did it tear away the beauty of the old city but it also ripped away many homes and a vibrant downtown community. Many residents were forced out of the city, and they now have to commute back in for their jobs. Curt wants to reverse this trend and bring back a thriving downtown, which will bring back residents and a strong sense of community. He is promoting the shalom of the city. Few mayors in the entire state of California have had such a dramatic effect on the life of the city. These dramatic changes have led to all the praise and accolades Curt has received over the past few years.

A few years ago I approached Curt about sharing what he has learned with other mayors and major builders in Southern California. He was excited about the idea. In March 2009 this dream became a reality. We held a conference called "The New Communities Conference." It was a daylong seminar to help mayors, city officials, architects and builders begin to dream about what it means to, in most cases, retrofit their cities for real community, beauty and lasting meaning. We even had a segment on the importance of sacred space for a healthy community. Our goal was to take the biblical vision for the shalom of the city and influence life in Southern California. In order to do this, we used common-grace language that nonbelievers could understand and find compelling. I think it happened.[32]

Curt Pringle is creating culture in Anaheim. Redeemer Church is doing its best to support him as an "undercover agent," someone who represents well the church as *organism*. It is exciting to watch this vision in reality. I strongly believe this vision—the church as institution and organism—can unify the evangelical church, bringing together the emerging and traditional church around a biblical view of culture.

CONCLUSION

Becoming the Deep Church

It is early morning, a week before Thanksgiving. The Santa Ana desert winds have descended on Southern California, sucking every ounce of moisture out of the air. Stoked by the dry winds, brushfires rage in different parts of Orange County. Dozens of houses have been destroyed. The air is thick with smoke. As I look out the Coco Restaurant's window onto Pacific Coast Highway in the town of Corona del Mar, I see people in their luxury cars and SUVs going to work. Life goes on. I am in a pensive mood, wondering, *What difference does the deep church make to them?* With million-dollar homes, fancy vacations and high-paying jobs, what do they care? Does what we do in church matter? And for those already in the church, I wonder if there is a need for a third way. I look around Orange County and there are so many big churches. Do we need something different? Will this book amount to anything? But no sooner have these thoughts crossed my mind than I think of Doug and Mattie.[1] The deep church saved their lives. Here is their story.

Up till four years ago, Doug and Mattie's life was comfortable. They had a beautiful home, nice cars, lots of friends. Doug was vice president of sales for a Fortune 500 technology company. They loved to cook and to travel. Although their life was not free of trials, they would say that life was going well. Doug said, "We went to church each week, but it was more like we went just so we could 'check the box' each week and go on with our lives. It really did not impact me that much."

Then one January day in 2005 their lives changed forever. Their only child, an adopted son named Nathan, was arrested. The charges were serious, and Nathan was looking at spending a long time in prison. An unspeakable nightmare had begun. The local news media were literally pounding on their door and peering inside their windows. Doug and Mattie had to cover their windows with paper to protect their privacy. They were devastated, humiliated. How could this be happening? What had gone wrong?

Shortly after the arrest a couple at our church reached out to them. They had met Doug and Mattie at a symphony function. They could see the shock, pain and loss in Doug's and Mattie's faces. For Mattie tears came easily. They still do. Soon this couple invited Doug and Mattie to their community group. The group welcomed them and brought them into their lives. As I sat with Doug and Mattie last week in their home, I asked what drew them to the group. Why did they keep going back each week? In spite of the devastating circumstances, Mattie said, "They immediately accepted us, loved us and comforted us. They shared in our suffering. They prayed with us. It was incredible. They literally saved our lives."

"One story sticks out," she said. "In the first months after the arrest, if we wanted to see Nathan, we would have to get in line at the jail around 2:30 a.m. and wait till the sign-up window opened at 7 a.m. If we did not do this, all the visiting slots would be taken for the day." It was a grueling, exhausting procedure. Almost cruel. After a few months of this, they were physically and emotionally drained. "One night," she said, "a member of our community group volunteered to help. He camped out in the lobby all night, holding a place in line until we got there at 7 a.m. Who does this kind of thing?" queried Mattie. "What would motivate someone who barely knows us and has never met Nathan to reach out with such kindness and compassion?"

A short while later, Doug and Mattie were invited to a midweek study on Romans that our church was offering. They were ready to take the next step. As they sat there the first week, the teacher was going through

Romans 3, talking about how God justifies sinners and adopts them into his family. He was in the middle of defining *justification* and *sanctification* when Doug leaned over to Mattie and said, "Why have I not heard of these terms before? They are right there in the Bible."

"Really?" I asked, as I sat in their living room. "All those years in church and you had never heard the word *justification* or even the concept behind it?"

"No, not really," Doug said. "Not only had we not heard those terms but we really did not understand the depth and breadth of the gospel. Over the years we heard lots of engaging pep talks on how to live better, improve our lives and serve God, but never was the gospel clearly and consistently taught."

For the first time in their lives they were hearing the good news that as sinners they are justified, forgiven through Christ and brought into God's marvelous kingdom. So simple, but so revolutionary. A few months later they finally began attending our worship service. Week after week, they heard the gospel preached from the Old Testament to the New Testament.[2] As Doug said, "It began to change the way we thought about all areas of life. We realized that the gospel impacted every aspect of our lives. Our lives took on new meaning. It was and is exciting."

At the same time the gospel was transforming Doug and Mattie's life, Nathan was going through a similar experience. As Steven, our associate pastor, met with him each week in jail, Nathan slowly came to grips with what he had done and began to take responsibility. He was accepting his guilt. He was no longer blaming others, the system or drugs. Each week Steven directed Nathan to the Scriptures, pointing out that the hole in Nathan's soul, his deep need for acceptance, could only be met by a relationship with his heavenly Father. Slowly Nathan began to see how he had met this need for years through sundry idols, all of them leaving him empty. He was broken, humbled by his crime, ready to admit his emptiness. What could he do?

Steven told Nathan to go to the only place that can give him the acceptance he craves—the gospel. Forgiveness comes through Jesus, who has paid for Nathan's crimes and sins. Nathan needed to receive what Jesus has done on his behalf and enter into God's marvelous kingdom. Over time this message sunk in. Nathan has stopped running. He has finally come home. He has received God's forgiveness. As he says, he now knows he is loved and accepted. This adopted boy, who struggled all his life with the gut-wrenching feeling that he was not acceptable, now knows he is part of God's family.[3] The change in Nathan has been dramatic. I don't know anyone whose circumstances are worse but who is more content. He is in prison but he has been set free.

> Amazing grace, how sweet the sound,
> That saved a wretch like me.
> I once was lost, but now am found,
> Was blind, but now I see.[4]

DEEP CHURCH CAN HAPPEN

The story of Doug, Mattie and Nathan clearly depicts the deep church. It reveals that evangelism often happens in community. It demonstrates the power of belonging before believing. And as this belonging takes place in supportive community, people are drawn closer to the Well. The gospel draws them, confronts their idols, offers forgiveness, justification, adoption into God's family and new life in his kingdom. Though we don't always know the exact moment, belief has taken place. In Doug, Mattie and Nathan's case, they continually moved toward the Well. They eventually became members of Redeemer Church, along with Nathan.

One of the most memorable "new members Sundays" we have had was when Nathan joined the church, from jail. Although he could not be present, we had a picture of him up on the screen in his orange jump suit, a big smile on his face. The joy was evident. When it came to the membership promises, we played a recording of him answering all the questions. Then we extended the "right hand of fellowship" to him as well as his parents.

Since that day, Doug has become a key church leader, serving for a short time as our part-time executive director and now as our our treasurer. Mattie has turned her grief into service, reaching out to other parents in similar situations, organizing a Bible drive that donated fifteen hundred Bibles to the Orange County jail system, and inspiring our congregation to write letters and cards to inmates who don't have family or who may be spiritually open. Doug and Mattie have been brought in only to be sent out. This is missional Christianity. Nathan shares the gospel with as many inmates as he can. He leads Bible studies. With Nathan's guidance, his cellmate, a former Buddhist, has come to Christ. Nathan has read through the Scriptures three times already with Mattie. Doug, Mattie and Nathan are growing in grace.

Deep church is a reality. Can it happen at your church? Yes. And it doesn't have to start with the pastor. Anyone can do it. Tim and Mary Beth Molnar prove it. They heard the call to be missional, to live as people who had been called into the kingdom in order to be sent out. They saw a couple in need and reached out to them. As they built a friendship with Doug and Mattie, supporting them through their trial, it was a natural extension to invite them to their community group, to experience what others in their group had every week, a wonderful family of believers. Doug and Mattie were moved by the visible love these people showed to them and their son. Soon they began attending our corporate worship on Sunday.

We can all be the deep church. God used the Molnars and their community group to show the love of Christ to profoundly hurting people. We don't have to wait until the church changes or the pastor adopts the deep church philosophy. You can begin right now.

We have discovered that living for the kingdom is contagious. As more people catch the vision, it begins to grow. The profound testimony of Doug, Mattie and Nathan has shaped other community groups. We now have groups ministering to women's shelters, the Orange County Rescue Mission, international students and inmates. And still others are making an impact for the kingdom in their callings, working in the fields of law, real estate, education, medicine, finance and politics. Together, we are becoming the deep church.

In conclusion, the following are seven suggestions for becoming a deep church.

1. Start or join a community group. Band together with other Christians who want to live their Christian life more intentionally and want to experience profound community. Along with praying for one another and sharing the burdens and joys of life, use the time to discuss that week's sermon (not to be critical of what the pastor said but to work hard at applying God's Word to your lives).[5] Create an environment that is exciting, hospitable and warm. Light some candles, build a fire in the fireplace, serve some food and make each event a celebration of togetherness. Expect God to do marvelous things. He will. If you need inspiration, read Dietrich Bonhoeffer's *Life Together*, Edith Schaeffer's *L'Abri* and Randy Frazee's *The Connecting Church*.[6] These books have profoundly influenced me, and they will you as well.

2. Keep the gospel of forgiveness and the kingdom at the center of your group. Community often starts with a bang and ends with a whimper. The honeymoon is great but the divorce is awful. What sustains a group over the long haul? Not enthusiasm, not mission and not sheer will. The only thing that sustains, renews and energizes a group is the power of the gospel. Jerry Bridges says we need to preach the gospel to ourselves every day, reminding ourselves that we are more sinful than we ever thought possible, but the gospel is more amazing than we can ever imagine.[7] This truth not only brought us into the faith, it sustains, motivates and empowers us to keep living faithfully, even heroically.

If this is true for the individual, it is even truer for a community. Nothing breaks apart community faster than selfishness, pride and hurt feelings. Only the gospel can break through and sustain a community built on forgiveness, reconciliation and other-centeredness.[8] When I asked Mattie why she thought the Molnars' community group was able to overcome its own self-interest and reach out to her family in their need, she answered, "Because they know they are forgiven. They have experienced it. And this makes them able to love others." She is right. The more we are affected by the gospel, the more our deep emotional and spiritual needs are met. We spend less time agonizing over our own hang-ups and past hurts, and have more energy for others. When our emotional bank is full, we have plenty to give away.

3. Become missional. Begin reaching out in mercy. Along with enjoying and caring for one another, begin to reach out to people in need. Spend time understanding how God calls his people into his family in order to send them out. He did this with Abraham, Joseph, Jonah, Daniel and Jesus' disciples. Learn to serve out of gratitude. Let the gospel impel you to care for others in need. As the apostle Peter says,

> You are a chosen race, a royal priesthood, a holy nation, a people for his own possession, that you may proclaim the excellencies of him who called you out of darkness into his marvelous light. Once you were not a people, but now you are God's people; once you had not received mercy, but now you have received mercy. (1 Peter 2:9-10 ESV)

Be people of mercy. Serve at a women's shelter, get involved in a crisis pregnancy center, adopt a fire station or local school. It is amazing what one community group can do to witness for the kingdom.

4. Become a shalom maker—someone who seeks the peace of the city through their vocation. Begin to understand your calling. Start a discussion in your community group about vocation and how God calls us to live every part of our lives to his glory. Read Al Wolters's book *Creation Regained* or Andy Crouch's *Culture Making*.[9] These will give you a good foundation for God's view on creation and our calling to make culture. Then in order to understand how your unique gifts affect your calling and God's role for you in his kingdom, read Os Guinness's *The Call* or Doug Schuurman's *Vocation*.[10] God wants us to be the organic church, but this won't happen until we are trained to be "undercover agents" for the kingdom. Can you imagine how different the world would be if each Christian understood his or her calling and passionately pursued it every day? We would turn the world upside down.

5. Become a deep worshiper. Begin to understand what deep worship is all about. Read some books on the history of worship.[11] Root yourself

in the ancient fathers.[12] Study the history of hymns.[13] Go deeper in your understanding of the Lord's Supper.[14] Become a better worshiper. You will find that the more you are excited about worship as a means of grace, the more others around you will be too.

In college, when I first began to understand the history behind some of the hymns, I began to appreciate them. This led to my enthusiasm in chapel whenever they were sung. My friends took notice. If I liked them, they thought, then maybe hymn singing is not just for old people. Over the years, I have been profoundly influenced by hymns.

The same is true for me with the Lord's Supper. My study of Communion has made weekly Eucharist one of the most profound moments of mystery and grace in my life. It has led me to a new understanding of the unity of the body of Christ and what it means to take the meal together as the covenant community of God. I can't imagine corporate worship without celebrating the Lord's Supper each week. I need the strength it provides; the church needs the glue of unity it applies.

6. Model centered-set thinking. Without being asked, reach out to guests. Invite them into the community. Don't put up unnecessary boundaries. Make them feel that it is safe to attend, to hang around and ask questions. Let the love of the community draw them to the Well. Include them in the life of the church. It is great to be friendly to guests, but unless they feel included they will not come back. Start new groups for them, host them at your house, and encourage them to belong. The difference this will make in your church will be profound.

7. Be the deep church first before you request it from your leaders. The goal of my book is unity, not division. Though I would love for you to give this book to your pastor, it will be received positively only when you are already modeling what is in it. As in any good marriage, we need to spend less time criticizing the other person and more time changing ourselves. My advice is to change yourself first. The pastor and leaders will notice. If you can give your pastor a copy and it can be received in a spirit of trust, then by all means do so. If the timing is right and your relationship is strong, suggest the church study the book together. Maybe

the leaders and elders will work through it together and reassess the ministry of the church. It may ignite a deep church movement.

MY FINAL WISH—UNITY

Let me add one more suggestion; this one is for scholars, professors and pastors. It is my hope that *Deep Church* will become a platform for working out a third way in the church, that pastors and scholars will use the seven protests I have outlined in this book to instigate conversations, build on my suggestions, do more research and strengthen the deep church. This will bring unity across denominations and theological persuasions.

Each week when I preach, I pray the "prayer of illumination." I ask God to illuminate our minds, and make our hearts teachable and our wills moldable as we dig into his Word. And at the end I pray this: "Heavenly Father, we pray for the one who preaches. They call him reverend but he is not. He has as much to learn from this text as those who listen—maybe more. We have come to see Jesus and him only and it's in his name we pray. Amen."[15]

Deep Church is as much for me as it is for its readers. It is as much for Redeemer Presbyterian Church as it is for others. My goal is that you have seen Jesus in this book. May God bless you and his deep church. As we say at the end of our service each week, and I recite to each of my four children when I pray over them at night:

The LORD bless you
    and keep you;

the LORD make his face shine upon you
    and be gracious to you;

the LORD turn his face toward you
    and give you peace. (Numbers 6:24-26)

ACKNOWLEDGMENTS

How does one thank a lifetime of people who have shaped, impacted and molded one's theology, character and philosophy of ministry?

I am grateful to InterVarsity Press for giving me this opportunity. My editor, Al Hsu, was the perfect editor for a first-time author. He was always patient, gave timely advice and direction, and kept me on task. I am grateful for everyone at IVP who helped edit and publish *Deep Church*. A special thanks goes to Joel Scandrett, formerly of IVP, who "discovered" me and brought my proposal to the attention of the editorial staff. Thanks, too, to Andy Crouch, who vouched for me, and to my outside readers who helped make this book so much better. Of course, as every writer says, I am ultimately responsible for the final product.

To Redeemer Church, its members and elders: thank you for letting me be your pastor and for encouraging me to try out so much of the deep church vision in our community. I first taught much of this matter in an adult discipleship class. Thank you, Redeemer, for letting me pursue my unique calling in your midst. I have to specifically thank Michael and Betty Carroll, who coached me early on through the proposal stage and edited my sample chapter, teaching me about creative nonfiction; Howard and Roberta for inspiring me every step of the way; Lela Gilbert for believing in my writing and pressing me to become better and find my voice; and Linda Parisi, who first got me thinking about writing the book.

I am grateful to the Huntington Group—Rob Bell, Brad den Dulk, Jim Denison, Mick Wilson, Dan Radmacher and Lars Rood—for teaching me to ask the right questions, sharpening my thinking and practice, and inspiring me to love the gospel. Thanks also to everyone from

Twenty-Something Fellowship; so much of *Deep Church* originated with you. And thanks to Mark Oestreicher, my former colleague and friend, for encouraging this book along the way.

To my mentors Rich Mouw and Tim Keller: no living men have taught me more about the deep church. Thanks for believing in me and being my friend. And thank you to John Armstrong for your willingness to travel this emerging journey with me and for being a sounding board at each stage of the process.

I am grateful to those long gone who have mentored me: St. Augustine, John Calvin, Richard Sibbes, John Newton, Abraham Kuyper, C. S. Lewis, J. R. R. Tolkien and Francis Schaeffer. Indeed, to the many men and women who have impacted me over the years by their writing and teaching, I am deeply indebted. I stand on the shoulders of giants.

I want to thank all those who allowed me to interview them and include them in the book. This book is better because of your participation.

Thank you to my endorsers for reading the manuscript and supporting my call for deep church.

Thank you to my mom and dad (who passed into glory in 2002) for your love and support. I enjoy and look forward to our call each week on my way up to Fuller Seminary for my day of study.

And most important, I want to thank my lovely bride of fourteen years, Michelle, and our four children: Jordan, Jonathan, Lindsay and Meghan. Without my wife's support and love, her belief in me, I could not have done it. And coming home after a long day of writing, meetings, sermon preparation and running a church is so much sweeter when I get to hear, "Hi Daddy! We missed you." In my home, I truly experience God's shalom.

Pursuing the peace of the city,
Jim Belcher
Costa Mesa, California

NOTES

Introduction

[1] Os Guinness, *Dining with the Devil: The Megachurch Movement Flirts with Modernity* (Grand Rapids: Baker, 1993); John Seel, *The Evangelical Forfeit: Can We Recover?* (Grand Rapids: Baker, 1993); Douglas D. Webster, *Selling Jesus: What's Wrong with Marketing the Church* (Downers Grove, Ill.: InterVarsity Press, 1992); David Wells, *No Place for Truth, or, Whatever Happened to Evangelical Theology?* (Grand Rapids: Eerdmans, 1993).

[2] Robert Webber, *The Younger Evangelicals* (Grand Rapids: Baker, 2002).

[3] I am well aware of the diversity within the camp and the fact that there are even reforming movements inside the traditional church.

[4] See for example John MacArthur, *The Truth War: Fighting for Certainty in an Age of Deception* (Nashville: Nelson, 2007); Gary L. W. Johnson and Ronald N. Gleason, eds., *Reforming or Conforming?* (Wheaton, Ill.: Crossway, 2008); Kevin DeYoung and Ted Kluck, *Why We're Not Emergent* (Chicago: Moody Publishers, 2008).

[5] See the Emergent Village website at <www.emergentvillage.com>.

[6] I want to thank my editor, Al Hsu of InterVarsity Press, for referencing this meeting on his blog, *The Suburban Christian*, at <http://thesuburbanchristian.blogspot.com/2008/05/john-piper-meets-tony-jones-two-views.html>.

[7] Piper is popular among the "young, restless and Reformed" crowd and in some ways represents a reforming element in the traditional church. Nonetheless, some of his theological views put him at odds with the emerging church. See Collin Hansen, *Young, Restless, Reformed* (Wheaton, Ill.: Crossway, 2008).

[8] John Piper and Justin Taylor, ed., *The Supremacy of Christ in a Postmodern World* (Wheaton, Ill.: Crossway, 2007), p. 155.

[9] Ibid.

[10] Tony Jones, *The New Christians: Dispatches from the Emergent Frontier* (San Francisco: Jossey-Bass, 2008), pp. 76-78.

[11] I do not want to be unfair to the pragmatic church, which often is the foil for both the emerging and traditional church. However, I will not spend much time critiquing or

defending the pragmatists. My focus is on the gap between the emerging and traditional camps.

[12]See "Willow Creek Repents?" *Out of Ur,* October 18, 2007 <http://blog.christianity today.com/outofur/archives/2007/10/willow_creek_re.html>.

[13]C. S. Lewis, "Mere Christians," *Church Times* 135 (1952). I want to thank Andrew Walker and Luke Bretherton, whose book *Remembering Our Future* (Carlisle, U.K.: Paternoster, 2007), reminded me of this quote.

[14]I want to thank Andy Crouch for this suggestion.

[15]I include in this group Redeemer Presbyterian Church, New York City, its many daughter churches around the country, the multisite Harbor Presbyterian Church in San Diego and scores of other churches that share a similar philosophy of ministry.

Chapter 1: There from the Start

[1]See Edith Schaeffer, *L'Abri* (Wheaton, Ill.: Crossway, 1992).

[2]*re:generation quarterly,* archived on the Christianity Today Library website at <http:// ctlibrary.com/rq>.

[3]Jim Belcher, "It's the Gospel, Stupid," *re:generation quarterly* 1, no. 2 (1995).

[4]Dieter Zander and Tim Celek, *Inside the Soul of a New Generation* (Grand Rapids: Zondervan, 1996).

[5]A Gen X 1.0 had been held earlier in Chicago.

[6]Mark Driscoll, *Confessions of a Reformission Rev.: Hard Lessons from an Emerging Missional Church* (Grand Rapids: Zondervan, 2006).

[7]Jim is currently church planting in Canterbury, England, with his wife and children. See <www.canterburyvineyard.com>.

[8]Mic Wilson helps his family run their vineyard, Wilson Creek, in Temecula, California. See the vineyard website at <www.wilsoncreekwinery.com>. Also, Brad den Dulk founded Corporate Computer Services in Orange County, California.

[9]The Mars Hill Bible Church website is <www.marshill.org>.

[10]See Michael Frost and Alan Hirsch, *The Shaping of Things to Come: Innovation and Mission for the 21st-Century Church* (Peabody, Mass.: Hendrickson, 2003), p. 51.

[11]In my travels to emerging churches, I have seen very few that had more than one or two generations represented in any significant numbers.

[12]Of course there is: In my short eight years in the Presbyterian Church in America, our presbytery has interceded and prevented two major church splits, restoring the congregations to health.

[13]See Tim Keller, *The Reason for God: Belief in an Age of Skepticism* (New York: Dutton, 2008).

Chapter 2: Defining the Emerging Church

[1]Eddie Gibbs and Ryan K. Bolger, *Emerging Churches: Creating Christian Community in*

Postmodern Cultures (Grand Rapids: Baker, 2005).

[2]Os Guinness, *Dining with the Devil: The Megachurch Movement Flirts with Modernity* (Grand Rapids: Baker, 1993). Also see *Modern Reformation* magazine at <www .modernreformation.org>.

[3]Mike Yaconelli, ed., *Stories of Emergence: Moving from Absolute to Authentic* (Grand Rapids: Zondervan/Youth Specialties, 2003).

[4]Gibbs and Bolger, *Emerging Churches*, p. 28.

[5]Scot McKnight, "What Is the Emerging Church?" lecture given at Westminster Theological Seminary, October 26-27, 2006 <http://tallskinnykiwi.typepad.com/ tallskinnykiwi/files/scott_mcknight_what_is_the_emerging_church.pdf>. Emphasis in original.

[6]Not every emerging author includes each of these seven criticisms, but overall these represent the most commonly held complaints against the traditional church. Each of these seven will be introduced and then discussed individually in later chapters. They will provide the major topics of dialogue between the emerging and traditional church. These seven will also be the basis on which I will build a third way, learning from the emerging and traditional churches but transcending some of their shortcomings.

[7]Dan Kimball <http://www.dankimball.com/vintage_faith/2006/04/origin_of_ the_t.html>.

[8]See Doug Pagitt, *Preaching Re-Imagined: The Role of the Sermon in Communities of Faith* (Grand Rapids: Zondervan/Youth Specialties, 2005).

[9]See C. Michael Patton's "Will the Real Emerger Please Stand Up?" <http://www .reclaimingthemind.org/blog/2008/08/will-the-real-emerger-please-stand-up/>.

[10]Ed Stetzer, "Understanding the Emerging Church," *Baptist Press*, January 6, 2006 <www.sbcbaptistpress.org/bpnews.asp?ID=22406>.

[11]Neil Cole, *Organic Church: Growing Faith Where Life Happens* (San Francisco: Jossey-Bass, 2005); Michael Frost and Alan Hirsch, *The Shaping of Things to Come: Innovation and Mission for the 21st-Century Church* (Peabody, Mass.: Hendrickson, 2003), p. 51; Frank Viola and George Barna, *Pagan Christianity? Exploring the Roots of Our Church Practices* (Ventura, Calif.: Barna Books, 2008).

[12]See the Emerging Pensees blog at <http://emergingpensees.blogspot.com/2006/ 09/what-is-emerging-church_25.html>.

[13]See the Emergent Village website at <www.emergentvillage.com>.

[14]Dan Kimball <http://www.dankimball.com/vintage_faith/2006/04/origin_of_ the_.html>.

[15]Chapter seven is an exception. It focuses on Dan Kimball, who fits in the relevants' camp, in my opinion.

[16]Michael Spencer, "Suggestions for Critics of the Emerging Church," *Next-Wave*, October 2006 <www.the-next-wave-ezine.info/issue94/index.cfm?id=17&ref= COVERSTORY>.

[17]See McKnight, "What Is the Emerging Church?"

Chapter 3: The Quest for Mere Christianity

[1]Thomas C. Oden, *The Rebirth of Orthodoxy: Signs of New Life in Christianity* (New York: HarperCollins, 2002).

[2]Each year Redeemer Church holds a joint dessert dialogue with the Reformed synagogue on whose campus we worship each Sunday. We call it "real dialogue." We affirm what we have in common, the Old Testament, but do not shy from or water down our differences. We have tackled the topics of sin, the sacrifice of Isaac, the Messiah and blood atonement. I have preached Christ in each of these meetings, holding nothing back. And each year the temple tells us afterward that the dessert was the highlight of their year. We are civil and loving friends. But our differences don't allow ecclesiastical union.

[3]John Stott, *Evangelical Truth: A Personal Plea for Unity, Integrity & Faithfulness* (Downers Grove, Ill.: InterVarsity Press, 2005), p. 116.

[4]Ibid.

[5]Ibid.

[6]Francis Schaeffer, *The Mark of the Christian* (Downers Grove, Ill.: InterVarsity Press, 2007).

[7]Oden, *Rebirth of Orthodoxy*, p. 58.

[8]Ibid.

[9]Ibid.

[10]Ibid., pp. 58-59.

[11]Ibid.

[12]Ibid., p. 31.

[13]Ibid., p. 32.

[14]Christopher Hall, "Ancient Church Fathers," a lecture given at Redeemer Presbyterian Church, Newport Beach, California, September 2008.

[15]C. FitzSimons Allison, *The Cruelty of Heresy* (New York: Moorehouse, 1993); Christopher Hall, *Reading Scripture with the Church Fathers* (Downers Grove, Ill.: InterVarsity Press, 1998); and Gerald L. Bray, *Creeds, Councils and Christ* (Fearn, Scotland: Christian Focus, 1997).

[16]Oden, *Rebirth of Orthodoxy*, p. 64.

[17]Ibid., p. 65.

[18]Bill Bishop, *The Big Sort: Why the Clustering of Like-Minded America Is Tearing Us Apart* (New York: Houghton Mifflin, 2008).

[19]Robert Greer, *Mapping Postmodernism: A Survey of Christian Options* (Downers Grove, Ill.: InterVarsity Press, 2003).

[20]Ibid., p. 174.

[21]Scot McKnight, *A Community Called Atonement* (Nashville: Abingdon, 2007).

[22]See Scot McKnight, "The Ironic Faith of Emergents," *Christianity Today Online*, October 3, 2008 <http://www.christianitytoday.com/ct/2008/september/39.62.html>, and "McLaren Emerging," *Christianity Today Online*, September 26, 2008 <http://www.christianitytoday.com/ct/2008/september/38.59.html>.

[23]Some kinds of postmodernism cannot affirm the top-tier view of truth. But others can. Thus to call the second group relativists or truth deniers is wrong. But finding common ground with the first group, the "hard postmodernists" or "anti-realists," may be hard if not impossible. But at least we would know what is on the table and what is at stake, something that is sorely lacking in the debate as it stands. So this two-tiered view will help the traditional church rebuild trust with those in the emerging church, the vast majority of which, I contend, can clearly affirm this new ecumenism.

[24]Greer, *Mapping Postmodernism,* p. 41. Also see John Frame, "Machen's Warrior Children," in *Alister E. McGrath and Evangelical Theology*, ed. Sung Wook Chung (Grand Rapids: Baker, 2003). Also found at *The Works of John Frame and Vern Poythress* <http://www.frame-poythress.org/frame_articles/2003Machen.htm>.

[25]Stott, *Evangelical Truth*, p. 116.

[26]C. S. Lewis, *Mere Christianity* (London: Collins, 1956), pp. vi, xi.

[27]I am well aware that it is often this first tier that is disputed, particularly around theories of atonement. I will look at this more in chapter five. For a third way on these disputes see Michael Bird, *The Saving Righteousness of God: Studies on Paul, Justification and the New Perspective* (Eugene, Ore.: Wipf & Stock, 2007).

[28]See Stanley N. Gundry, ed., *Three Views on Eastern Orthodoxy and Evangelicalism* (Grand Rapids: Zondervan, 2004).

[29]Paul Marshall with Lela Gilbert, *Their Blood Cries Out* (Dallas: Word, 1997).

[30]See Vigen Guroian, *Tending the Heart of Virtue: How Classic Stories Awaken a Child's Moral Imagination* (New York: Oxford University Press, 2002), and *Rallying the Really Human Things: Moral Imagination in Politics, Literature, and Everyday Life* (Wilmington, Del.: ISI Books, 2005).

[31]I am well aware that there are those who think we differ on the top tier as well. For a fine discussion on Eastern Orthodoxy, see Stan N. Gundry, ed., *Three Views on Eastern Orthodoxy and Evangelicalism* (Grand Rapids: Zondervan, 2004).

[32]John Frame, *Evangelical Reunion: Denominations and the One Body of Christ* (Grand Rapids: Baker, 1991).

Chapter 4: Deep Truth

[1]See The Ooze website at <www.theooze.com>.

[2]See James Glenn Belcher, *John Calvin and the Renewal of Our Times* (Ann Arbor, Mich.: UMI Microform, 1996).

[3]See Roger Lundin, *The Culture of Interpretation: Christian Faith and the Postmodern World* (Grand Rapids: Eerdmans, 1993).

[4]Brian McLaren, *The Church on the Other Side* (Grand Rapids: Zondervan, 2000); Tony Jones, *Postmodern Youth Ministry* (Grand Rapids: Zondervan/Youth Specialties, 2001).

[5]See Robert Bellah, *Habits of the Heart: Individualism and Commitment in American Life* (Berkeley: University of California Press, 2007); and Charles Taylor, *The Ethics of Authenticity* (Cambridge, Mass.: Harvard University Press, 1992).

[6]Stephen Toulmin, *Cosmopolis: The Hidden Agenda of Modernity* (Chicago: University of Chicago Press, 1992).

[7]Charles Taylor, *Sources of the Self: The Making of the Modern Identity* (Cambridge, Mass.: Harvard University Press, 1992); Kenneth Gergen, *The Saturated Self: Dilemmas of Identity in Contemporary Life* (New York: Basic Books, 2000).

[8]Charles Colson, "The Postmodern Crackup," *Christianity Today*, December 1, 2003 <www.christianitytoday.com/ct/2003/december/24.72.html>.

[9]I should confess my bias. Chuck, until the age of ten or twelve, grew up with my dad on the hard streets of Winthrop, Massachusetts, on the outskirts of Boston. My dad used to tell the story of how, in 1946, when the Red Sox faced the Cardinals in the World Series, Chuck and my dad played hooky from school (with the help of my grandpa) to go to Fenway Park. Good practice for Watergate!

[10]See the Prison Fellowship website at <www.prisonfellowship.org>.

[11]Brian McLaren, "An Open Letter to Chuck Colson," December 2003 <www .brianmclaren.net/archives/000018.html>.

[12]Crystal Downing, *How Postmodernism Serves (My) Faith: Questioning Truth in Language, Philosophy and Art* (Downers Grove, Ill.: InterVarsity Press, 2006).

[13]With so many critical voices railing against postmodernism in the mid-1990s, I wanted to know why so many young Christian thinkers and church practitioners developed a positive view of postmodernism. Someone (I can't remember who) recently said that many of the younger thinkers in the church were told to stay away from postmodernism. It is bad. And it therefore became the forbidden fruit. So they picked the fruit and when they bit into it, they liked the taste. In fact, they realized that it was not bad but was very close to the Christian view of things. As I read Tony Jones, Brian McLaren, and philosophy professors like James K. A. Smith and Merold Westphal, I found they read Jacques Derrida and Jean-François Lyotard, two high priests of postmodernism, *not* as examples of hypermodernism but as strong critics of the Enlightenment project. They see postmodernism not as a continuation of modernism but as its chief critic. These postmodern authors are allies, in part, in the fight against the Enlightenment, thinkers who can serve the Christian faith, even though they are not believers. See Gene Veith, *Postmodern Times: A Christian Guide to Contemporary Thought and Culture* (Wheaton, Ill.: Crossway, 1994); James Smith, *Who's Afraid of Postmodernism? Taking Derrida, Lyotard, and Foucault to Church* (Grand Rapids: Baker Academic, 2006); Heath White, *Postmodernism 101: A First Course for the*

Curious Christian (Grand Rapids: Brazos, 2006); Merold Westphal, *Postmodern Philosophy and Christian Thought* (Bloomington, Ind.: Indiana University Press, 1999).

[14]See Abraham Kuyper, *Lectures on Calvinism* (Grand Rapids: Eerdmans, 1943); C. S. Lewis, *Mere Christianity* (New York: HarperCollins, 2001); Cornelius Van Til, *Christian Apologetics* (Phillipsburg, N.J.: P & R, 2003); Herman Dooyeweerd, *In the Twilight of Western Thought: Studies in the Pretended Autonomy of Philosophical Thought*, Collected Works of Herman Dooyeweerd (Lewiston, N.Y.: Edwin Mellen Press, 1999); and Nicholas Wolterstorff, *Reason Within the Bounds of Religion,* 2nd ed. (Grand Rapids: Eerdmans, 1984).

[15]Stanley J. Grenz and John R. Franke, *Beyond Foundationalism: Shaping Theology in a Postmodern Context* (Louisville, Ky.: Westminster John Knox, 2001).

[16]Wolterstorff's most famous book is probably his *Lament for a Son* (Grand Rapids: Eerdmans, 1987), which he wrote after the accidental death of his son.

[17]He called this third way Reidianism, from Thomas Reid's thinking, the first "postfoundationalist" as Nick says. See Nicholas Wolterstorff, *Thomas Reid and the Story of Epistemology* (Cambridge: Cambridge University Press, 2000).

[18]Wolterstorff, *Reason Within the Bounds,* p. 56.

[19]Ibid., p. 57.

[20]Ibid.

[21]See Nicholas Wolterstorff, *Justice: Rights and Wrongs* (Princeton, N.J.: Princeton University Press, 2007).

[22]See Nancey Murphy, *Beyond Liberalism and Fundamentalism: How Modern and Postmodern Philosophy Set the Theological Agenda* (Philadelphia: Trinity Press International, 1996).

[23]Jones, *Postmodern Youth Ministry*, p. 26.

[24]Ibid., p. 26.

[25]Ibid.

[26]Ibid., p. 39.

[27]See Alasdair C. MacIntyre, *Whose Justice? Which Rationality?* (South Bend, Ind.: University of Notre Dame Press, 1989); and Richard Mouw and Sander Griffioen, *Pluralisms and Horizons* (Grand Rapids: Eerdmans, 1993).

[28]Smith, *Who's Afraid of Postmodernism?* p. 123.

[29]Lesslie Newbigin, *Foolishness to the Greeks* (Grand Rapids: Eerdmans, 1986), p. 7.

[30]Miroslav Volf, "Soft Difference," at <www.twine.com/item/116clsm9y-vpf/soft-difference-by-mirslav-volf>.

[31]In chapter three I placed them in the reconstructionist camp of the emerging movement.

[32]Michael Frost and Alan Hirsch, *The Shaping of Things to Come: Innovation and Mission for the 21st-Century Church* (Peabody, Mass.: Hendrickson, 2003), p. 47.

[33]The church Tony is a member of, Solomon's Porch, is a good example of a relational-

set church. I examine Solomon's Porch in chapter nine on preaching.

[34]The woman's name has been changed to protect her identity.

Chapter 5: Deep Evangelism

[1]Edith Schaeffer, *The Tapestry: The Life and Times of Francis and Edith Schaeffer* (Nashville: W Publishing, 1985).

[2]The man's name has been changed to protect his identity.

[3]See the Emmaus Way website at <www.emmaus-way.com>.

[4]See Brian McLaren, *More Ready Than You Realize: Evangelism as Dance in the Postmodern Matrix* (Grand Rapids: Zondervan, 2002); Brian McLaren, *The Church on the Other Side* (Grand Rapids: Zondervan, 2000); Michael Frost, *Exiles: Living Missionally in a Post-Christian Culture* (Peabody, Mass.: Hendrickson, 2006); and Alan Hirsch, *The Forgotten Ways* (Grand Rapids: Brazos, 2006).

[5]Tim Conder, *The Church in Transition: The Journey of Existing Churches into the Emerging Culture* (Grand Rapids: Zondervan, 2006), p. 146.

[6]Ibid., p. 148.

[7]Ibid., p. 147.

[8]Ibid., p. 148.

[9]Ibid., p. 149.

[10]Ibid.

[11]Ibid., pp. 151-52.

[12]D. A. Carson, *Becoming Conversant with the Emerging Church: Understanding a Movement and Its Implications* (Grand Rapids: Zondervan, 2005), p. 152.

[13]Carson says church discipline can be traced back to Jesus himself (Matthew 18), but can also be found in various other parts of the New Testament (e.g., 1 Corinthians 5; 10–13).

[14]Carson, *Becoming Conversant,* p. 149.

[15]Ibid., p. 152.

[16]Redeemer's pastoral team at the time was assistant pastor David Juelfs, director of worship Dan Myers and myself. For more on the Christian Community Development Association see their website at <www.ccda.org>.

[17]See John Perkins, *Let Justice Roll Down* (Ventura, Calif.: Regal Books, 2006).

[18]See <http://harborpc.org>.

[19]Her name has been changed to protect her identity.

Chapter 6: Deep Gospel

[1]Gordon MacDonald, *Ordering Your Private World* (Nashville: Thomas Nelson, 2007).

[2]For an introduction to Kuyper, see James D. Bratt, ed., *Abraham Kuyper: A Centennial Reader* (Grand Rapids: Eerdmans, 1998); and John Bolt, *A Free Church, a Holy Nation: Abraham Kuyper's American Public Theology* (Grand Rapids: Eerdmans, 2001).

[3]For a good summary of a Kuyperian view of creation see Albert M. Wolters, *Creation Regained: Biblical Basics for a Reformational Worldview* (Grand Rapids: Eerdmans, 2005); and Cornelius Plantinga, *Engaging God's World: A Christian Vision of Faith, Learning, and Living* (Grand Rapids: Eerdmans, 2002).

[4]See "What's ASP all about?" American Studies Program <http://www.bestsemester .com/asp/overview/>.

[5]Brian McLaren, *The Secret Message of Jesus: Uncovering the Truth That Could Change Everything* (Nashville: W Publishing, 2006).

[6]Brian McLaren, *A Generous Orthodoxy* (Grand Rapids: Zondervan/Youth Specialties, 2004), p. 48.

[7]Ibid., pp. 79, 49.

[8]Ibid., p. 49.

[9]Ibid., p. 99.

[10]Whenever I read Brian's description of privatized Christianity, I hear the echo of missiologist Lesslie Newbigin, whose writings have had a dramatic impact on me. Brian also acknowledges that Newbigin is a major influence. After forty years as a missionary to India, Newbigin tells us, he returned to "Christian" England to find that secularism had triumphed. Christianity was still around but it had become so privatized as to become inconsequential. Newbigin thinks this happened when the church thought it could make peace with Enlightenment secularism or modernity. Modernity, based on individual reason, contended that only scientifically verifiable facts were public truths. Everything else was a value, not a fact. Values were for the private realm. In an attempt to survive, the church, says Newbigin, agreed to these terms and retreated to the private realm. Over the years this armistice turned Christianity into a private religion. It was relegated to the realm of individual values that could no longer speak to the public sphere. The church lost its public influence, and the public square became naked. Christianity became merely therapeutic, helping people cope with life, offering religious goods and services, but not having much to say about the marketplace, government or culture. Newbigin credits this capitulation to a loss of will; the church no longer believed its own story, that Christianity is indeed universal history, public as well as private. I think Brian would agree. But he would go even further. Whereas Newbigin blames individualism in Christianity on the fact-value split, Brian would see this—if I am reading him correctly—as just one more symptom of a much greater problem. The church did not merely stop acting in the public realm; privatized salvation is at the heart of its theological message.

[11]McLaren, *Secret Message of Jesus*, p. 10.

[12]Ibid.

[13]See Mark Husbands and Daniel J. Treier, eds., *Justification: What's at Stake in the Current Debate* (Downers Grove, Ill.: InterVarsity Press, 2004); Steve Jeffery, Michael

Ovey and Andrew Sach, *Pierced for Our Transgressions: Rediscovering the Glory of Penal Substitution* (Wheaton, Ill.: Crossway, 2007).

[14]Darrell Guder, *The Continuing Conversion of the Church* (Grand Rapids: Eerdmans, 2000), pp. 120-41.

[15]Many critics will point to Brian's 2007 book, *Everything Must Change*, as proof of his social gospel liberalism.

[16]It is not just the traditional church that needs to listen. Scot McKnight challenges Brian McLaren to listen better to his critics: "Despite his many proposals in these last two books, McLaren would rather ask a question and create a conversation than propound a solution. This style is an attribute of a good teacher. Yet having said that, I want to voice the frustration of many: McLaren's willingness to muddy the waters, which is characteristic of *Generous Orthodoxy*, goes only so far. Many of us would like to see greater clarity on a variety of questions he raises. McLaren grew up among evangelicals; we'd like him to show the generosity he is known for to those who ask theological questions of him. The spirit of conversation that drives much of his own pastoral work urges each of us to answer the questions we are asked, and the Bible encourages those who ask those questions to listen patiently and to respond graciously. The lack of the latter has so far inhibited the former. This can be taken as a plea on behalf of all concerned to enter into a more robust, honest conversation" (Scot McKnight, "McLaren Emerging," *Christianity Today Online*, September 26, 2008 <www.christianitytoday.com/ct/2008/september/38.59.html>.

[17]Guder, *Continuing Conversion of the Church*.

[18]Ibid., p. 121.

[19]As Brian said on Scot McKnight's blog, *Jesus Creed*, "I certainly believe in the need for saving faith, for forgiveness, for hope beyond death, for the pursuit of orthodox articulations of belief, for overcoming the damning effects of sin, for rejecting wholeheartedly the idea that we can be saved by our own efforts or through religion, and so on. I'm not attacking those beliefs."

[20]Charles Wesley, "And Can It Be That I Should Gain?" (1738).

[21]Of course many would disagree that the penal-substitution theory of the atonement is central. N. T. Wright contends, "I find myself compelled toward one of the well-known theories of atonement, of how God deals with evil through the death of Jesus, not as a replacement for the events or the stories nor as a single theory to trump all others, but as a theme which carries me further than the others toward the heart of it all. I refer to the *Christus Victor* theme, the belief that on the cross Jesus has won the victory over the powers of evil. Once that is in place, the other theories come in to play their respective parts" (*Evil and the Justice of God* [Downers Grove, Ill.: InterVarsity Press, 2006], pp. 94-95).

[22]See Scot McKnight's book *A Community Called Atonement* (Nashville: Abingdon, 2007) for how the kingdom can be linked to penal atonement without slipping into reduc-

tionism in either direction. Penal atonement and union with Christ bring us into the
kingdom and community.

[23]McKnight, "McLaren Emerging."

[24]Ibid.

[25]Hans Boersma, *Violence, Hospitality, and the Cross* (Grand Rapids: Baker Academic,
2004).

[26]Cited in ibid., p. 113.

[27]Ibid., pp. 113-14.

[28]McLaren, *Generous Orthodoxy*, pp. 61-62.

[29]Brian McLaren, "Brian McLaren on the Kingdom of God," *Pomomusings*, January 14, 2008
<http://pomomusings.com/2008/01/14/brian-mclaren-on-the-kingdom-of-
god>.

[30]McLaren, *Secret Message of Jesus*, p. 123.

Chapter 7: Deep Worship

[1]Robert Webber, *The Younger Evangelicals* (Grand Rapids: Baker, 2002), p. 187.

[2]Ibid.

[3]"But the problem is," says Tim Conder, "the word *traditional* is meaningless without
a frame of reference." He continues: "What is tradition to one person is an innovation, a whim, a distant memory, or an oddity to another." In our diverse, multicul-
tural world, "even most racially and culturally homogenous churches are far too diverse to use the term *tradition* in any more than a local sense." Unless it is defined
better. Normally, when someone bemoans the loss of tradition what they mean is
that we are losing the way things used to be done around here. What is ironic about
Tim's discussion is that he is describing the pain created by worship wars at his
church as it transitioned from a contemporary worship format to an emerging one.
In this sense, then, *tradition* meant the recent past, the last twenty years. (See Tim
Conder, *The Church in Transition: The Journey of Existing Churches into the Emerging Culture* [Grand Rapids: Zondervan, 2006], p. 102.)

[4]Chris Armstrong, "The Future Lies in the Past," *Christianity Today Online,* Febru-
ary 8, 2008 <www.christianitytoday.com/ct/2008/february/22.22.html>.

[5]See the Vintage Faith Church website at <www.vintagechurch.org>.

[6]See Dan Kimball, *Emerging Worship* (Grand Rapids: Zondervan, 2004); Dan Kimball
and Lilly Lewin, *Sacred Space: A Hands-On Guide to Creating Multisensory Worship Experiences for Youth Ministry* (Grand Rapids: Zondervan/Youth Specialties, 2008).

[7]Kimball, *Emerging Worship*, p. 5.

[8]Ibid.

[9]Ibid., p. 79.

[10]Ibid., p. 81. See also Kimball and Lewin, *Sacred Space*, pp. 14-15.

[11]Over the past year Dan has shied away from using the word *emerging* and distanced

himself from parts of the emerging movement. See <http://www.dankimball.com/vintage_faith/2009/04/scot-mcknights-words-made-me-want-to-cry-in-a-good-way-.html>.

[12]Kimball, *Emerging Worship*, p. 34.

[13]According to Kimball, the way we guard against this is to focus on the purpose of worship. Worship is about the saints gathering to live out Psalm 95:6, which says, "Oh come, let us worship and bow down; / let us kneel before the LORD, our Maker!" (ESV). It is a multisensory experience of bowing, kneeling, listening, learning, looking, singing, caring, touching and loving with our minds, our hearts and our bodies. Such worship produces a greater love for God and for people (Matthew 22:37-39). "God forbid that we teach the people in our churches to view emerging worship as anything else" (ibid., p. 11).

[14]Andy Crouch, "The Emergent Mystique," *Christianity Today*, November 1, 2004 <www.christianitytoday.com/ct/2004/november/12.36.html>.

[15]Ibid.

[16]Ron Gleason, "The Death Knell of the Emerging Church Movement," unpublished paper, p. 2.

[17]Ibid., p. 3.

[18]There is a good bit of anticreational rhetoric in this criticism. We will look at this temptation to run down all aspects of culture in chapter ten, "Deep Culture."

[19]Many in the emerging church are more into being culturally relevant than biblical. I think Kimball is aware of this danger and would agree that some in emerging circles have mimicked the worst parts of evangelicalism. This saddens him. He would agree with his critics that if the emerging church has become just a cooler, hipper version of the seeker church, then they have lost their way. Has this happened at some emerging churches? I am sure Kimball would admit as much. What I find promising about Kimball's book is that he is calling the church beyond consumer-driven, emotional-high-producing, thin content to worship that has depth.

[20]D. H. Williams, *Retrieving the Tradition and Renewing Evangelicalism: A Primer for Suspicious Protestants* (Grand Rapids: Eerdmans, 1999), pp. 6-7.

[21]See Brian McLaren, *Finding Our Way Again: The Return of the Ancient Practices* (Nashville: Thomas Nelson, 2008).

[22]Williams, *Retrieving the Tradition and Renewing Evangelicalism*, pp. 10-11. Furthermore, Williams says, "but these vestiges of the early faith are just that, *vestigia*, i.e., footprints or tracks that speak of a doctrinal and confessional past which has been peripheral for so many evangelicals that it has ceased to guide the direction of many present-day congregations and in some cases, is forgotten" (p. 11).

[23]Jonny Baker and Doug Gay, comps., *Alternative Worship: Resources from and for the Emerging Church* (Grand Rapids: Baker, 2003), p. 27.

[24]Ibid.

[25] Ibid.

[26] I agree with Williams who says it so well: "While there is a growing hunger for a rediscovering of the essentials of what it is to think and live Christianly that goes beyond the moments of high-powered 'praise and worship' experiences, the formation of a distinct Christian identity in years to come will not be successful unless we deliberately reestablish the link to those resources that provide us with the defining 'center' of Christian belief and practice" (Williams, *Retrieving the Tradition and Renewing Evangelicalism*, p. 13).

[27] Thomas Oden, quoted in Chris Armstrong, "The Future Lies in the Past."

[28] I would say that when it comes to worship, the traditional church looks to the Bible and recent tradition, largely ignoring the postmodern context. The emerging church, on the other hand, also appeals to the Bible but it has a much deeper desire to connect with the culture, to make its worship relevant to the postmodern context. In having this desire, it has sampled the traditions of the church to help it appeal to the culture which craves mystery, ritual and sacred space. The problem as I have said is that while it appreciates the fruit of the tradition it does not embrace the Tradition. In fact, its free-church ancestry makes this difficult.

[29] Tim Keller, "Reformed Worship in the Global City," in *Worship by the Book*, ed. D. A. Carson (Grand Rapids: Zondervan, 2002), p. 198.

[30] See, for example, the Red Mountain Music website at <www.redmountainchurch. org/rmm>; the Indelible Grace Music website at <www.igracemusic.com>; and Sandra McCracken's website at <www.sandramccracken.com>.

[31] See Horton Davies, *The Worship of the English Puritans* (Orlando, Fla.: Soli Deo Gloria, 1997).

[32] See the Redeemer Presbyterian Church website at <www.redeemerpres.com> for our worship bulletin.

[33] See the Redeemer Presbyterian Church, New York City, website at <www .redeemer.com>.

[34] No book on the Lord's Supper has influenced me more than Keith A. Mathison, *Given for You: Reclaiming Calvin's Doctrine of the Lord's Supper* (Phillipsburg, N.J.: P & R, 2002).

Chapter 8: Deep Preaching

[1] They are just as harsh about seeker-driven topical preaching.

[2] See the Solomon's Porch website at <www.solomonsporch.com>.

[3] Dan Kimball, for example, told me his views on preaching are very different from Doug's.

[4] Doug Pagitt, *Preaching Re-Imagined: The Role of the Sermon in Communities of Faith* (Grand Rapids: Zondervan, 2005), pp. 87, 74, 76, 82, 88.

[5] Ibid., p. 52.

[6]Ibid., p. 134.

[7]Ibid., p. 138.

[8]Ibid., p. 139.

[9]Ibid., p. 175.

[10]Ibid., p. 133.

[11]Doug Pagitt, "The Emerging Church and Embodied Theology," in *Listening to the Beliefs of Emerging Churches*, ed. Robert Webber (Grand Rapids: Zondervan, 2007), p. 127.

[12]Ibid.

[13]Ibid., p. 126.

[14]Ibid., p. 125.

[15]Since Kevin DeYoung writes the chapters that are critical of Doug, I will only mention his name when presenting their critique.

[16]Kevin DeYoung and Ted Kluck, *Why We're Not Emergent: By Two Guys Who Should Be* (Chicago: Moody Publishers, 2008), p. 78. The problem, thinks DeYoung, is that emergents have adopted a view where the Bible is only derivatively and indirectly God's Word. The authority of the Word is not in the actual text of Scripture "but in Him who speaks through the words of the text" (p. 79). DeYoung says this view comes from Karl Barth. The emergents have, whether they realize it or not, adopted this neo-orthodox view of Scripture.

[17]Ibid., p. 80.

[18]Ibid., p. 118.

[19]Ibid.

[20]Ibid.

[21]After all, he says, aren't pastors to follow Paul's advice to Timothy and Titus to preach and teach, rebuke and encourage, guard against false doctrine, and train other men to do likewise (2 Timothy 2:1-2; cf. 1 Timothy 4:6, 11, 13; 5:17; Titus 1:9)? As Paul says, "In the presence of God and of Christ Jesus, who will judge the living and the dead, and in view of his appearing and his kingdom, I give you this charge: Preach the Word" (2 Timothy 4:1-2).

[22]DeYoung and Kluck, *Why We're Not Emergent*, p. 160.

[23]Ibid.

[24]Dan Kimball, response to "The Emerging Church and Embodied Theology" by Doug Pagitt, in *Listening to the Beliefs of Emerging Churches*, ed. Robert Webber (Grand Rapids: Zondervan, 2007), pp. 151-54. According to Dan, Doug does not believe there are theological conclusions that remain valid whether we are living in the third or the twenty-first century. "No matter what the time period or personality or cultural context, when examining the Scriptures and what God has revealed to us, we would still eventually come up with the same conclusion," Dan states (p. 153). Dan's struggle with Doug is his rejection of the need for this first-tier foundation that is so well

articulated in Nicene Christianity; "through time," Dan says, "people have wrestled with and tested these core doctrines in the Nicene Creed, and they apply in any culture of any time period" (Dan Kimball, "The Emerging Church and Missional Theology," in *Listening to the Beliefs of Emerging Churches*, ed. Robert Webber [Grand Rapids: Zondervan, 2007], p. 92). It is these statements, says Kimball, that we need "to cling to and hold onto firmly."

[25]When I asked Dan about it in person, he said that if he knew the direction Doug was taking in his theology he would have come out even stronger in his opposition than he does in this chapter.

[26]Doug Pagitt, response to "The Emerging Church and Missional Theology" by Dan Kimball, in *Listening to the Beliefs of Emerging Churches*, ed. Robert Webber (Grand Rapids: Zondervan, 2007), p. 113.

[27]Regarding the loci of authority, Doug rejects Dan's claim that the Nicene tradition is in any way normative today. "Creeds," says Doug, "were never meant to be the end of our thinking on such issues; they were meant to be expressions to engage with, or within, as we consider these and other issues to our day" (ibid., p. 114). In sum, the creeds were just "cultural theological responses" that hold no more weight than anything Solomon's Porch comes up with. Creeds are not timeless but time bound. Therefore they are not to be the "floor" for our foundation. We need to be free to explore, to dance, with all kinds of new theological partners and not be constrained.

[28]Even the Reformers appealed to tradition in taking on the Roman Catholic Church. They wanted to reform the tradition, not reject it. They called the Roman Catholic Church back to the true tradition, free from so many human customs that had been appended to the church fathers. This is what *ad fontes* ("back to the sources") meant.

[29]In response to Mark Driscoll's essay in *Listening to the Beliefs of Emerging Churches*, Doug makes a telling comment. He says, "I think much of our difference comes from the fact that in many ways we are telling different stories of Christianity. We seem to be calling for different starting and ending points" (Doug Pagitt, response to "The Emerging Church and Biblicist Theology" by Mark Driscoll, in *Listening to the Beliefs of Emerging Churches*, ed. Robert Webber [Grand Rapids: Zondervan, 2007], p. 42). This gets to the heart of some of the real differences in the emerging camp.

Even the most sympathetic observer must conclude that Doug's book *A Christianity Worth Believing* takes positions that are at odds with the Great Tradition, as laid out in chapter 3. In the introduction to *A Christianity Worth Believing*, he says he no longer believes in "the versions of Christianity that have prevailed for the last fifteen hundred years" (Doug Pagitt, *A Christianity Worth Believing* [San Francisco: Jossey-Bass, 2009], p. 2). His book bears this out. Although there is much to affirm in the book, particularly the way it points out abuses in fundamentalism, he has major issues with the Great Tradition's historic views on atonement, the cross, the wrath of God, separation from God, the Fall, depravity, the Creator-creature distinction, God's sovereignty, election, the requirement for enabling grace to obey, and heaven and hell. He makes this clear throughout.

[30]See Herman N. Ridderbos, *Paul: An Outline of His Theology* (Grand Rapids: Eerdmans, 1997).

[31]Eugene L. Lowry, *The Homiletical Plot: The Sermon as Narrative Art Form* (Louisville, Ky.: Westminster John Knox, 2001).

[32]Michael Frost and Alan Hirsch, *The Shaping of Things to Come: Innovation and Mission for the 21st-Century Church* (Peabody, Mass.: Hendrickson, 2003), p. 47.

[33]Kimball, "The Emerging Church and Missional Theology," p. 99.

[34]Ibid., p. 98.

Chapter 9: Deep Ecclesiology

[1]See Eugene Peterson, *Under the Unpredictable Plant: An Exploration in Vocational Holiness* (Grand Rapids: Eerdmans, 1994).

[2]C. John Miller, *Outgrowing the Ingrown Church* (Grand Rapids: Zondervan, 1986).

[3]See Neil Cole, *Organic Church: Growing Faith Where Life Happens* (San Francisco: Jossey-Bass, 2006).

[4]Pete Ward, *Liquid Church: A Bold Vision of How to Be God's People in Worship and Mission: A Flexible, Fluid Way of Being Church* (Peabody, Mass.: Hendrickson, 2002).

[5]See the Presbymergent website at <http://presbymergent.org>; the Anglimergent website at <http://anglimergent.ning.com>; and the Luthermergent website at <http://Luthermergent.org>.

[6]See also Emergent Village's "Values and Practices" at <http://emergentvillage.com/about-information/values-and-practices>, which endorses a deep ecclesiology. It says, "We are committed to honor and serve the church in all its forms—Orthodox, Roman Catholic, Protestant, Pentecostal, Anabaptist. We practice 'deep ecclesiology'—rather than favoring some forms of the church and critiquing or rejecting others, we see that every form of the church has both weaknesses and strengths, both liabilities and potential."

[7]Ward, *Liquid Church*, p. 2.

[8]Ward, unlike those influenced by Anabaptism, did not build his call for a networked church on the "fall of the church" paradigm that is so popular these days. Not once in his book does he mention Constantine or Christendom and blame it for all the problems in the church. Not once does he call the church back to the first-century ecclesiological paradigm. Not once does he castigate the solid church for trying to contextualize to culture by taking on parts of the world around it. I found this interesting.

At about the time I was working on this chapter, George Barna and Frank Viola came out with a book titled *Pagan Christianity? Exploring the Roots of Our Church Practices.* Calling for an organic church made up of house churches, the authors base their argument on the "fall of the church." This fall took place after the first century when the church started adopting wholesale practices of the pagan culture. Because of this the contemporary church in its present institutional form "has neither a biblical nor a historical right to function as it does." The only hope of the church is to return to the first-century church. "I believe," says Viola, "the first century church was the church in its purest form, before it was tainted or corrupted" (George Barna and Frank Viola, *Pagan Christianity?* [Carol Stream, Ill.: Tyndale House, 2008], p. xviii).

Although Ward shares with *Pagan Christianity?* a negative view of institutionalism and the desire for a more organic Christianity, he sees in the biblical record much more fluidity and freedom in adapting the way the church is structured to the environment it finds itself in. In other words, the mission dictates the structure. For Viola and Barna the biblical record is all we need. We don't need culture to help determine the church or what is relevant. Once we move beyond what is in the first-century church, we become pagan. Ward, surprisingly, does not take this route, probably because he comes from an Anglican and not an Anabaptist background, and thus does not have the same suspicion of adapting the Bible to the surrounding culture as some Anabaptists and heirs of the Radical Reformation do.

[9]See also George Barna, *Revolution* (Carol Stream, Ill.: Tyndale House, 2005).

[10]He mentions three main ways that solid churches adapt. The first attempt he calls the "church as heritage site." The second is to become a refuge for those wearied by the culture. The third is to become a nostalgic community (Ward, *Liquid Church*, pp. 26-27).

[11]See The Mission House Church website at <http://subversiveone.blogspot.com>.

[12]John S. Hammett, "An Ecclesiological Assessment of the Emerging Church Movement," *The A-Team Blog* <http://ateam.blogware.com/AnEcclesiologicalAssessment.Hammett.pdf>.

[13]Ibid., p. 11.

[14]See my series on the book of Daniel at <www.redeemerpres.com>.

[15]Hammett, "Ecclesiological Assessment," p. 11.

[16]In fact, the emerging church, says Hammett, is following in the footsteps of seeker churches, which focus on meeting felt needs. The megachurch model has positioned itself to meet the needs of the consumer, and the emerging church is simply extending this problem, albeit newly contextualized for this generation. George Barna is an example; for years he trumpeted the church-growth model but now has rejected it in favor of the house-church model. Traditional church critics point out the logical nature of his move.

[17]As Miroslav Volf comments, "complete spontaneity . . . is impossible within a com-

munity of love, at least within human community. . . . [I]n order to love one must at least implicitly acknowledge and follow quite specific rules of interaction." On this side of God's new creation, we cannot do without rules of interaction that are at least partially external to every member. And these rules need to develop "along institutionally prescribed lines" (Miroslav Volf, *After Our Likeness: The Church as the Image of the Trinity* [Grand Rapids: Eerdmans, 1998], p. 237). Without these institutionally sanctioned rules, laws and structure, there will be little accountability to reign in a maverick leader who is intent on abusing the community.

[18]Ed Stetzer and David Putman have recognized this danger. Stetzer and Putman straddle the line between traditional and emerging, working within the Southern Baptist Convention. Commenting on Barna's book *Revolution*, which describes many in the emerging church, they write: "we think that those he describes show an undeveloped idea of what church is—as described by Scripture, not by the modern notion of church. These revolutionaries are often the children of the Anglo megachurch who are looking for something meaningful and authentic. Yet in the process of rejecting what we agree is in trouble (modern evangelicalism), if they fail to take God, Scripture, and church with them, they will become too tied to the world. In short, they become syncretized" (*Breaking the Missional Code: Your Church Can Become a Missionary to Your Community* [Nashville: Broadman & Holman, 2006], p. 57).

What Stetzer and Putman are saying is that the "revolutionaries"—though they have the gospel message and a strong call to contextualize this message to reach the culture around them—have combined this with a faulty view of the church. Or more scary still, they have no concept of the church at all. What they need to do is spend more time working out a biblical view of the church.

[19]I am well aware that some in the reconstructionist camp would disagree. See Frank Viola, *Reimagining Church* (Colorado Springs: David C. Cook, 2008). Let me also add that retreating to the position of Viola, who not only rejects the Great Tradition (classical orthodoxy) as nothing but pagan accretions but also claims that all we need is the Bible and the record of the first-century church, is not the answer. Besides being dangerously dismissive of two thousand years of accumulated wisdom and the oversight of the Holy Spirit in his church, which testifies to God's faithful care and protection of his church, this view wrongly posits that there is a "golden age" of the church that we can and must return to.

[20]See D. G. Hart, "Whatever Happened to Office?" in *Recovering Mother Kirk* (Grand Rapids: Baker Academic, 2003), pp. 107-16.

[21]As Volf says, drawing on the long history of our tradition, "to survive as a church at all, every church must act internally or externally, must secure its own foundations in its confession of faith in Jesus Christ, and celebrate the sacraments. For this, it also needs leaders, teachers and deacons. . . . [O]ffices are a necessary part of ecclesial life" (Volf, *After Our Likeness*, p. 248).

[22] Hart, *Recovering Mother Kirk*, p. 113.

[23] See Alan J. Roxburgh's chapter "Pastoral Role in the Missionary Congregation," in *The Church Between Gospel and Culture: The Emerging Mission in North America*, ed. George Hunsberger and Craig Van Gelder (Grand Rapids: Eerdmans, 1996), pp. 319-32.

[24] Luke Bretherton writes, "Thus, de-traditionalism, because it allows believers to pick and choose beliefs and practices amenable to them, means Christianity comes to involve nothing too difficult" (Andrew Walker and Luke Bretherton, eds., *Remembering Our Future* [London: Paternoster, 2007], p. 17). The sad thing is that when we avoid the difficult things like discipline and admonition, we are like children who resist discipline at all costs. But the book of Hebrews tells us that we should not resist the discipline of the Lord. It is a sign of his love for us. Since God has entrusted the elders with this authority, not for abuse but for godly correction, avoiding their discipline is avoiding the loving discipline of the heavenly Father. The results can't be good.

[25] Hart, *Recovering Mother Kirk*, p. 115.

[26] See Thomas C. Oden, *After Modernity . . . What?* (Grand Rapids: Zondervan, 1990).

[27] I took it that they wanted second-tier tradition alone. Over the course of the year I attempted to explain the vision of the church, but to no avail. I did my best to lead organically, empowering my leaders, but this didn't help either.

Chapter 10: Deep Culture

[1] See John Frame, "Machen's Warrior Children," in *Alister E. McGrath and Evangelical Theology*, ed. Sung Wook Chung (Grand Rapids: Baker, 2003). Also found at *The Works of John Frame and Vern Poythress* <http://www.frame-poythress.org/frame_articles/2003Machen.htm>.

[2] Steve Taylor, *The Out of Bounds Church? Learning to Create a Community of Faith in a Culture of Change* (Grand Rapids: Zondervan/Youth Specialties, 2005), p. 138.

[3] T. M. Moore, *Culture Matters: A Call for Consensus on Christian Cultural Engagement* (Grand Rapids: Brazos, 2007), p. 12.

[4] See Shane Claiborne and Chris Haw, *Jesus for President: Politics for Ordinary Radicals* (Grand Rapids: Zondervan, 2008).

[5] Moore, *Culture Matters*, p. 146.

[6] Taylor, *Out of Bounds Church?* p. 137.

[7] David Kinnaman and Gabe Lyons, *unChristian: What a New Generation Really Thinks About Christianity . . . and Why It Matters* (Grand Rapids: Baker, 2007).

[8] There is no question that the Bible warns against the world and worldliness and the need to flee them. But extremism and legalism come from confusing two biblical usages of the word *world*. On the one hand, God has created the world and deemed it "good" (Genesis 1). And as the apostle John says, "For God so loved the world" (John 3:16). On the other hand, due to the Fall, there is a part of the creation that has re-

belled and has produced a rebellious system of thinking and acting that stands opposed to the kingdom of God. So when the Bible says "Do not love the world" (1 John 2:15), it does not mean "don't care for the environment" or "avoid all connection with the culture." It really means "don't embrace anti-God thinking, acting and systems."

[9]In other words, the Bible tells us to be all things to reach all people. There are areas of life where we are supposed to look like the world around us. I think this includes large aspects of culture. But there are also areas where we are to "flee from idols," as the apostle John says. Ironically, many in the traditional church look nothing like the world in the areas they are supposed to, and they have embraced areas—pride, arrogance, judgmentalism and an unloving attitude—they are to stand apart from. No wonder the younger generations see the church as un-Christian.

[10]Taylor, *Out of Bounds Church?* p. 68.

[11]Ibid., p. 70.

[12]John MacArthur, *The Truth War: Fighting for Certainty in an Age of Deception* (Nashville: Thomas Nelson, 2007), p. 139.

[13]Ibid., p. 140.

[14]Ibid.

[15]Ibid., p. 199.

[16]Ibid., p. 200.

[17]Can it be the traditional church bought into the public-private split, when they are so involved in politics? Over the past twenty-five years the traditional church, particularly the more fundamentalist wing, has become involved in politics. The Moral Majority, the Christian Coalition and the Family Research Council are examples of this. They have encouraged evangelicals to get involved in the political process, to take back America. Yet, at the same time, others in the camp, writers like Ed Dobson and Cal Thomas, have called Christians to retreat from political entanglements and return to the church. Who speaks for conservative Christians? I am not sure, but I think Dobson and Thomas are being more consistent with the history of fundamentalism. I would even make the case, if I had the time and space, to say that even when traditionalists have been involved in politics, it has been mostly as a defensive posture, to protect their own safety and communities, and to take back areas that have been lost. It is one of reclaiming or protecting but not one of proactively constructing or cultivating on a broad scale. This is why they have often been accused, with some truth, of being single-issue focused. Moreover, I would argue that if America returned to a bygone era, when America was "Christian," they would exit politics altogether. They would not be needed and would retreat behind their own protective walls, living their lives, building their families and churches. They don't have a broad-based biblical view of political philosophy or cultural engagement. It is purely defensive not constructive. Thus Dobson and Thomas are calling traditionalists to

return to their long-held belief that culture is not changed by laws and politics, but by transforming one heart at a time through the church. So the Christian Right still holds to the sacred-secular dualism that has characterized the movement since the 1920s.

[18]This has begun to change. More emerging writers have begun to look at politics and economics. But they still do not have a well-worked-out view of the state.

[19]On Anabaptism and culture see Robert Webber, *The Church in the World* (Grand Rapids: Zondervan, 1986); Robert Friedmann, *The Theology of Anabaptism* (Eugene, Ore.: Wipf & Stock, 1998); and J. Budziszewski, *Evangelicals in the Public Square: Four Formative Views on Political Thought and Action* (Grand Rapids: Baker Academic, 2006).

[20]See Stanley Hauerwas and William H. Willimon, *Resident Aliens* (Nashville: Abingdon, 1989).

[21]John Bolt, *A Free Church, A Holy Nation: Abraham Kuyper's American Public Theology* (Grand Rapids: Eerdmans, 2001), p. 427.

[22]Ibid., p. 428.

[23]Ibid., p. 429.

[24]Calvin called common grace the *sensus divinitatis* or *semen religionis*.

[25]Although Kuyper would not subscribe to a full-blown natural-law ethic, that is, that a nonbeliever has access to large amounts of truth on which to build his ethical foundation (in this sense Kuyper was a nonfoundationalist), he would not go to the other extreme and say that a nonbeliever is incapable of knowing any truth or justice whatsoever (Kuyper was not an anti-realist). Reality could be comprehended on some level, however minimal. He followed Calvin, who commented that the nonbeliever is like a philosopher walking through a field during a pitch-black night when lightning strikes, and for just a split second the philosopher is able to describe what he saw. While the nonbeliever may not be able to totally describe reality, he or she is able to get some of it right.

[26]Christian Smith, cited in D. Michael Lindsay, *Faith in the Halls of Power: How Evangelicals Joined the American Life* (New York: Oxford University Press, 2007), p. 122.

[27]See Andy Crouch, *Culture Making: Recovering Our Creative Calling* (Downers Grove, Ill.: InterVarsity Press, 2008).

[28]Dallas Willard, *The Great Omission: Reclaiming Jesus's Essential Teachings on Discipleship* (San Francisco: HarperOne, 2006).

[29]Lesslie Newbigin, *Truth to Tell: The Gospel as Public Truth* (Grand Rapids: Eerdmans, 1991), pp. 83-85.

[30]Using Andy Crouch's book *Culture Making*, we explain to our members that "culture is what we make of the world" (p. 23). As Crouch maintains, "Culture is . . . the name for our relentless, restless human effort to take the world as it's given to us and make something else. . . . Culture is all of these things: paintings (whether finger

paintings or the Sistine Chapel), omelets, chairs, snow angels. It is what human beings make of the world" (p. 23). Motivated by the cultural mandate in Genesis 1, we
are called to be culture makers in every sphere of daily life.

[31]"Pringle is probably the single most influential elected official in Orange County. He
is Mayor of OC's most dynamic large city, influential in county public policy as an
Orange County Transportation Authority director, owner of an influential public
affairs company—and head-and-shoulders above the elected official crowd in terms
of vision and sheer political talent" (Scott W. Graves and Matthew Cunningham,
"OC's Top 40 Influential Politicos," *Red County Magazine*, March 3, 2008 <www
.redcounty.com/magazine/2008/03/ocs-top-40-influential-politic.php>.

[32]Over four hundred people attended, including elected officials from twenty-seven
different municipalities. Speakers included Joel Kotkin, professor at Chapman University and author of *The City: A Global History* (New York: Modern Library, 2006);
New York Times columnist David Brooks, author of *On Paradise Drive* (New York: Si-
mon & Schuster, 2005); journalist Roberta Green, coeditor of *Blind Spot: When Journalists Don't Get Religion* (New York: Oxford University Press, 2008); Philip Bess,
author of *Till We Have Built Jerusalem: Architecture, Urbanism, and the Sacred* (Wilmington
Del.: ISI Books, 2006); and Andres Duany, coauthor of *Suburban Nation* (New York:
North Point Press, 2001). See <www.restoringcommunityconference.com>.

Conclusion

[1]Their names have been changed to protect their identities.

[2]See Craig G. Bartholomew and Michael W. Goheen, *The Drama of Scripture: Finding
Our Place in the Biblical Story* (Grand Rapids: Baker, 2004); Michael D. Williams, *Far
as the Curse Is Found* (Grand Rapids: Baker, 2004); and Christopher J. H. Wright,
Knowing Jesus Through the Old Testament (Downers Grove, Ill.: InterVarsity Press,
1992).

[3]See C. S. Lewis's essay "The Weight of Glory," in *The Weight of Glory* (San Francisco:
HarperOne, 2001).

[4]John Newton, "Amazing Grace" (1779).

[5]See Larry Osborne's case for sermon-based discussion groups in *Sticky Church* (Grand
Rapids: Zondervan, 2008).

[6]Dietrich Bonhoeffer, *Life Together* (San Francisco: HarperOne, 1978); Edith Schaeffer, *L'Abri* (Wheaton, Ill.: Crossway, 1992); and Randy Frazee, *The Connecting Church*
(Grand Rapids: Zondervan, 2001).

[7]Jerry Bridges, *Transforming Grace: Living Confidently in God's Unfailing Love* (Colorado
Springs: NavPress, 2008).

[8]See Lewis Smedes, *The Art of Forgiving: When You Need to Forgive and Don't Know How*
(New York: Ballantine, 1997).

[9]Al Wolters, *Creation Regained: Biblical Basics for a Reformational Worldview* (Grand Rap-

ids: Eerdmans, 2005); Andy Crouch, *Culture Making: Recovering Our Creative Calling* (Downers Grove, Ill.: Intervarsity Press, 2008). See also Richard Mouw, *When the Kings Come Marching In: Isaiah and the New Jerusalem* (Grand Rapids: Eerdmans, 2002).

[10]Os Guinness, *The Call: Finding and Fulfilling the Central Purpose of Your Life* (Nashville: Thomas Nelson, 2003); Douglas Schuurman, *Vocation: Discerning Our Callings in Life* (Grand Rapids: Eerdmans, 2004).

[11]See Horton Davies, *Christian Worship: Its History and Meaning* (Nashville: Abingdon, 1957); idem, *The Worship of the English Puritans* (Orlando, Fla.: Soli Deo Gloria, 1997); Howard G. Hageman, *Pulpit and Table* (Eugene, Ore.: Wipf & Stock, 2004); and Bard Thompson, *Liturgies of the Western Church* (Philadelphia: Fortress, 1980).

[12]See Gerald Bray, *Creeds, Councils & Christ* (Downers Grove, Ill.: InterVarsity Press, 1984); Christopher A. Hall, *Learning Theology with the Church Fathers* (Downers Grove, Ill.: InterVarsity Press, 2002); and Christopher A. Hall, *Reading Scripture with the Church Fathers* (Downers Grove, Ill.: InterVarsity Press, 1989).

[13]See Kenneth W. Osbeck, *101 Hymn Stories* (Grand Rapids: Kregel, 2002); and Steve Turner, *Amazing Grace: The Story of America's Most Beloved Song* (New York: Harper Perennial, 2003).

[14]See Keith A. Mathison, *Given for You: Reclaiming Calvin's Doctrine of the Lord's Supper* (Phillipsburg, N.J.: P & R, 2002).

[15]I learned this prayer from Steven Brown, longtime pastor of Key Biscayne Presbyterian Church.

ABOUT THE AUTHOR

Jim Belcher (M.A., Fuller; Ph.D., Georgetown) is founding church planter and lead pastor of Redeemer Presbyterian Church in Newport Beach, California <www.redeemerpres.com>. He is coproducer of the docudrama *From Earth to Heaven: The Life and Art of Vincent Van Gogh*. He is on the steering committee for the Restoring Community Conference: Integrating Social Interaction, Sacred Space and Beauty in the 21st Century <www.restoringcommunityconference.com>, an annual conference for city officials, planners, builders and architects.

Jim previously led the Twenty-Something Fellowship and cofounded The Warehouse Service at Lake Avenue Church in Pasadena. He has served as adjunct professor at Azusa Pacific University and was cofounder of the Renaissance Project Skateboard Company. He has been published in *Leadership Journal* and *re:generation quarterly*, and he and his wife and four children live in Costa Mesa, California.

You can learn more about *Deep Church* and Jim's ministry at <www.thedeepchurch.com>.